The Millennial Woman in Bollywood

A New 'Brand'?

MAITHILI RAO

OXFORD
UNIVERSITY PRESS

Oxford University Press is a department of the University of Oxford.
It furthers the University's objective of excellence in research, scholarship,
and education by publishing worldwide. Oxford is a registered trade mark of
Oxford University Press in the UK and in certain other countries

Published in India by
Oxford University Press
22 Workspace, 2nd Floor, 1/22 Asaf Ali Road, New Delhi 110002, India

© Oxford University Press India 2022

The moral rights of the author have been asserted

First Edition published in 2022

2nd impression 2023

All rights reserved. No part of this publication may be reproduced, stored in
a retrieval system, or transmitted, in any form or by any means, without the
prior permission in writing of Oxford University Press, or as expressly permitted
by law, by licence or under terms agreed with the appropriate reprographics
rights organization. Enquiries concerning reproduction outside the scope of the
above should be sent to the Rights Department, Oxford University Press, at the
address above

You must not circulate this work in any other form
and you must impose this same condition on any acquirer

ISBN-13 (print edition): 978-0-19-013047-3
ISBN-10 (print edition): 0-19-013047-4

ISBN-13 (eBook): 978-9-35-497459-5
ISBN-10 (eBook): 9-35-497459-7

ISBN-13 (OSO): 978-9-35-497460-1
ISBN-10 (OSO): 9-35-497460-0

DOI: 10.1093/oso/9780190130473.001.0001

Typeset in Minion Pro 10.5/14
by Newgen Knowledge Works Pvt. Ltd.
Printed in India by Replika Press Pvt. Ltd.

*To my daughter and other young women—pre, post, and deemed
millennials.*

Contents

Foreword—Shabana Azmi   v
Preface—A New Brand?   ix

Introduction: A Changing Ecosystem Births the Millennial Woman as a Brand   1

1. No Means No   31
2. Rom com Revamped   42
3. Non-conformists Are the New Cool   75
4. Woman the Hero   109
5. Woman at Work   137
6. Sisters under the Hood   173
7. The Subversives   197
8. Subversion in Retro Mode   212
   Afterword   224

Select Filmography—Chapterwise   227
Sources of Quotes—Chapterwise   267

Foreword

'Main Chup Rahungi' (I shall remain silent) was considered a virtue for Indian women in the sixties. Little wonder then that it became the title of a popular Hindi film starring Meena Kumari.

You know a society from the way its cinema portrays women. Popular culture, cinema included, prefers the easy option of peopling its story with familiar stereotypes. This is undemanding entertainment where the audience knows what to expect, of course with minor tweaks for novelty. But there has always existed another way of making films, where characters and situations reflect the overt and covert changes in society—attitudes, deeper concerns, and acceptance of what was once considered risky if not taboo. Our cinema once had this alternative to the mainstream. The Parallel Cinema in which I grew as an actor and person had space for real women and wider social concerns, all told with honesty and in a realistic style. I remember being advised against doing *Ankur* because Lakshmi (the character I played) steals rice! 'You will be stamped to play negative characters if that shot is not removed' said the know-alls. Of course it was not and I remember feeling empathy for Lakshmi rather than condemnation. What fills me with new hope for a better cinema now is the large number of films that are engaging, intelligent, and give women agency. This has happened in the last two decades. Thankfully, these films have wider reach because of multiplexes and good marketing. Whether it was the birth of a new millennium bringing with it expectations of hope for the better, or the sweeping changes brought in by globalization, there is greater skill and sophistication in how we tell our stories now.

More important are the women who tell their own stories—as directors, writers, and actors. They are the face and voice of the educated urban woman all around us, making her mark in many fields. Speaking of Hindi cinema, there is now a thriving group of women making films that speak in original voices, with a new sensibility that has found its personal expression. Zoya Akhtar, Meghna Gulzar, Kiran Rao, Konkona Sen

Sharma, Reema Kagti, Alankrita Srivatsava, Leena Yadav... they all have a track record to be proud of.

Indie filmmakers, Anurag Kashyap, Anubhav Sinha, Farhan Akhtar, Vikramaditya Motwani, Tigmanshu Dhulia, and other new directors injected energy and vision that has transformed mainstream films. Who would have ever thought that someone would dare subvert iconic classics *Devdas* and *Sahib Bibi Aur Ghulam*? They did it in their own distinct idiom that resonated with contemporary audience. It is astounding how characters like Paro, Chandramukhi, and Choti Bahu have been transformed into contemporary women with their own attitude to self-identity, sexuality, and power. This generation of filmmakers have recast mainstream tropes in their narratives, so that present day audience relates to them.

Earlier too there were many women centric films starring Nutan, Mala Sinha, Meena Kumari, Nanda, etc. but these were largely within the stereotype of the quietly acquiescing wife, the loving sister, the sacrificing mother. Occasionally a *Guide* came along way ahead of its times and immortalized Waheeda Rehman with her robust portrayal of Rosy performed with vigour and a rare abandon. But it was an exception rather than the rule.

By the mid-eighties Indian society was changing. The women's movement had started planting its roots in the world of the Arts. Women were expressing themselves more freely and striking out of the traditional moulds imposed on them by a patriarchal society. The film producers started realizing that a newer avatar of the heroine was needed. But Indian society was not sure of how much 'freedom' could be 'accorded' to a woman without disastrous consequences for the social order: So a spate of films followed with an eye firmly on the box-office. Heroines gave the impression of having agency but copped out in the end. An assertive woman had to eat humble pie! There were also the avenging angels made of cardboard—*Zakhmee Aurat*, *Khoon Bhari Maang*, *Insaf ki Devi*, etc. As Shyam Benegal famously says, 'First we had Rambos now we have Rambolinas,' it was only a decade ago that women with complexity, contradictions, and strength started finding acceptance in Bollywood. The distinction between the Madonna and the whore started to blur. The vamp has said her last goodbye.

Today the sheer number of women centric films is amazing, spanning a variety of themes and styles. *Queen, Kahani, The Dirty Picture, Panga, Thappad, Manmarziyan, Tumhari Sulu, Badla, Raazi, Chhapak* are a few of recent landmark films. Of course, the path-breaking *Pink* and *Anarkali of Aarah* said a loud, reverberating No to unwanted sexual overtures. Even the staple Romantic comedy was reworked to present a modern woman who is not a shrinking violet but game for live-in relationships and did not agonise over pre-marital sex. This is the greatest change that is so remarkable in our patriarchal society. It reflects the spirit of the millennial woman who confronts patriarchy in her own way. We have actors—Vidya Balan, Tabu, Kangana Ranaut, Priyanka Chopra, Deepika Padukone, Taapsee Pannu, Anushka Sharma, Alia Bhatt, and others—to bring these characters alive on the screen. They are all truly millennial women.

Maithili Rao explores the millennial woman in all her facets in this book. Her book celebrates this new freedom and analyses the compromises demanded by the particular genre and its narrative style. Rao has had an abiding interest in the portrayal of women almost from the time she started writing on cinema. It is a feminist perspective without arcane academic rigidity.

I enjoyed reading it immensely. I'm sure you will too.

Shabana Azmi
March 2020.

Preface—A New Brand?

The answer to the subtitle of this Preface lies in the question itself…

Bollywood looks for means to brand itself anew, reflecting its response to new challenges. We think Bollywood is too much with us and have a love-hate relationship with its overwhelming presence in our lives. We are often guilty of dismissing it as mindless entertainment. Cinema has to evolve beyond escapism to survive in a world brimming over with alternate, edgy content that you can see on your smartphone. That is incentive enough for Bollywood to move with the zeitgeist. Globalization has seen the zeitgeist change at a pace never felt before; what took a couple of generations earlier now happens in less than a decade.

According to economists, the world has seen de-globalization post 2008 crisis. However, culturally, globalization seems immune to these market forces. It is an irreversible, ongoing process. Bollywood continues to imbibe cultural values and narrative modes from trusted Hollywood while European and Korean cinema seems to be the new flavour for those in search of something different—what Bollywood calls *hatke.* Directors with eclectic tastes and more artistic sensibility derive inspiration from wherever they find it: the Hindi heartland for auteur Vishal Bharadwaj's Shakespearean adaptations, to the latest live-in relationship caper *Luka Chuppi* (2019); avant-garde Europe, for thrillers *Badla* (2019) from the Spanish *Contratiempo* (2016) and *Andhadhun* (2018) from the French short *L'Accordeur* (2010); Salman Khan's super hit *Bharat* (2019) remade from the huge Korean crowd pleaser *Ode to My Father*(2014). The refreshing difference today is either the remake rights are bought or the inspiration acknowledged in the credits. It is very different from the blatant plagiarism—of scenes, or whole stories, music—so rampant before satellite TV came to our skies. Copycats are easy to catch. Our own regional cinema is a source for remakes—could be a delectably different rom com like *Shubh Mangal Savdhan* (2017) from the Tamil original *Kalyana Samayal Saadham* (2013) to the toxic misogyny of the violent hero *Kabir Singh* (2019) based on the Telugu megahit *Arjun Reddy* (2017). Fox and

Disney entered into co-productions in India with enthusiasm and it is true that they have not anticipated or adjusted to the vagaries of the fickle box office. These Hollywood studios are retreating from producing Bollywood films but they have not totally given up. The film industry survives on hope: it did, it does, and will continue to do so.

Audiences are hooked to a smorgasbord of content to choose from and it is difficult to wean them off variety. Never before have we lived in such a connected world. In the pre-internet and satellite television days, popular cinema used to filter changes leisurely, sifting through chaff for the kernel that would suit the cultural norms and aesthetic taste of its consumers. Popular cinema has followed trends, has never aspired to be the trendsetter (except for fashion). The financial stakes are too high for an industry seeking the Holy Grail: the unfailing formula for a box office hit. As an industry wag once said, if he found the formula he would bottle it and the sales would make him a billionaire.

The adventurous breed of indie filmmakers has energized Bollywood with the surprising success of films that tweaked genres like rom coms to feature an equal, if not even more prominent, role for the woman. Unnoticed by the larger society and film industry for a long time, the presence of working women and their influence on consumption has made inroads into interconnected industries: advertising, television, and cinema. The millennial woman is everywhere in urban India. Her visibility may not be prominent in rural areas. The scene is changing in small town India and semi-urban places. Educated young women are aspirational, want economic independence and personal freedom to choose life partners and most recently, own their sexuality even if society considers it taboo. This of course does not mean that the entrenched caste system has ceased to make a difference in life choices. In fact, with the greater freedom the young want, the reaction is to impose the old restraints with even more authority by families and institutions like Khap Panchayats[1] and their equivalents in other parts of India. Radical change in the status and ambitions of women inevitably invites resistance by patriarchy. That is a given. What many of the post-feminist generation want is personal freedom to get ahead in a career of choice, live the way they want, and marry the person they choose. Choice is the key word.

---

[1] Village councils dominated by patriarchal elders. It specifically refers to Haryana.

There are outstanding examples of exceptional women who have made brave choices.

The newest heroine for millennials is Dutee Chand, India's 100 metre sprint queen who came out of the closet, declared she was gay and in a relationship with a female relative. She has faced her immediate family's disapproval but Chand's openness about her sexual preference has won the support of the LGBHTQ community and the media lionized this athlete who was born in a below poverty line tribal family. Chand qualified for the 2016 Summer Olympics and won the Silver at Jakarta Asian Games, 2018. She survived the prolonged ordeal of being dropped from the Indian contingent after accusations of female hyperandrogenism, until the Court of Arbitration for Sport ruled in her favour against the Athletics Federation of India & International Association of Athletics Federations. Her gutsy fight and achievements cry out for a biopic. Gay men have been portrayed with empathy (underlining the hostility of conservative society) in *Aligarh* (2015), based on true-life story after years of demeaning depictions as effete figures of ridicule.

As reflective of a lesbian's right to love, *Ek Ladki Ko Dekha To Aisa Laga* (2019) is a rather vapid, dramatic comedy about a young man smitten with Sweety Chaudhary (Sonam Kapoor Ahuja), the poor little rich girl who is a closet lesbian, there is more emphasis on the hero Sahil Mirza's (Rajkumarr Rao) unrequited love than Sweety's loneliness that confines her to diary outpourings, and finally her courage in coming out with the help of Sahil, failed playwright who dons the gender rights activist mantle. Non-heterosexual choice is grudgingly accepted when it is a man while a film about a woman's choice of a gay partner needs all kind of extraneous padding, to jazz up the salability quotient. *Ek Ladki's* ... USP is Anil Kapoor and Sonam Kapoor Ahuja reprising real life to play gregarious father and reticent daughter. The title tries to recreate the magic of R.D. Burman/Kishore Kumar classic; the iconic song by Javed Akhtar is a rhapsodic tribute to ethereal innocence. The updated version comes nowhere near the original's lyricism: a masterly melding of melody, poetry and image. All one can say is that Bollywood tentatively broke a long-standing taboo.

Things have changed rather radically in the last two years. *Badhai Do* (2022) centres on a lavender marriage of a gay man Shardul Thakur (Rajkumarr Rao) and lesbian woman Suman/Sumi (Bhumi Pednekar).

Shardul Thakur is a harassed police officer: posted at an all-woman station and hounded by his extended family (characters are fleshed out beyond generic types: overbearing aunt, grumpy cousins, henpecked uncle) to get married. He is the only son, the *kuldeepak*, in short, burdened with carrying forward the family name. He is into body-building, an aspirant to Mr. India title. The writing makes it a point to show a gay man as a specimen of muscular masculinity. Rao bulks up impressively, hiding vulnerabilities under his macho uniform. Bhumi Pednekar, the actor game for roles that break the stereotype, is a physical training teacher in a school. Sumi is on the shelf, going by small town standards. The locale swings between Uttarakhand small town and Dehra Dun. The couple live like roommates and have their same sex partners hidden under the guise of a cousin/business acquaintance, etc. Sumi's partner is so obviously from the North East with her petite frame and distinct features. It causes a lot of frantic humour but embedded in it is the deep emotional bonding of the women who nurture each other's desire to mother a baby. Sumi's character is developed with more nuance and depth, revealing her frustration, anger, and longing for motherhood while Shardul maintains a façade of bravado. It is Sumi's coming out of the closet that finally emboldens him to come out to his family. No preachy and passionate sermons but a sincere reaching out for understanding and acceptance. The reconciliations are not facile but they do finally accept this lavender marriage. Sumi and Shardul adopt a baby after a year's waiting and their sexual partners take their place at the family ceremony.

If a strong lesbian heroine is long delayed recognition, a transwoman in a love story is a daring first for Bollywood. *Chandigarh Kare Aashiqui* (2021) plumps for the new template of a bodybuilder hero. Manu Munjal with more brawn and volatile heart than brains is a Punjabi stereotype rescued from predictability by Ayushmann Khurana who is willing to be ridiculed. Into this rather provincial ambiance wafts in the svelte, sexy Zumba teacher, Maanvi (Vaani Kapoor) who speaks impeccable English to go with her polished manners. When two hot bodies are thrown together in the heated gym, can desire be far behind? There is a lot of earthy humour and broad innuendo reeking of frustrated libidos. Abhishek Kapoor wastes no time in bedding the two but the insuperable problem is Maanvi's confession: she is a transgirl. It takes Manu's thick head and preconceived notions of masculinity to even entertain the idea of sex change: that someone born a boy houses a girl waiting to come out of the physical body's confines and free the woman inside. Manu's sensitization is rather cursory and the writing doesn't delve into the transwoman's psyche with any degree of depth. The film goes through the predictable arc of a sports competition to imbue some sensitivity into the stud who embraces his ladylove in public, ignoring sniggers and snide comments.

It is difficult to pin down patriarchy's attitude to gender stereotypes and non-heterosexual preference: are gay men more dangerous to its dominance and lesbians less so? This soft focus portrayal of a lesbian heroine perhaps reflects the film industry's noncommittal attitude to potentially explosive subjects. On the other hand, OTT platforms have inserted lesbian relationships into multitrack series whether the story really needs it or not. Perhaps the two trends will learn from each other's mistakes and reach a deeper and more realistic understanding of queer sexuality. Right now, Bollywood's portrayals mirror the assumed non-political individualism of this generation.

The last sentence demands a drastic revision in view of the tumultuous change, just as 2020 was to start. December 2019 is a watershed month in independent India. After the BJP government passed the Citizenship Amendment Act, unprecedented protests swept across the country against what many liberals (of all religions), civil society activists, and the largest minority in India, Muslims, think is an unconstitutional provision. This Act goes against secularism, enshrined in the Preamble to the Constitution. The short but significant Preamble, that spells out the basic principles of the Constitution we the people have given ourselves, has become the mantra of protestors: reading it aloud at civic meetings, carrying copies along with portraits of Dr Ambedkar and Mahatma Gandhi. And of course, the national flag. The effort is to repudiate the government's branding of protest as anti-national. These protests were spontaneous, not led by any political party. Young people, young women being more than an equal part, were at the forefront on college campuses, public meetings, and vocal on the social media. Women standup comics—again a new phenomenon—posted their defiantly satiric acts and parody of popular Bollywood hits on YouTube and other social media, shared by thousands across the country. The significant revelation was that the millennials who were assumed to be apolitical, a self-centred generation now led the movement on campuses and streets of metros and small towns. Women were at the forefront of these marches—millennials and post-millennials holding out roses to the cops and flaunting witty, creative banners. There were so many anonymous heroines standing shoulder to shoulder with the young and not so young men. Cheeky young women in Kolkata sang with gusto the Bengali version of the Chilean protest anthem *You are the rapist*.

Another very poignantly transformative change caught people by surprise. Young people had discovered the romance of rebellion. Faiz Ahamd Faiz—the iconic Pakistani poet of revolution—was reclaimed in India as its own legacy. *Hum Dekhenge*—a long poem that celebrates courage and assurance of change—was the anthem sung and recited across many campuses and civil society gatherings. Even the apolitical IIMs and IITs and the prestigious IISC—where the elite of the student community have no time for things other than their demanding academics—joined the *Hum Dekhenge* chorus of support to their beleaguered cohorts of liberal bastions, JNU(Jawaharlal Nehru University) and Jamia Milia Islamia—both in Delhi and assured of a national impact—which were sites of protest that invited brutal police reprisals and vandalism. JNU's student union is Left Liberal and their long-standing demands for hostel fee reductions and other issues provoked counter-violence from rival student body affiliated to the RSS. This simmering discontent at one of India's premier institutions culminated in violence against students and some faculty members by masked and armed hoodlums while the police stood by passively. No one has been arrested so far even though there are many videos of the event in circulation. JNU has the reputation of giving space to dissent and civilized intellectual debate of issues. The sight of Aishe Ghosh, president of the JNUSU with bandaged head and fractured arm in a sling, sparked a large section of Bollywood into vocally condemning the violence attributed to the right-wing students and holding the biggest rally seen in Mumbai in recent memory. Directors, writers, actors, lyricists—mostly associated with Indie cinema and veterans like Shabana Azmi and Javed Akhtar known for their support to liberal-secular causes—were unequivocally supportive of the many anti-CAA protests. The culmination was Deepika Padukone's visit to the JNU campus, standing in silent support beside the injured Aishe Ghosh. If ever an image spoke more than a thousand words, it was this stunning, wordless message of solidarity. Bollywood's highest paid actress spoke truth to power with her mere presence. Of course Padukone's silent support invited both admiration and an avalanche of malice from troll armies calling it a publicity stunt on the eve of *Chhapaak*'s release (her first film as producer in which she played an acid attack survivor). Trade pundits concur that she risked far much more by her support to the students than any PR gain. Even Raghuram Rajan, former RBI governor wrote on his Twitter post without naming Padukone: 'When a Bollywood actress registers her silent protest by meeting with the victims of the attack on JNU, even though she puts attendance at her latest movie at risk, she inspires us all to take stock of what is truly at stake.' Days of somnolescent indifference was put behind by the newly woke Bollywood.

This was so significant that non-film eminent persons were moved to comment on it. From celebrity support to the extraordinary courage and determination shown by ordinary women is the most important part of this upsurge of dissent. The popularity of *Hum Dekhenge* even in non-Urdu proficient regions is testament to the enduring appeal of a language that expresses love and revolution with equal felicity. The famous Kaifi Azmi *nazm* written decades ago when the poet was a young man comes to mind to describe the ethos of poetry-inspired sense of true camaraderie and inspirational call to walk together on the path of progress: *Uth meri jaan mere saath hi chalna hai tujhe*.[2]

India had never seen the presence of ordinary women gathered in protest against the violence perpetrated on Jamia Students—many of them were like family to the residents of Shaheen Bagh, a locality close to the University. Muslim women, old grandmothers, young women with babes in arms and little children in tow and articulate students have been the talisman and symbol of this protest. Delhi's assembly elections, marked by high decibel, incendiary anti-Muslim rhetoric, have come and gone, followed by the worst communal riots in Delhi in three decades. Many commentators called it a tinder-box waiting to be lit, inciting a pogrom against Muslims, provoking retaliation in densely populated localities.

Before the Covid-19 pandemic forced the shutdown (the entire country was in lockdown) of defiant women after 100 days of protest on 24 March 2020, Shaheen Bagh had become a place of pilgrimage for liberals. This sit-in sustained itself against motivated calumny and

---

[2] Rise my love, you have to walk with me.

feeble counter protests. There were mini Shaheen Baghs all over India—predominantly peopled by Muslim but also joined by concerned citizens of other faiths. The commentariat, of the instant variety and dispassionate academics, examined this phenomenon from a variety of perspectives. This is valid even after Shaheen Bagh became a cherished memory in a society grown indifferent to protest in an atmosphere where dissent is equated with being anti-national.

The observations of serious journalists and academics are both immediate responses as well as searching exploration of the significance of this protest. Some delve deeper into history to understand and explain the relevance to the present and its parallels with the past. Amulya Gopalakrishnan, a columnist with deep understanding that relates events to a wider cultural context, commented. 'The political is the personal too. It comes down to deep-down emotions like fear and love, just played on a larger scale .... But now, something about the emotional climate is really changing. The nationwide protests against the discriminatory Citizenship Amendment Act and the threat of the NRC, and the student demonstrations have also been an outpouring of love and indignation and sadness and comradeship. If you haven't been to these protest marches, it is hard to convey the collective effervescence one feels there ... May be that's why there has been so much poetry, which gives words to heightened emotions' (from *Those who resist 'new India' have found their voice, passion and community. Sunday Times*, 12 January 2020).

Gyan Prakash (eminent historian who teaches at Princeton University) observed in the same issue of the *Sunday Times*. 'India is astir with ground-level protests ... what is remarkable about these protests is their organic nature. Muslim students took the lead ... the courageous initiatives at Aligarh and Jamia struck a chord beyond the Muslim community and spread at electric speed. Students and youth, the civil society, and even sections of Bollywood have joined the protest .... this calls to mind what Mahatma Gandhi attempted in the Khilafat movement, which used a Muslim grievance to launch a nationalist movement against the British' (*Why the protests remind us of Gandhi's Khilafat movement*. 12 January 2020). The kind of cultural and sub-cultural syncretism commentators found in the spirit of the protests soared to song in the voice of the iconoclastic musician from the South, T.M. Krishna. He sang at Shaheen Bagh and rendered Tamil, Kannada, and Malayalam versions of *Hum Dekhenge* making Faiz's poetry pan Indian. Interestingly, the concert Artists Against Communalism was on the *shethepeople*, The Women's Channel.

If feminists of the 80s bemoaned the lack of activism on part of millennials—dubbed the Me generation—the overwhelming presence of young women in this sustained protest restored faith in this generation's political potential and sincere adherence to the spirit of our Constitution. The women who oppose the protest are equally, if not more, vehement. The times may be polarized and the debate shrill but it cannot be said it is unexciting. Yes, the very air we breathe—before Covid-19 spread panic—was cacophonous. It was also vibrantly alive. The heady thrill of debate is not ephemeral like the latest fad. Millennials have tested its power and will not relinquish it easily even if fear of Covid-19 spelt hiatus (and closure) for the warriors of Shaheen Bagh. The fundamental struggle to reclaim India's secularism will not lose its strength or sheen. It is a landmark movement by women for the greater good of a liberal society and nothing will diminish its historic significance even after the ruling regime and the judiciary called the protesters to vacate public space. It is even more important for many millennial women who drew inspiration from it.

This late blooming of the millennial women, resulting in an exhilarating plunge into urgent contemporary issues, validates the faith Indie filmmakers put into crafting so many facets of this emerging face of a woke Indian woman. They intuitively grasped this changing attitude and made an engaging *Queen* (2013) or a subversive cult film like *Dev D* (2009). Indie directors have a vision and sensibility that is influenced by world cinema. They use mainstream elements of song, dance, and melodrama with finesse and bring to the narrative a deeper understanding of young people caught in the flux of change. It is an old cliché but true: India lives in different centuries simultaneously. This is a challenge Bollywood faces when it wants to maintain its pan-India appeal. India's most famous brand, synonymous with Indian cinema abroad, has to take into account the societal change brought about by the entry of women in much larger numbers in media, corporate world, IT, and other fields. To continue with the old tried and tested formula does not work.

Popular media can least afford not to reflect the changes happening at a dizzy pace. Bollywood with the infusion of indie filmmakers is in tune with the changes in technology that gives films a narrative edge. They are aware that attitudes and expectations of the young are altered by the world outside. They form the largest segment of audience. This is true of other countries as well. Films must reflect this change and even be the agents of change. We see films with unconventional themes succeed because they are not too experimental and use the advantages of a flexible formula to appeal to the millennials. A film like *Gehraiyaan* (2022) divided the audience but it could not be ignored. Deepika Padukone played a challenging role that shocked conventional morality. Alisha is a Yoga trainer, in a live-in relationship with a writer who soon proposes to her at a party. She has just met her US-based younger cousin's fiancé Zain Oberoi (Sidhant Chaturvedi) and it is lust at first sight for both. She has a troubled childhood—her mother committed suicide and the father is emotionally distant. She is looking for investors to back her idea of an app for Yoga. Passion, guilt, vulnerability, and ambition—they churn her emotional life and Zain professes love but defers commitment. A Woody Allenesque scenario where pleasure and sin cohabit demands a lot from actors and Padukone plunges into its amoral depths without holding back. The film ends as a noir thriller, and Alisha the accidental survivor of a murder attempt overcomes blackmail and moves on. After family skeletons tumble out of claustrophobic cupboards, Alisha regains her innate poise. A near-death experience makes her appreciate life anew. Moral ambiguity and ambivalence chasten a deeply troubled woman to emerge erect after her ordeal, so much of it self-inflicted. Alisha could belong in Manhattan as much as Mumbai.

Paradoxically, millennials, both men and women, have aspirations that are influenced by the West and yet, there is a desire to be rooted in Indian soil and ethos. The anomie of alienation is frightening for the young of a society that has grown up in the embrace (often suffocating) of authoritative patriarchy and the safety net of the extended family. Often, this instinct to have a rooted identity is not given the importance it merits because of modernity's dazzling allure. It is perhaps one of the reasons why the young voted overwhelmingly for Narendra Modi's second term because he personified (for the converted) pride in being Indian—more importantly, being Hindu. A disquieting trend that negates the secular ideal so many liberals hold as the fundamental principle of Indian democracy. That is a different subject. The pervasive Hindu ethos of the 1990s blockbusters like *Hum Aapke Hain Kaun, Dilwale Dulhaniya Le Jayenge, Maine*

Pyar Kiya, etc. is undeniable. What we see now is an attempt to synthesize the new millennial aspirations with a comforting and comfortable cultural familiarity: the importance of faith and in this case Hindu, and respect for family bonds. The eternal conflict between individualism and tradition takes a sharper edge now. We see its refraction and reflection in the media. Cultural deracination is not really an option because it flies in the face of box office safety. Filmmaking finally is a business that will take 'safe risks' (an oxymoron) and push the envelope only thus far and no further. After parallel cinema's high watermark, portrayal of the millennial woman is testing the limits of departure from formulaic storytelling.

Millennial is not just a buzzword currently bandied about in every context. Millennials are setting the agenda for entertainment. Even though the film industry continues to be male dominated, the representation of women in films has become truer of changing social and cultural reality. Even Ekta Kapoor, the TV czarina who made Saas Bahu unending sagas the ruling genre, has produced non-formulaic films: Diwakar Banerjee's avante-garde triptych *Love Sex Aur Dhoka* (2010), Milan Luthria's *The Dirty Picture* (2011) that made Vidya Balan a huge star. Kapoor backed the release of *Lipstick under My Burkha* (2016) when a hidebound Censor Chief tried to ban it in India after the film won accolades abroad. Call it a canny producer's instinct for backing a potential blockbuster but this is happening with establishment giants like Yash Raj Films too. The largest number of rom coms with a difference—premarital sex, live-in relationships that were once taboo—were produced under its aegis.

The number of women working in the industry has proliferated. There have never been so many women directors in Bollywood. Gauri Shinde debuted with *English Vinglish* (2012) with diva Sridevi coming back to cinema. It was unthinkable a decade ago to make a stay-at-home mother of two the protagonist. She works hard to learn spoken English to win the respect of her husband and daughter who were dismissive of her for her lack of fluency in English. Zoya Akhtar crossed over into a league of her own with *Gully Boy* (2019), the slum to celebrity story of a Rap singer. Meghna Gulzar's *Raazi* (2018) is a sensitive story (based on real life) of a Kashmiri young woman who spied for the country by marrying into a Pakistani military family. Gulzar made it a humanistic story where the other side of the border is not demonized as Bollywood tends to (by male directors especially), catering to the hyper-nationalism that is assiduously fostered today. There are other successful women directors making films of their choice without succumbing to stereotypical stories with stereotyped characters.

There are women working as editors, writers, cinematographers, production designers, and marketing professionals. Their presence encourages women-centric films. It is the entertainment industry that first spoke of sexual harassment—Bollywood's worst-kept secret—and started India's Me Too movement. This enabled women from other fields to speak up. Whatever course this movement takes, it initiated a very significant conversation. It produced *Pink* (2016), a reaffirmation that No means No.

Women have partially freed themselves of stereotyped roles they are still mired in. Socialization is an entrenched process that tries to impose older, traditional role models, a permanent feature of the girl child's upbringing. This is challenged with quiet certitude by *Thappad* (2020) making it a landmark film. The millennial woman's evolution is a fascinating work in progress. It is exciting to watch and analyse for a long time viewer and critic of Bollywood, exploring significant changes that have made Hindi films vibrant and relevant.

The introductory chapter sets the change in context, relating cinema to the larger forces at work. Subsequent eight chapters group films by theme and examine both continuity and departures. The power of saying No; revamping of the staple romantic comedy; woman the hero; woman at work; sisterhood and female bonding; the subversives who reinterpreted classics. Finally, the unexpected ripples that brought back older divas into limelight again. Each chapter examines important films of the particular genre. Most of the films are familiar to regular Bollywood watchers so that connections are easy to make and follow the argument.

Introduction

A Changing Ecosystem Births the Millennial Woman as a Brand

The evolution of the 'new woman' can be traced in films from the late 1930s until the present within Bollywood, Parallel Cinema, and Indie films. The transformation of archetypes like 'the mother' or the 'rebel' illustrates the ways in which early constructs of womanhood and femininity have been shed or retained. Films like *Dev D* (2009) and *Sahib Bibi Aur Gangster* (2011) reference old classics while subverting icons popularized by them. The feminization of the industry through women directors and writers has sparked fresh narratives on womanhood.

Some commercially successful films have also broken social barriers. New gender norms are being pushed, aided by access to global media and brave new-age Indie and Bollywood films. However, the now dominant Hindutva discourse on womanhood exerts a push towards a regressive past. The path has been bumpy as filmmakers have had to contend with these contradictory forces.

The larger ecosystem continues to be patriarchal. Female writers and directors in recent years have discarded patriarchal plot structures and challenged the male gaze. Female protagonists embrace and flaunt their sexuality but the 'item number' continuous to objectify the female body. As the analysis of films over the years has shown, the millennial woman in Bollywood and in society at large is a work in progress as she constantly remakes herself within her social milieu.

The millennial woman—she is the medium and the message

Bollywood carries the heft of India's soft power. May be unacknowledged by culture theorists but its growing presence even in non-traditional markets and the respectability conferred by academia is validation enough. Bollywood has outgrown its adolescent angst to step out as a confident adult. Over time, we were resigned to foreign, specifically Western perception of Bollywood being synonymous with a meretricious idea of Indian popular culture. Bollywood has shrugged off the slings and arrows of culture purists with the swag of an arriviste. Even proud flag bearers of Hindi cinema's long and honourable legacy are reconciled to Brand Bollywood. The term that started with pejorative, rather condescending connotation of a derivative upstart, is now flaunted with no apology and much pride.

Now Bollywood is a global brand that endorses other brands. It facilitates the process of creating new brands. This process of branding is embedded in the entire process of filmmaking: from a feasible story idea to full-blown screenplay, to casting saleable stars (who are brand ambassadors of a range of consumer products that promote the myth of a lifestyle that's desired—lusted after, to be honest) followed by the marketing blitz on every platform available (and affordable). Celebrity valuation is measured by her/his brand equity. 'Only Virat Kohli and Deepika Padukone had a brand value of over $100 million in 2018', according to *Times Business* dated 15 May 2019. Top cricketers in India are on par with Bollywood stars for brand value. Advertising hits the jackpot when it combines cricketers and Bollywood for the wow impact. The trend now is to have real-life couples as brand ambassadors for the Aww-so-cute factor: like the Virat Kohli–Anushka Sharma ads as the real couple at someone else's wedding and Deepika–Ranveer Singh basking in post-marital comfort. These are consummately crafted mini-stories that reinforce the combined impact of star pairs. It reinforces Bollywood's brand equity.

Coming back to selling a film, it involves professionals who try to read the pulse through focus groups. The advertising budget of a reasonably big movie can finance a small offbeat film. Another inexorable fact follows: the fate of a film is decided over the opening weekend. Blockbusters carpet bomb theatres, edging out smaller films that survive through word of mouth, and wait for television release. Streaming giants (Netflix and Amazon) who have entered the Indian market, and now make locally tailored content free from the whimsical unpredictability of the censors, are more alluring avenues.

Female stars are integral to the marketing exercise. They are the seductive influencers while male actors strut their machismo. The men are from Mars and women are from Venus cliché persists in the way they promote the film and themselves. Promotion of the film is written into the contract. The heroine's projected persona is the desirable millennial woman, be it on talk shows anchored by comedians, talent shows across channels, social media, print, and electronic interviews. The millennial woman is both the medium and the message, in visible and subliminal ways. The impact of the screen image is sought to be extended through every available platform. She is the new brand, targeting susceptible young girls and women to embrace the implicit change in ambition, attitude, and achievement, along with the external image. The three A's are the millennial signature. The millennial woman may be a small fragment of a billion plus population but the concerted media effort makes her visibility and impact far in excess of the demographic size she represents. The millennial woman often stands out alone in carefully crafted ads, selling a dream that could be attainable. The product on sale? Hard to recall. That has caused concern to advertising theorists and practitioners. The burnished, seductive image beckons like a beacon of change, promising a possible makeover for other millennial and post-millennial women.

Mourning the loss of memorable ads of the past, like the Nirma jingle that made Hema, Rekha, Jaya aur Sushma part of collective memory, social commentator and advertising guru Santosh Desai writes: 'There is something quite unique about advertising, particularly on television, as a mode of communication. It is a compressed, highly stylised form of storytelling that implants desire directly and intrusively into our everyday lives… Advertising, seen one way, is a lie that speaks the truth. It exaggerates, embellishes and reframes reality in order to speak to desires that we are often unable or unwilling to articulate. It connects the banal with the lofty, embedding higher orders of meaning into small everyday actions of little consequence' (*Times of India*, 2 July 2018). Desai concludes that now, there are no ads that have mass appeal like the 1990s Nirma, for example. It is a Deepika, Priyanka, and Anushka holding centre stage, radiating luminous star charisma selling dreams and diamonds.

It is not just on a traditional medium like television that brand consciousness is sought to be imprinted. Digital platforms personalize the message, more so for the young who consume alternate media. The message is magnified from different sources and finds a fertile soil to implant new desires and definitions of desirability. The image of the millennial woman beams from large hoardings, infiltrates through intimate videos and films that use new technology with enviable élan. It is a package that has in-built room for individualization. Global meets local is the idea that has permeated urban life. Fusion is the new mantra: fashion, films, food, festive celebration where ethnic is eroticized and presented as the new chic. It is a fascinating, evolving process that sets the purist's teeth on edge. However, it marches on, relentless. Since the argument goes back and forth, finding connections across media and our engrossing film history, and social changes that are mirrored in Bollywood, the introduction is divided into sub-heads.

Is the millennial woman more than a media myth?

The buzz has not been shorn off the millennial, a portmanteau word that has been with us for two decades. The beginning of any century comes with its own wish list of hopes, ambitions. The desire to break from the past is implicit. True. Yet, there is something even more potent about the start of a new millennium, a more potent fin de cycle syndrome. (The phrase invites extension beyond its original meaning, to denote the cusp between the 19th and 20th centuries.) Entry into a new century is a mix of optimism, excitement, and also nostalgia, of bidding goodbye to the past—immediate and not so distant. An ethos ripe for experiment: a watered-down *Amrit Manthan*[1] of sorts, new images and norms rising from the churn where winds from the West speed up the internal turmoil.

---

[1] The mythical churning of the primeval ocean by gods and demi- gods to obtain nectar among other treasures

The millennial is not just something only the West is engaged with—culturally, economically, and politically. Undeniably, the millennial woman is part of an influential demographic in the US. She formed a crucial part of young voters in the US. Most young Democratic women chose Bernie Sanders over Hillary Clinton at the fiercely contested primaries. Feel the Bern, was the cry though older feminists like Gloria Steinem chided them for not backing a woman candidate. If not politically, this irreversibly globalizing paradigm has come to our shores too, at least the metropolitan areas, rapidly urbanizing small towns and even pockets of the hinterland. The millennial woman is a fact of Indian society, however minuscule the segment. When pop culture discovered this new potent image and incorporated it in its narrative, it demands exploration of all its facets and meanings, both significant and trivial.

Any new trend in the narrative doesn't exist in a vacuum, born of Immaculate Conception. It is an evolution from the past, tethered to some of the older concepts from which it seeks to break free, put down new roots, and take it into the future. Women have been honoured—burdened is more accurate—as keepers, custodians, and disseminators of tradition. Centuries of conditioning have made them internalize a legacy they are expected to pass on to the next generation. Patriarchy feels smug that they have made women, who are often victims, custodians. No longer, at least for a vocal minority that questions this legacy and asserts her right to self-hood, equality of choice, and opportunity. The keyword is choice. Choices offered by the information age to urban educated women are far more than any in the recent decades.

We are said to be on the move from the information age to the Imaginative Age according to futurist Rita J. King. The value adders in this projected future are imagination and creativity, more than analysis of data-based knowledge. Gautam Dalmia, chairman of the Dalmia Group, points out that 'this is evidenced by the entertainment industry top ladder making as much as the business elite' (*We Are the World, Times of India*, 3 May 2018). Though films have been awarded industry status, it has not made financing easy and transparent. In spite of it, industry Mughals and charismatic stars wield influence that is immeasurable, beyond financial clout.

Cinema and the on-going social change

Cinema works subliminally, altering perceptions, changing attitudes the way dripping water wears away resistance. These transitions are happening at a faster pace and visibly so. However, the important fact is that transitions are rooted, easing from the past to the present with the future embedded. Cinema draws upon many sources—collective memory, social reality, folklore, mythology—while minting new mythologies that absorb and reflect the flux of change. Most media are not trendsetters but quick to catch the trend. Cinema meets this constant challenge with varied degrees of success, which is both artistic and commercially viable. To quote Dalmia again: 'Each transition has the same challenge: the previous era's thinking lingers because individuals are hard wired with evolutionary instincts of the past' (*We Are the World, India Undergoes Multiple Transitions at Once, Leading It Is a Roller Coaster Ride. Times of India*, 3 May 2018).

It is difficult to predict where this rollercoaster is headed. It is not only because we are a young nation inhabiting an old civilization. We have learned to live with its contradictions over the years, if not centuries. In addition, the old adage, that India lives simultaneously in different centuries, can't be banished into the limbo of history by waving the millennial wand. We now live with the Me Too movement that has not lost momentum after the initial shock to pillars of the establishment: from cinema and television, journalism, and the corporate world. The year 2019 started with a shocking allegation. The phenomenally successful Raju Hirani, hailed as the new Hrishikesh Mukherjee for combining social message with wholesome entertainment, is the most famous of all accused celebrities. How the sexual harassment charge played out was the acid test for Bollywood. A test that Bollywood shirked. The question foremost in our mind was: will it act on it, or close ranks when the powerful is threatened? As expected, Hirani escaped unscathed. In spite of Bollywood's abject surrender to its powerbrokers, the Me Too movement can't be banished from the national conversation.

Yet, a paradox stares us in the face. How do we reconcile these empowered women who call out the famous and powerful men with the Shabarimala impasse? When devotees of the celibate deity deny entry to women of menstruating age? That too after the Supreme Court granted women this right? The result of the review petition is still awaited. The most discomfiting fact is that many of the devotees resisting court orders are women who have internalized the stigma of menstruation as unclean. This divide, between faith and a woman's right of entry, has made menstruation the subject of debate at prime time. Therefore, we have two groups: Happy to Bleed and Willing to Wait locked in ideological opposition. Neither side will yield an inch.

The change has been coming in steady dribbles. Even staid Indian TV, at the mercy of TRP chasing channels and ad revenue, opened up to hitherto taboo subject most visibly in advertisements. Even the racist Fair and Lovely ads spoke of its advantage in terms of getting a good job and the consequent self-confidence it gives a woman. The stress is not on her desirability in the matrimonial market. The underlying racist message persists, in a new guise of getting ahead in career. Implied is romance culminating in marriage. This ad is not limited to women now. It has crossed the gender divide and there is a Fair and Handsome version for dark-skinned men.

There are other changes in the all-pervasive Ad space. The sanitary pad was earlier discreetly positioned, with Anushka Sharma revelling in wearing white during 'those days'. Now there is Akshay Kumar chastising a husband smoking a 10-rupee cigarette while his wife is in hospital for *auratowali bimari* (women's disease). Kumar, post-*Padman* (2018) that did not do well at the box office because of its preachy narrative, harangues the man for letting his wife suffer from using unclean cloth during menstruation instead of giving her a non-branded sanitary pack for the price of two cigarettes. Then there are candid stories of young girls' awkwardness in school with homemade cloth pads and reminding mothers about the benefits (hygienic and psychological) of using sanitary pads. Menstrual health is advocated in press, TV, and ads in film theatres.

The Oscar for best documentary *Period; End of Sentence* is validation on the world stage of how Indian society has shaken off the shackles of shame. Menstrual health is part of the national conversation. The horrific gang rape of Nirbhaya in Delhi in 2012 forced parents to discuss the sensitive topic of rape and its brutality with young children who were hitherto shielded from this ugly truth. For better or worse, taboo topics are aired for discussion and debate. The morality police, however, had their way in banning condom ads from 6 AM to 10 PM. But sexually suggestive songs and dances get a free pass.

There have been a slew of liberal judgements from the proactive Supreme Court: decriminalizing same-sex relationships, striking down an anachronistic colonial law; adultery is not a criminal act anymore, again striking down a bequeathed colonial law that held the wife to be a possession of her husband whom another man wronged. The law has restored agency to women. How she exercises it in a conflicted society is the question. The answers could be influenced by media portrayals of contemporary women. Cinema and advertising are the prime influencers of change. Women in workplace settings are common. What is uncommon is the ad for a well-known brand of cement is a woman engineer in a hardhat at the construction site. The working woman is no longer confined to a desk job—even if the said desk has a state of art computer.

We are at a crucial junction of transition now because of a confluence of factors: globalization and liberalization of our economy that made Western entertainment accessible to anyone with a set-top box and dish antenna. Change is and was inevitable. It is a continuum. That is why millennial is more than a buzzword. No more a novelty, it has come to stay and become part of the conversation/discourse. The millennial woman is more than an aspirational image conjured up by marketing mavens amidst the constant thrum of consumerism.

So who is the millennial? Though definitions vary, it speaks of, for, and to a generation that has come to adulthood, or on the way to it, post-2000. There are neat generational divisions in the US: broadly post-war to baby boomers, flower power wielding hippies, feminists, millennial, and now post-millennial, a term coined by the Pew Foundation in a new research project. We have no identifiable replications in India. Pre- and post-Independent, Nehruvian, pre- and post-Emergency, the coalition age of regional parties, the beginning of liberalization leading to market economics, globalization of not just our economy but the influence of media through satellite TV, and then the internet are our broad categories.

To these markers we need to add the rise of Hindutva—religious, cultural, and political—culminating in the demolition of the Babri Masjid (6 December 1992) and the rise of triumphalist Hindu Right that resulted in unapologetic majoritarianism. In its wake came Love Jihad, anti-Valentine day vigilantism, mob lynchings of Muslims suspected of eating beef or transporting cows. It is a continuing attempt to impose a homogenous culture on a multi-cultural, multi-religious, and multi-ethnic society. We got mixed messages from Bollywood: soft Hindutva and assertion of Hindu family values from the Rajashri brand of films in the face of growing fascination that popular series like *Friends* and *Sex and the City* exerted on large sections of young and not so young audiences exposed to the multiplicity of bewildering choice offered by the magical set-top box. And now, by streaming platforms. The sexual freedom and autonomy of the young, more so of the women working in exciting New York, has had a subterranean effect over a generation and a half. The Punjabified imitation hit our screens as *Veere Di Wedding* in 2018.

Something even more radical happened in 2003. Mahabano Mody-Kotwal staged Eve Ensler's *Vagina Monologues* in Bombay to the utter shock of regular English theatre patrons, some of whom assumed it was a raunchy bedroom farce. Well-known names, Dolly Thakore for instance, were proud to be part of the ensemble cast. Initially, audiences did not know how to react and many squirmed in embarrassment but over time, the shock wore off. The words shouted from the stage were part of female vocabulary, no longer taboo. Since then, Mody-Kotwal has taken English and Hindi versions of the play (some modified for local sensibilities) to major metros and small cities. *Vagina Monologues* became part of the young woman's education. The play was also performed in Bengali (a dramatized reading) and Marathi, titled *Yoni Chi Guntavnuk*. It wouldn't be an overstatement to say that *Vagina Monologues* was this generation's simplified equivalent of *The Female Eunuch*. Most significantly, this was not confined to the English-speaking elite of the big cities who could speak about their sexuality, own and explore it without having to be evasive or apologetic. Taking the Hindi version of this radicalizing play to smaller towns gave women there a chance to have a conversation about what was a taboo subject.

The Millennial woman has arrived: Economically and culturally

The millennial woman here has grasped opportunities with greater alacrity than the man, because men born to an entrenched patriarchy have always been privileged and take their advancement for granted. The deprived seizes the moment with greater hunger and far more quickly than the privileged. We see the unfolding change in Bollywood. The more exciting, path-breaking films have been about women with new actors who have broken free of a mouldering stereotype. This rise of new kind of films—content-driven and entertaining—with the woman at the heart of the narrative has been steady and significant. Interestingly, the same period saw the decline of the Khan Triumvirate, forcing them to reinvent themselves and energize a different narrative vehicle. Even more remarkable has been the acceptance and subsequent popularity of a posse of extremely talented actors: Irrfan, quickly followed by Rajkumarr Rao, Nawazuddin Siddiqui (he is now set to play romantic hero), Ayushmann Khurrana, Vicky Kaushal. They are not conventional hero material but they have gone on to become successful heroes, both critically and commercially. Actresses breached conventional expectations first—a much more difficult and rare achievement in the exclusive boys' club that is Bollywood.

CNN 18's yearend conclave, the Actresses Roundtable 2017 rose above the usual platitudes floating on the optimism created by a mutual congratulatory mood. Women seem to be having all the fun, started off experienced anchor Rajiv Masand. They chorused an enthusiastic yes. Women who made the most noteworthy films of the year (*Lipstick under My Burkha, Tumhari Sulu, Shubh Mangal Savadhan, Toilet, Mukkabaaz, Secret Superstar*) concurred that it was women who made the difference while men stayed in their safe zones. (They acknowledged an exception in Ayushmann Khurrana who risked playing a young man with erectile dysfunction.) The stars at the table, Ratna Pathak Shah (*Lipstick under My Burkha*), Vidya Balan (*Tumhari Sulu*), Bhumi Pednekar (*Shubh Mangal Savdhan/Toilet*), Zoya Hussain (*Mukkabaaz*), Zaira Wasim (*Secret Superstar*) argued that this was a reflection of what was happening out there in society. They were adventurous in their choices and agreed that what they confronted was primarily patriarchy. It was spelt out with conviction and sardonic wit by Ratna Pathak Shah, doyenne of theatre and film. She challenged you to accept the older woman's right to her sexual fantasies, and what is more radical, to pursue them. Vidya Balan's unexpectedly wholesome hit, *Tumhari Sulu*, validated a middle-class suburban homemaker's late-blooming. She proved that there is nothing sleazy in hosting a late-night chat show, purring a sexy hello to all the lonely men out there longing for some sort of female company—even just a sympathetic voice over the radio. The film deconstructed the received image of the wife and mother to venture into and make a success of an unconventional career. The youngest Zaira Wasim was equally outspoken and analytical. She played a small-town Muslim teenager who not only becomes a singing sensation on YouTube, hiding her identity behind a burkha, but also catalyses her timid mother to walk out of an abusive marriage. Her film *Secret Superstar* was also a huge hit in China.

That was just a sneak peek into 2017. The year 2018 found two women at the directors' Round Table. Earlier years were remarkable too. Sunny Leone, adult film star, migrated from the US to India in 2012 and has acted in half a dozen films with a sexual slant but in no way soft porn. Leone has been featured in the media, minus the nudge-nudge wink-wink innuendoes. When a male TV anchor on a major channel turned offensively patronizing while interviewing Leone, he became the target not only of trolls but many Bollywood voices spoke up in defence of the star who conducted herself with dignity. This attitude is a vast change from the way the media interacted with and portrayed Mallika Sherawat, who thumbed her pert nose at the notoriety brought on by kissing her co-star Emran Hashmi (he was dubbed the serial kisser) many times over in many films. She was at her prime from 2003 to 2008. To what do we attribute such a noticeable change in attitude in under a decade? That our society, where Tinder is the favoured dating App, has become more broadminded? Dating and live-in relationships are not so uncommon in a society where arranged marriages are still the norm for a vast majority.

The past decade and a half have seen a remarkable emergence of the new post-feminist woman in society and thus in Bollywood. They are the daughters of India's feminist pioneers who fought on specific issues like custodial rape, equal pay for equal work, dowry deaths, right to inheritance, education, and work. The post-feminist generation takes these rights for granted, at least the urban minority privileged to have access to most of these rights. An accusation against the millennial generation in general is that they come to the workplace with a sense of entitlement and expect a special pat on the back for work they are routinely expected to do. This observation, made in the West where most of this generation will not get well-paying jobs as easily as their parents did, may not apply to the

Indian millennial. Jobs are few and applicants many. There has been no study of their attitude at the workplace.

The trend has grown out of a new globalized India where the educated working woman has become more self-assertive and unapologetic about life choices. This new feminism is different from the 70s pioneering feminism, which sometimes denied women their femininity in the pursuit of finding themselves, often through work. The millennial comes with a capital M—Me. It is as if she seeks to navigate through our collective schizophrenia as an individual of her time, not burdened with larger societal concerns and her obligation to right the wrongs that are all around her. She seems to shake it off with an elegant shrug. As a survival strategy to get ahead in life that poses its own particular challenges to her. The community of sisters united for a cause is so 80s for this self-centred woman. She represents, in a way, the selfie-obsessed generation. Narcissism doesn't feel the need to apologize.

But of course this image was transformed in the last month of 2019 and has spilt over into the dawn of the new decade. Young women are at the forefront of protests against a discriminatory Citizenship Amendment Act. It is a youth-led movement across the country demanding that the secular nature of our constitution be maintained by a government in a hurry to impose a Hindutva agenda that sees minorities, especially Muslims, as the Other—distrusted if not openly hated. This is an exciting new chapter in our social and political history that needs to be examined at great length. The predominantly Muslim women (women and men from other religions have also joined them) sitting in protest over two months in Delhi have made Shaheen Bagh the symbol and inspiration of similar sit-ins across the country.

Now to return to Bollywood of the first two decades. The film industry, even the Indie section, is run by the numbers game. Though the stars deny that ranking matters to them, and espouse bonhomie, there is no denying the hunger for the top slot in the pecking order. It is not enough to be just part of the A-lister club. Newfound confidence is engaged in subduing old inherited insecurities. The most revealing portrayals of this complex being have coalesced into Bollywood's emerging brand. Very soon, this millennial woman created a niche for herself and niche seeks a way to merge into mainstream. The glass ceiling still remains but this new image of the heroine is insulated from the censure of conservatives. *Queen's*

Rani is everybody's darling. And yet, old fears and new expectations gnaw at this hard-won confidence. Even indie cinema is a commercial venture. This dilemma adds an intriguing layer to the new heroine. It makes empathy and identification easier for the uneasy perch the heroine is poised upon. Into this state of uncertainty came a resounding, unequivocal validation of a working woman's right to befriend a man at a concert but say No when he tries to go further. *Pink* was a moment of truth for not only millennials but older generations too: No Means No. Nothing can take that right away from a woman. It needed to be said a long time ago but its time had come now. It left a lot of people confused about the mixed messages coming from popular cinema.

This rather unstable equilibrium was further shaken by tremors set off by the Me Too movement. Initially, the upheaval was mostly seen and articulated on social media. The ethos it has created has compelled both male and female actors to come out in support of the brave women who have spoken out. There won't be room for fence sitters and carefully couched generalities in the future. Willing to wound and yet afraid to strike is the perennial dilemma the acting sorority is caught in. Will this be fundamentally transformative? That is the insistent question that won't go away anytime soon.

This question has already emboldened a few actresses to get off the shaky perch. From pious generalities to condemnation of pervasive sexual harassment has been a big step for women in a male-dominated industry that operates like a cabal most of the time. Deepika Padukone, Priyanka Chopra, Kangana Ranaut, Alia Bhatt, Vidya Balan, Kalki Koechlin, Swara Bhaskar (the last two are the most forthright of them all) have spoken up in defence of women who have led the Me Too movement, as have director Meghna Gulzar and actor/director Konkona Sen Sharma. They have all spoken when asked for an opinion, not volunteered to set forth as latter day Amazons fighting for women's cause. At least, it nudged the actors to face and addresses a paradox that has long been part of Indian society. While priding ourselves on marching in step with modernity, we continue to be haunted by our entrenched schizophrenia when it comes to media portrayals of women, especially in mainstream cinema feared for its reach and influence. We are heirs to a deadly combination of Brahminical puritanism and Victorian prudery that has crippled generations with warped ideas of sexuality, more specifically female sexuality.

Modernity confronts its old enemy yet again. There is a primitive fear of unbridled sexually free women, threatening the very foundations of patriarchy. Like the Madonna and Whore binary of early Hollywood, we have the Devi and Devadasi binary to conveniently package women into safe pigeonholes. It also makes for easy storytelling with stereotypes the audience recognizes and responds to. It is convenient for moviemakers and comforting to the audience: their conservative values are not threatened.

Changing these inherited stereotypes is an on-going process, for both mainstream and alternative cinema, and its auteurs. The evolution of the millennial woman is where this journey is at now. It is an exploration of how to infuse the new social reality into acceptable images of modern women without alienating an audience looking for validation of their own deeply held, often subconscious, beliefs. Bollywood of the new millennium has ventured into this contentious zone with unexpected assurance, even savoir-faire. Even more gratifying is the acceptance from audience following this new genre's critical success. This is a story worth detailing. As for the future, the question is: will the millennial woman cut free from the moorings that are mired in patriarchal norms?

***

From Mother India to Badhai Ho!

Given the fact that film history is full of echoes from the past, iconic films and characters obviously offer a reference point for similarities and departures. To return briefly to the past to place the contemporary in context, the most enduring images of women of Hindi cinema flow from two fountainheads: the archetypal mother and the rebel looking for a cause. From *Mother India* (1957) to *Godmother* on the cusp of 2000, these have been unforgettable women as part of our pantheon. Radha of *Mother India* who becomes the site of nationalism and ironically, the matriarch who upholds Dharma that is basically patriarchal, is an enduring archetype. An archetype dwindles into a comforting stereotype over time like the weepy, self-sacrificing mother symbolized by Nirupa Roy in her many avatars. She is Radha transplanted to an urban ghetto in *Deewar*

(1975) in her most powerful role. Karishma Kapoor in *Fiza* (2000) takes on the mantle of moral conscience-keeper as the older sister of a teenage brother who has succumbed to Islamic terrorism post the Bombay riots of 1992–1993.

The archetypal Maa for all seasons has come a long way—from the deified *Mother India* to the coy, still attractive mother of the bride of *Hum Aapke Hai Kaun,* engaged in a demurely suggestive sing-off with the groom's uncle. He is an old admirer. The de-sexualized mother has now regained her femininity, but safely encased in traditional virtues. This 90s trend of young love ensconced in stifling family bonds and waiting for parental approval was Bollywood's instinctive answer to the first exposure to globalization. *Maine Pyar Kiya* (1989), *Hum Aapke Hain Kaun* (1994), and *Dilwale Dulhania Lejayenge* (1995) celebrate, not merely comply with, the supremacy of the family over the autonomy of young love. In *DDLJ*, Farida Jalal as the heroine's mother urges the beleaguered daughter Simran to run away with Raj, her determined suitor who has followed her from London to Punjab. She offers her jewellery to make this possible. She had suffered discrimination as a young girl when her brother's education took priority over hers. But the besotted lovers (Raj and Simran are the phenomenally popular pair admired and quoted as iconic lovers) are adamant that they will unite only with the father's approval. The girl's hand has to be bestowed by the father, a cherished possession to be passed on into another man's keeping. This reassertion of Indian patriarchal values was Bollywood's answer to combat the threat of indiscriminate Westernization.

This coincided with the rise of militant Hindutva, politically and culturally. Hindutva espoused the supremacy of Hindus and sought to homogenize a people divided by ethnic, linguistic, and cultural differences into a monolithic group to take on India's perceived 'Other'—the minorities. Christians are regarded as agents and disseminators of Western culture and Muslims are the hated invaders who subjugated Hindus. It is a historic memory that is not allowed to fade with time, but distorted and reviled as hate objects. Exponents made no effort to hide their political agenda and tried to infiltrate media to further this end through the garb of cultural nationalism. The humongous success of Bollywood hits of the 90s speaks of its acquiescence to, if not complicity with, cultural Hindutva. These films remain landmarks, to be quoted and paid homage, because they used all the big bazookas: charismatic stars at their peak, emotionally strong narrative, songs, dance, and strategic use of melodrama.

Now we have a new age mother in *Ki & Ka* (2016), where roles of husband and wife are reversed (superficially) for a contemporary Rom com. The self-contained, sophisticated mother of the ambitious career woman asks: did you have sex? It is spoken normally, similar in tone to a routine question: did you take your vitamins? The couple is dating and the mother wants to know if they are sexually compatible, without in the least sounding judgemental. The film tried too hard to portray a new kind of marriage to become a box office hit. But it did show how far the Indian mother has travelled in time. As does the earnest mother in *Shubh Mangal Savadhan* (2017), who tries to explain what happens on the wedding night with an elaborate metaphor that generates more laughs than sex education (which the girl really did not need!). The mother who triumphs over all stereotypes is Babli of *Badhai Ho!* (2018). The middle-class homemaker, given to hosting Mata ki Puja and Housie games, becomes pregnant when her older son is of marriageable age, and has a girlfriend in tow. She is ready to face the inevitable embarrassment but not to the extent of having an abortion. She believes it is wrong. *Badhai Ho!* forced us to confront the unspeakable: parents have sex. It also resurrected Neena Gupta's career in unexpected ways. A fine actress had to wait for this new openness about sex to find a role that matched her talent.

The rebel has always been with us: In both mainstream and parallel cinema

Against the archetypal mother, no doubt attenuated now, we had the first true rebel against societal oppression. Nirmala of *Duniya Na Mane* (1937) is Indian cinema's first domestic guerrilla who will not accept as husband the old man she is forced to marry. There are other rebels who follow and each rebel is unique, and rebels in her own way. There is specificity to her rebellion. She is not a rebel without a cause. These are individuals—unlike the spurt of women as dacoits in the 80s when there was a paucity of good roles for heroines while the Angry Young Man towered over the screen. The interesting, complex roles—played by Shabana

Azmi, Smita Patil, Deepti Naval, Rohini Hattangadi—all belonged to India's New Wave. In this vacuum, heroines from Rekha to Sridevi and others in between rushed to get into leather pants, jackets, and boots, wielded a whip and a gun, donned midriff-baring lehengas for a song, and dance to entice the villains. They were the female dakus, becoming outlaws to avenge wrongs done to their family. They were female counterparts of the male dacoits, oestrogen replacing testosterone, with no room for individuation of any sort.

Diffused angst of a generation is not part of the larger Indian ethos, which seeks a tangible relationship between cause and effect. Not for her the brooding angst of the Angry Young Man of the 70s. Even the recurring Amitabh Bachchan's angry hero was interpreted as symbolising post-Nehruvian disillusionment with the establishment, followed by the betrayal of the Emergency. Allied to this is the distinct, epic link with Karna's tragedy, of the hunger for legitimacy to halo the anti-hero with tragic grandeur. In its own way, the popular imagination demands logic, even as it happily laps up the illogicality of a Manmohan Desai's brand of lost and found brothers: another Indian paradox—great or trivial.

To return to the most haunting rebel of Indian cinema, we must seek the Guru Dutt oeuvre. He generously gives his female protagonist the same depth of despair and complexity as he did to the poet of *Pyasa* (1957) and filmmaker of *Kagaz Ke Phool* (1959). Choti Bahu of *Sahib Bibi aur Ghulam* (1962) is not content to remain cloistered in the *zenana* of a late 19th-century *zamindari* family while her husband spends all his time in the company of a *tawaif*.[2] To win him back, she goes against her values to drink with him in a futile effort to hold him. The tragedy of Choti Bahu is her descent into alcoholism even as her husband becomes partially paralysed. True tragic grandeur is denied the Indian film heroine. Sentimental suffering is her ordained fate, as the noble discarded mother or patiently waiting wife holding on to her *pativrata*[3] dharma, the harassed daughter-in-law meekly bearing her lot. Choti Bahu is the truly flawed tragic woman enshrined in Hindi film history.

As for other notable rebels, Nutan's Kalyani in *Bandini* (1963) leaves her village home to find the revolutionary she loves and ends up in jail

---

[2] Tawaif is Urdu word for a courtesan, accomplished in poetry, music, and dance.
[3] A chaste devoted wife.

for murder after she kills the lover's wife in a fit of rage. She seeks absolution for her crime in selfless service to a TB patient in jail. Waheeda Rehman's Rosie in *Guide* (1965) was a role she was warned against. She entered the skin of the dancer who walks out on a suffocating marriage to a self-centred archaeologist with no time for her or her art. Rosie is emboldened to take this revolutionary step in a small-town setting (where as a visitor, she is the object of much gossip and curiosity) by the local guide, a born charmer with questionable morals. Shabana Azmi's Rambhi of *Godmother* (1999) grows in stature and ambition from the hapless widow of a slain politician to become a skilful, amoral politician herself. The violent reaction from an outraged patriarchy targets Rambhi but she is aware of her own wrongdoing while pursuing power before a heroic death. Azmi's Pooja of *Arth* (1982) refuses to take back her repentant, unfaithful husband when she learns to stand on her own feet and finds her personhood. All these films use the mainstream idiom and narrative structure with supreme artistry. *Godmother* and *Arth* are the exceptions because they reveal the influence of parallel cinema.

Parallel cinema was more austere, and mostly neo-realistic in its approach. It avoided narrative elements like song and dance to mark out its difference from the mainstream. Most filmmakers used the woman protagonist both as a metaphor for the larger socio-political theme and as an individual in all her complexity. The remarkable women of parallel cinema had a bigger cause by implication; the personal was part of the larger political. But the millennial makes it solely personal. It is about her personal life. Is the personal political? Not in the ideological sense but at the broadest definition of political, it could be called the politics of personal choice because the world has gone beyond Francis Fukuyama's *End of History* thesis. We in India might question the triumph of Western liberal democracy but large sections of urban middle-class India have been converted to consumerism and left the big social battles to NGOs. Our films reflect this lack of ideological moorings, even of the easy pro-poor rhetoric that is so convenient to flaunt as serious intent.

Mainstream does not reflect the million mutinies—to use Naipaul's phrase—going on in our society. But it does notice and reflect the more manageable protests that are easy to accommodate in its favoured brand of storytelling. Bollywood ventured into the woman-with-a-cause film by Raj Kumar Santoshi, a director known for valorizing angst-ridden machismo through Sunny Deol's persona in *Ghayal* (1990). He amplified the theme with high-powered melodrama. *Damini* (1993) the eponymous middle-class heroine, risks her marriage and in-laws' reputation to get justice for a raped maidservant. Humiliation and every form of cruelty are heaped upon the brave heroine, till she converts the naysayers at the end. *Damini* followed the logic of self-righteous melodrama. *Lajja* (2001) was an overtly dramatic celebration of women's collective effort to confront oppressive social evils from dowry to female foeticide across India, from a small town to regressive badlands of the Hindi belt. The four women in the film bear names that are variations of Sita, the revered epic heroine. Obviously, the symbolic names are satirical by intent.

Public taste has since moved on—palatable realism or soft focus symbolism is the favoured option of filmmakers and audience. We now have candlelight vigils for anything from the memory of demanding justice for a murdered Jessica Lal and commemorations of Nirbhaya. Identity politics, the new battlefield in most of the world, is hardly acknowledged, let alone addressed. In this ideological vacuum, it is the personal life of *Queen*'s (2014) Rani or Reshma's struggle to make it big in *The Dirty Picture* (2011) that engages us. That's entertainment. With a purpose. We root for the individual woman, and if in the process, we also endorse an embedded feminist/political cause, that is collateral gain of sorts.

Indie films and the millennial woman

The millennial woman is an island of hard-won selfhood and agency in a country ranked almost at the bottom when it comes to the safety of women. The number of gang rapes and horrific incidents of child abuse—not sparing even infants—is the miasma through which the educated urban girl claws her way to self-hood. Pop culture, especially Bollywood that usually works like an anodyne to overwhelming social problems, celebrates the positive and buries insuperable social ills under an avalanche of pious clichés, when it deigns to acknowledge this discomfiting reality. It is easier to give more space to the woman in a traditional genre like the Rom com and sometimes invest in a female hero making her the centre of the narrative. It is fair to acknowledge that this needs conviction on the part of the filmmaker and not little courage, because Bollywood has not shed its patriarchal spots—the male leopard still struts through the commercial landscape and doesn't allow the rules of the entertainment game to change radically.

It is the indie film that has given birth and validation to the millennial woman. It is mainstream in form, adapted and reinvented, and parallel cinema in spirit and vision. A winning combination, when the mix is seamless and organic. The indie and mainstream are in a tentative embrace today, each borrowing from the other's strength. Indie needs the industry framework. Mainstream needs an invigorating injection of creativity from the new auteurs who know what appeals to the millennials. Today, filmmakers like Anurag Kashyap who started out as an avant-garde director, use music in innovative ways, as a separate track that has its own meaning and resonance. It seems they are more comfortable with music and traditional narrative tropes than their illustrious predecessors. The edgy style, of say *Dev D* (2009) and *Sahib Bibi Aur Gangster* (2011) makes irreverent homage a part of the narrative and they are not afraid to subvert classics of Bimal Roy and Guru Dutt. The way they portray iconic women like Paro, Chandramukhi, and Choti Bahu is crucial. Subversives across decades will be explored in a separate chapter.

Globalization is an on-going force

We overlook the fact that popular culture is never static or stagnant at our own peril. It reflects the zeitgeist, unless it wants to be banished into irrelevance and then extinction. Bollywood sets the tone, content, and limits of popular culture in India even in face of competition from television and content made for digital streaming platforms. Bollywood not just defines popular culture but is a monopoly with regional clones jostling for space in smaller markets.

This has to be amended as three recent megahits from the South made between 2020 and 2022: *KGF 1 & 2*, *Pushpa the Rising* and *RRR*—now glory in the new pan-Indian tag. Non-stop choreographed action, foot-tapping music, strong underdog heroes who rise to be mafia bosses (*RRR* is the exception, since it valorizes the bromance of two historical freedom fighters who had never met) have made them superhits in their dubbed version. Bollywood feels threatened. Hindi warriors have jumped into the

fray. Hindi, along with being Hindu, is proclaimed as markers of Indian nationalism. A language war erupted briefly till conciliating statements cooled tempers roused by linguistic pride. What is most notable in the Telugu and Kannada films are swaggering heroes who define machismo (bordering on toxic) with luxuriant locks and excess facial hair. They see women as objects of desire who can be abducted or only provide entertainment and the women internalize this demeaning depiction without even token protest. Bollywood of old has to change its formula and embrace the small, delightfully authentic auteur films that show a sustained growth. The definition of success has to be redefined. Is the Hindi film industry ready to face this challenge?
Bollywood has already embraced the malleable Indie into its fold by funding their films with a canny sense of what the audience is ready for and wants, even if doesn't exactly know what it wants. Just like a discerning niche audience was waiting for the parallel cinema, Hindi film audiences were ripe for something new, real, and relatable.

Change is essential for its survival and Bollywood has absorbed changes, from within and without. The most apparent change is the vanished dress code that was almost sacrosanct in the 60s through to 80s. The good girl wore Indian clothes—sari or salwar kameez while the bad girl flaunted her body in tight Western outfits. The virtuous heroine, who was unaware of her own sexuality, often got into ethnic exotica—clingy, blingy dancer's costume that bared the midriff rather generously—for the song/dream/fantasy sequences. Even if the 'misguided' heroine was initially Westernized, she turned into demure biddable wife material at the end. Sari clad, *mangalsutra,* and *sindur* in place. This dress code was understood by all and operated as the *lakshman rekha.*[4]

This *lakshman rekha* was practically obliterated by globalization. It began in the 90s. Kajal's Simran of *DDLJ* alternates between Western clothes outside and salwar suits at home. Now, the heroine mostly wears Western clothes, unless the milieu is traditional, but jeans have breached the iron code. When the star promotes her film or preens at award shows and other events, designer gowns are de rigueur. Except for Vidya Balan—who had to battle fashion police for years before success emboldened her to be herself—the sari, even at its sexiest, is largely absent.

---

[4] The line of rectitude drawn for the epic heroine Sita.

For years, Balan was the victim of body shaming until she rebelled to be herself. Body shaming shows no sign of being shamed out by political correctness. Fashionistas deem themselves above political correctness—here and the world over.

This makeover of the woman is fallout of globalization's pervasive secondary effect. Is it a coincidence that along with economic reforms of 1991 and the opening of the market, Indian women were frequently crowned Miss World and Miss Universe in the 1990s? Cynics ascribed this to the entry of cosmetics for the brown skin in India and beauty queens endorsed, in a subliminal way, the magical properties of these new brands made freely available in India. Women no longer had to hoard dollars and pounds to spend on lusted after cosmetics on a rare trip abroad, or cajole, flatter and beg homecoming NRI cousins, aunts, friends to bring them.

What was even more transforming was the new compulsion: women had to fit the slim, aerobicized body shape to carry off Western clothes. In long and mid shots, it was difficult to make out who the actress was—was it Raveena, Karishma, Twinkle, Shilpa, or any other rising starlet? They all seemed to roll off a conveyor belt. The voluptuous woman, a legacy from temple sculptures and celebrated in literature and erotic poetry, is not only inherent to the Indian concept of female beauty. It validates the basic fact: the normal Indian woman is broad hipped and heavy breasted, artfully draped in a sari that could both heighten sex appeal or modestly cover extra kilos. The preference for Western wear is not limited to films alone.

The other role model of how a professional woman ought to carry herself was and is the television anchor. Gone forever is the image of Salma Sultana on Doordarshan, in her impeccably draped sari with the border precisely in place across the torso with geometrical precision and the signature rose peeking from behind her ear. Other well-known newsreaders like Dolly Thakore, Luku Sanyal, Rini Simon Khanna, Usha Albuquerque, Neethi Ravindran were all dressed in saris. Now, anchors are almost uniformly in fitted jackets over blouses, business suits (even Hindi channels), Kurtas over pants. Sometimes salwar suits are acceptable. The sari is an exception. A dressy sari is reserved for Diwali and other such occasions to usher in a festive spirit.

This is the external change. Internal change is more subtle and almost insidious. The woman is allowed to be modern with a career and freedom to choose her partner. Yet, there are invisible but powerful limits to her freedom. That is because filmmakers don't want to rock the morality boat so vigorously that the film sinks. India is still a patriarchal country and the film industry is male-dominated. So this newly freed millennial woman walks gingerly between personal aspiration and societal approval. It is an old journey that this generation has embarked on anew. The gains are significant primarily because the millennial woman has been not only accepted but is almost the norm across genres. Public perception and commercial success riding in tandem are taking her to the winning post.

Indie cinema: Echoes from parallel cinema

The new heroine is not relegated to ploughing a lonely furrow like the brave revolutionaries of parallel cinema. The brilliant actors of the movement turned into stars courted by mainstream filmmakers but the films that propelled them into prominence were confined to niche audiences and festival circuit. This is borne out by the careers of Smita Patil, Shabana Azmi, Deepti Naval and their male co-stars, Naseeruddin Shah, Om Puri, Farooq Sheikh, and many others. These critics' darlings were the routine winners of National Awards and feted at film festivals. Theirs was the glory of New Wave cinema's artistic achievement but the dazzling superstardom with its attendant financial bonanza was denied them. We admire the richness of our rooted regional cinemas and sympathize with its stranded auteurs (when the parallel cinema movement faded away after its brief incandescence) who struggle to survive in a market-driven by bottom lines and box-office numbers. That is a different story that needs to be told because parallel cinema and its auteurs continue to be perceived as more authentic voices of Indian reality by discerning watchers at home and abroad.

Indie cinema is now filling this critical divide. Indie cinema's steady growth and increasing success have infiltrated the mainstream—except for diehard resistors—and demands to be taken on par, if not more seriously, than the star and formula-driven mainstream and male superstar vehicles of tailored entertainment. Indie is no longer niche and its influence is far more pervasive and visible than that of its predecessor, the parallel cinema of 70s and 80s. It speaks to, for, and of the millennial generation: shaping the narrative, and gaining acceptability of the new post-feminist woman.

There are intriguing similarities and departures in the way the two movements have affected the mainstream. Both have acted as disruptors, subversives, and iconoclasts, as will be explored in subsequent chapters. *Bhumika* and *The Dirty Picture*, *Mirch Masala* and *Lipstick under My Burkha*, *Arth* and *Queen*—this pairing gets more intriguing. This brings us to the millennial woman, her predecessors and the burgeoning post-millennial generation that has yet to arrive on Indian shores.

Indie filmmakers have not totally eschewed traditional narrative tropes as a matter of principle. Songs, unless it is a festive/wedding, club/party scene, are mostly in the background to underline mood and complement emotion. This frees the actor to explore other facets of her craft. It is not an exaggeration to say that the Indie film has made actors independent of the expected given image and acting style that goes with it; they have the luxury and leeway to bring nuance to conformity. The primacy of engaging the audience is never lost sight of. This audience is not confined to the big cities—they have other avenues of entertainment—actually, it is the B and C towns that fill the coffers in the long run. Yes, multiplexes in metros are the initial indicators of box-office returns and they are the first acid test. Small town viewers are equally important because they sustain the film's longevity. Even more crucial is their acceptance of the heroine who seems to be breaking norms. Some films of course do better in metros than small towns. Things do even out in the long run.

Though the millennial woman is automatically equated with an urban, Westernized woman, she can inhabit the small town, with more traditional roots but the big change is the attitude. The strong rural woman—*Ishqiya* (2010), *Anarkali of Aarah* (2017), *Parched* (2015)—reflects this change. Even in *Band Baaja Baraat* (2010), an early trendsetter, Anushka Sharma's Shruti is a typically lower-middle-class Delhi girl but she has big dreams. Attitude is the crucial difference that makes her transcend her particular milieu and life situation.

A reverse process, different from parallel cinema, is at work now. Parallel cinema stars were welcomed by the mainstream, though the roles a Smita or Shabana played were different from those of Hema Malini or Rekha. Established stars now venture into new terrain, though the narrative is not avant-garde as some parallel films were. The line between mainstream and indie films is blurry. These films and their makers are personal, not in the auteur sense that set apart Shyam Benegal or Govind Nihalani or Adoor Gopalakrishnan or Girish Kasaravalli from the mainstream formula then prevalent. Indie auteurs are personal in the way they use familiar tropes, songs, and dances, to express a modern sensibility that wants to reinvent the formula. Unlike the larger social concerns that were driving forces of parallel films even when they told stories about individuals, a large section of Indie films concentrates on the concerns of the Me generation. Both the men and women of these films are all about I, Me, Myself. The interesting, telling impact of films like *Queen, The Dirty Picture, Band Baja Baraat* et al., is the ease with which they connect with the viewer. That all important audience identification gives these Indie and mainstream offshoots their validity: emotional and societal.

One brief comparison encapsulates the essential difference. *Chakra* (1981) told the story of Amma (Smita Patil), a widow with a teenaged son, caught in two relationships with two very different men: a steady truck driver who treats her like a wife, and with whom she finds security; the other is the cocky, show off small-time crook whose dalliance is undependable, and more worrisomely, holds an irresistible attraction for her dazzled son. Amma's precarious existence reflects the grimy truth of a Bombay slum at the mercy of bulldozers at any time. In *Manmarziyan* (2018), Taapsee Pannu's Rumi is torn between two men. You could call the first man the love of her life: a wannabe strutting musician with whom she has great sexual chemistry and she has a roaring affair with him, unmindful of the gossip endemic to an Amritsar mohalla. The DJ has nothing but his swag and unrealistic ambition. He cannot settle down and runs from commitment. The NRI banker who she marries makes no demands and waits for her to make the marriage work. He is older, more understanding, and pragmatic. The open end, after they annul the marriage, hints at a possible reconciliation through a tentative friendship is a classic throwback to the attractions of ambiguity. Ambiguity is truer of contemporary mores and admission that a woman can be attracted to two very different men at the same time.

The social settings are poles apart and Rumi has more agency than Amma. Yet there is a connection across decades and situations. Rumi has the luxury of choice, something she has to resolve for herself. *Manmarziyan* was not a commercial hit but was liked by Anurag Kashyap loyalists. The significance lies in the growing audience for such non-conformist films. It is an ethos that encourages stories that would have outraged conservatives in earlier times.

The making of the millennial woman

We now inhabit a film landscape where Bollywood towers as the sole identifiable brand even when thriving mainstream regional films offer tough competition. The all-India tag that comes with the brand gives it an unbeatable and rather unfair advantage. What goes into making the Indian millennial woman? A transplant from the West or an evolution rooted in native soil that had been seeded with global ideas? A bit of both: influenced by the West and yet, a natural progression of changes over the past few decades that telescope history and social change in a remarkably short period of the vast span of history. What took a century earlier now seems to happen in a couple of decades. The all too palpable result of globalization and the speed of information are self-evident facts.

The evidence is all around us, more obviously in the metros and other large cities. Social changes—rapid ones for an ancient civilization inhabiting the core of a modern nation-state—percolate into popular media is the conventional belief. Trickle Down effect, so to speak. Something different—almost radical and instant—seems to be happening in the age of internet and social media outreach when the young are addicted to their phones. Facebook and Instagram are a large part of this wired existence. Changes are more horizontal, spreading out from metros to small towns and semi-urban places. So what is au courant in Bombay or Bangalore is part of the social discourse in Satara and Nanjangud almost instantly though the sophistication of the urban elite gives way to wide-eyed wonder and hesitant imitation, something social scientists see and not yet theorize perhaps.

What is not so apparent is how this change has infiltrated into small towns. The change is visible in the externals—dress, demeanour, and deportment—which are easy to dismiss as superficial, and not affecting the fundamental bedrock of tradition and socialization that has gone on for generations. That is a facile assumption. The bedrock is being shaken by new ideas and aspirations. The number of young working women in metros, cities, and small towns is increasing. Social and attitudinal change can't be measured in cold numbers and statistics. It is a reality that is palpable and can be experienced in a variety of ways. Take Thomas L. Friedman's *The Earth Is Flat*. He is fascinated by the small-town young women who throng to IT hubs like Bengaluru, Pune, Gurgaon and live on their own, away from parental supervision. Men have always migrated for education and jobs to the cities. What is remarkable now is the number of women who have gravitated to where the jobs are.

This is something the world has noticed. *The World Is Flat: A Brief History of the Twenty-first Century*, Thomas L. Friedman's 2005 international best-seller validates what has been happening in India, specifically Bengaluru. His thesis is that globalization has made the world a level playing field in the early 21st century. He uses the anachronistic title as a metaphor for opening up developing economies to commerce, giving all competitors equal opportunity. Friedman has appeared in documentaries where he interviewed young women from small towns who came to India's Silicone City. They share apartments and are thrilled with the new freedom their jobs have given them. This transformation is happening in not just metros but also large cities with a hinterland teeming with the young, restless, and ambitious.

This visibility in the cities contradicts the data of decrease in the number of employed women. The few that have got the desired jobs have pulled families out of lower to middle-class professionals. Women are in the media (print, electronic, television, and film in various capacities), hospitality, travel, marketing, advertising, banks, teaching, IT. It is true they are at entry and mid-level. Very few, if any, break the glass ceiling. The minority of successful career women enjoy the coverage given by lifestyle supplements of the pink papers. *Panache,* in early January 2019 highlighted the freedom of handpicked single women who travel solo, choose to remain single and enjoy a life that is far better than that of their mothers. This is the tiniest of a tiny fragment. Numbers of such women are growing.

The following employment trend carried by *Economic Times* is sourced from Employment and Unemployment Survey, NSSO (various rounds).

'While several recent studies have highlighted low female WPRs in urban India, we present evidence to show that urban women are beginning to enter the labour market in greater numbers.'

'The number of women working and seeking work grew by 14.4% annually between 1991 and 2011, even though the population of urban women grew at only 4.5% during the same time period, according to the total number of women *in the workforce* increased more than three-fold, from 9 million in 1991 to 28 million in 2011, while the number of women *seeking or available for work* increased more than eight-fold, from 1.8 million in 1991 to 15.5 million in 2011.': Census 2011.

The article goes on to say: 'This means that the number of women in the workforce in 2011 would have been higher by more than 55% if these 15.5 million women were able to find jobs. In comparison, the male workforce would have increased by only 13% if the 14 million men seeking or available for work found employment. This indicates a significant shift in women's participation in the labour market in urban areas since 1991.' The projected numbers may or may not come true but the trend is undeniable.

The millennial is here to stay

The trend, of the veneer of Westernization that has filtered down to hitherto conservative segments, is there for all to see. Something as clichéd as the near universality of jeans and kurta/T-Shirt even in small towns where the norm for college girls and young women was the salwar kameez, sari and (half sari in the South) does merit more than a cursory acknowledgement. Anything connected with the reach of films in general and Bollywood in particular is first manifest in clothes. It is still the trendsetter. Attitude follows in its wake, as ripples on the surface. Some of the deeper effects take time to percolate into this fertile ground. Television, social media, and the smartphone—which is almost a physical extension—have prepared the ground.

The ecosystem—a promiscuously used word for anything and everything—is a necessary cliché to describe the paradox of dizzy change coexisting with outworn tradition that describes Bollywood of the last two decades. More women behind the screen enhance the confidence and sense of self-worth of the heroine. Gayatri Rangachari Shah and Mallika Kapur's *Changemakers* profiles 20 women who now work not only as directors, scriptwriters, editors (these numbers are impressive) but in fields as diverse as cinematography, stylists, lyricists/dialogue writers, market and studio executives, producers, art directors. There is even a gaffer and script supervisor. The successful women directors are more visible and greater in number than any time in Indian cinema: Zoya Akhtar, Farah Khan, Meghna Gulzar, Gauri Shinde, Ashwini Tiwari Iyer, Alankrita Shrivastava, Leena Yadav, Konkona Sen Sharma, and Kiran Rao (the last two with one film each so far). Kangana Ranaut, always doing the unexpected, took over the directorial reins halfway through her ambitious *Manikarnika*.

Scriptwriter Juhi Chaturvedi has revolutionized what is acceptable in entertainment: a sperm donor, or a constipated old man as heroes. Bhawani Iyer is the co-writer of *Raazi*, a small film that crossed the new benchmark of 100 crores for a film to be considered a hit. Sanyukta Chawla Sheikh wrote *Neerja* and *Parmanu: The Story of Pokhran*. Women producers like Ekta Kapur and Priti Shahani backed departures from the formula. A-listers Priyanka Chopra and Deepika Padukone have turned producers of non-formulaic films. It is a trend started by Anushka Sharma with an impressive track record of making strong content-driven films, some of them veering off into quirky whimsy. The adventurous spirit is alive. Whether it is part of, or reflective of the political and social churn of the times, is a moot question.

There is another remarkable change. The received wisdom that held true from the time of feminist critique of the media is the all-prevailing male gaze. It is time to move on from the set definition because there is also the female gaze and homoerotic gaze that is part of the viewing process. Women have internalized the male gaze and many are comfortable conforming to it. For consumers of visual pleasure, the entertainment industry satisfies and panders to a complex of demands: the sculpted male body offered to frenzied fans, both male and female (Salman Khan's shirtless state in every film, now Tiger Shroff offers a younger body) and it also meets the narcissism of male stars flaunting gym-toned abs. Thus the male gaze seems to have come full circle but only superficially. Because you don't see the camera splintering the star male body into so many body parts as it does to the actresses be it a starlet or a superstar.

The portrayal of woman as a sex object is a given in Bollywood. The only difference now is the in-your-face packaging of top heroines rushing to do hyped item numbers in films where they have no acting roles.

Earlier, the vamp gyrated to cabaret numbers while the heroine remained chastely demure. Then came the era of Sridevi and Madhuri Dixit. They swung a hip and heaved the bosom 'as part of their screen role'. Whether it was *Choli Ke Peeche* or *Dhak Dhak karne laga*, the song was part of the narrative, which told us something about the woman who danced for our delectation. Along with the disappearance of the well-defined dress code, the line of acceptability has fallen in inverse proportion to the rising hemline and expanse of bare midriff. Be it *Kajra Re* or *Chikni Chameli* or *Fevicol*, neither Aishwarya or Katrina or Kareena had any other part to play in the film. The race among top heroines to perform these raunchy numbers confers glitzy, if questionable, respectability on obscene gyrations that leave nothing to the imagination—be it in lyrics, movements or hardly—there costumes that vie with the camera for fragmenting the female body. This is the most objectionable part. When the woman's body is split into various body parts, it denies autonomy, let alone agency. As a footnote, Karan Johar who produced *Agnipath* (2012) of which *Chikni chameli* was the highlight, has apologized for it.

When you now see Swara Bhaskar masturbating in *Veere Di Wedding* (2018) without any qualms of modesty—she imperiously puts out a hand to stop her shocked husband when he unexpectedly comes home—the special item song really has no place in the narrative. It has morphed into the whacky video of *Stree* (2018) that was on TV as an advertising hook months before the release. Kriti Sanon's invitation *Aao kabhi haveli pe* to a skeleton out of boredom with her dating App is not part of the film *Stree*, a horror comedy with a feminist angle. The spooky spoof was an instant success. So, even the good old sales prop is in for a remake as a sign of the times.

Has the millennial woman truly arrived? Or is she a work in progress? The next decade looks promising. We may get our answers then.

1
No Means No

This was a long time coming. Finally, we had two films, *Pink* (2016) and *Anaarkali of Aarah* (2017) *very* different in locales and narrative style, that declared that when a woman says no, she means no. A syllable that is a whole, irrefutable sentence. It is more than simple semantics. A familiar phrase gains immense weight and magisterial gravitas in Amitabh Bachchan's baritone. *Pink* states this without clouding it with any ambiguities and apologies that a woman can at any point of time say No to sexual advances—even if she had engaged in friendly banter, smiled, touched his arm briefly during conversation, dined and drank with him, accompanied him to his room but when he tries to go further, it is her inalienable right to refuse with one word: NO. These are all the 'encouraging' signals Minal Arora (Taapsee Pannu) is accused of by the lawyer who knows how to insinuate immorality. His tone, choice of words, and arguments are all calculated to imply that this is what society at large believes. And that includes all those present in the courtroom—except for the three women in the dock and their lawyer. These are brilliantly written and enacted scenes, especially by Prashant Mehra (Piyush Mishra) to reveal how the victims of molestation and death threats are portrayed as high-class prostitutes. That is the very reason the victim does not go to the police because she will be verbally raped in public.

Pink is the corrective to how our popular cinema has portrayed the whole wooing and mating game in film after film with a subtext that is insulting and demeaning to women. For ages, our audiences have been bombarded with the subtextual message that when a girl says no, she is actually signalling yes. Only modesty and cultural conditioning prevent her from saying yes. All the so-called wooing by the loutish hero is actually sexual harassment through song, gesture, arrogant body language, and dialogue loaded with double entendre, or couched in flowery avowals of love. This was the norm in popular films through the 60s and 70s. It lingered on until the language and idiom of romance changed in the 90s. Even as the independent, urban working girl was a social reality, at some subliminal level, it was a challenge to patriarchy. There was, and still is, an uneasy coexistence between this independent woman and conservative society that appropriates the right to judge her character, morals, and availability through the lens of her clothes, the time she gets back home, and the way she interacts with men. The lens gets into zoom mode if the girl is living alone. If three young women share a flat, the implied speculation goes further to suggest a brothel.

Director Aniruddha Roy Chowdhury calibrates the narrative precisely to counter these assumptions. *Pink* follows the thriller format: economic with details of what exactly happened at a concert where the three young women Minal Arora, her roommates, Falak Ali (Kirti Kulhari) and Andrea (Andrea Tariang) meet Rajveer (Angad Bedi, a privileged young man with a powerful politician for uncle) and his friends—all seemingly civilized young men. Like a thriller, we are not privy to all the details of the incident that has disturbed the girls to such an extent that they do not want to talk about it, even with each other in the privacy of their home. Home is a flat in a gated enclave small enough for some neighbours to keep track of their comings and goings and irregular timings. That is enough to flag suspicion, indicated by a few faces at the window. A mysterious senior citizen who walks in the park nearby, his prominent black mask (thanks to Delhi's pollution) contrasted with a shock of white hair and a laser stare make him look like an alien from sci-fi for a startling instant. He watches Minal on her morning jog and later sees her dragged off into a car and driven away in the gloom of the night. He cannot stop this abduction but notes the car details. Minal is dumped back at her gate, frightened out of her wits by their roughing her up and threats to withdraw the police complaint she lodged. Even for making the complaint, she has to overcome police apathy and evasion, considering Rajveer's connection. The scene in Surajkund police station is full of implied threats in a matter of fact way. The tone in which the cop says Madamji to Minal's older colleague and his words 'you seem more experienced' are loaded with insults. From petitioner, Minal is made an accused for solicitation and lethal assault. She is taken away by the cops, and her friends are left bewildered. The mystery man, now revealed as retired ace lawyer Deepak Sarin (Amitabh Bachchan), tries to get Minal bail but can't since it is Friday and you can't apply for bail during the weekend. An arrest precisely timed, as he notes.

These details and perfect casting make for brilliant content (written by Ritesh Shah, producer Shoojit Sircar, and director Roy Chowdhury) perfectly executed. Sarin initially lets go of cross-examination to the bewilderment of his clients. Rajveer's lawyer Prashant Mehra pillories Falak as a girl who has been borrowing money from an older divorcee (they were in a relationship). Innuendoes come down like a ton of bricks on Minal who doesn't live in the Karol Bagh home of her parents because her uncertain timings (she is a dancer with an entertainment group) might disturb them. Not a word or gesture and behaviour of that eventful night are spared from expert milking for innuendo. On the stand, they are all uncertain and vulnerable because they have not been subject to coaching. Now, Sarin wants yes or no answers to questions that sound like an inquisition. Are you a virgin? Minal is speechless. He establishes she is not a virgin and had sex at nineteen with her boyfriend. Was she forced? No, because I liked him, she mumbles in a low faltering voice. Her father leaves the court at this time.

Earlier, the judge wants to know if these questions are relevant and if so, the session could be in camera. Sarin insists they are relevant and need to be asked publicly. Sarin's purpose is now clear. He wants to establish that she had sex because she liked her boyfriend and when she stopped Rajveer with No, she meant it. Time now for Bachchan's purple patch that nails our double standards and the latitude given to boys from 'good' families. His indictment is precise and cutting; sarcastic in his feeling sorry for the poor misguided young men and a set of rules for girls that curtails her independence. It is an indictment that is a resounding slap in society's face. Any woman, be it a girlfriend, an acquaintance, or even a wife, cannot be touched against her will. A long poem recited in Bachchan's reverberating baritone is heard in voice over. To quote one of the lines: '*Tu khud ki bojh mein se nikal, Tu kis liye hataash hai*'.[1] The time to unburden women of their despair has come.

Pink is a landmark in our cinema because it establishes that a woman, even if she is a modern working woman wearing Western clothes and socializes with men, is not to be molested or sexually assaulted. *Pink* is

---

[1] Emerge out of your self-imposed burden, why do you despair?

our equivalent of *The Accused* (1988), the Jonathan Kaplan classic. Jodie Foster is the victim of gang rape at a bar. *The Accused* affirms that whatever her profession, however short her skirt, however many drinks she has had, why she was in the wrong place at the wrong time doesn't mean she can be the victim of gang rape by a bunch of horny men who think she is asking for it. Jodie Foster's Oscar winning performance nailed the patriarchal excuse. Broody, bipolar Sarin comes back from retirement to fight this just cause. There is an implied criticism that Minal and her friends needed a male saviour. If they had a lawyer, say like Indira Jaisingh, would *Pink* be more significant? There are many committed and capable women lawyers for the filmmakers to draw upon. There is a counter to this valid feminist argument: the most damning indictment of patriarchy is most effective when it comes from an eminent patriarch. By patriarch, I mean a most eminent actor who is a legend in his lifetime, not that he is a spokesperson for patriarchal values. Whether Mr Bachchan holds the same views in personal life is not relevant to the argument. The fact that the many TV awards for best actor were won by Amitabh Bachchan for *Pink* speaks of his credibility with the general audience. It accepts his stature as the industry's patriarch. To take the comparison with *The Accused* further, Kathryn Murphy, the district attorney who prosecutes the rapists, is played by Kelly McGillis. Hollywood did not need a Jane Fonda or Meryl Streep. *Pink* needed Amitabh Bachchan to send the message home to an audience steeped in patriarchal values.

Minal's No is not confined to *Pink*. Taapsee Pannu who plays Minal, the girl in the dock, becomes a lawyer taking on society at large in *Mulk* (2018). Here, she is Aarti, the Hindu daughter-in-law of a Muslim joint family living in Varanasi. Murad Ali Muhammad (Rishi Kapoor) is the head of the family, a well-respected lawyer living in perfect amity with his Hindu neighbours. When his nephew is caught and shot as part of a terrorist group, the family is not only ostracized by erstwhile friends but Murad Ali and his brother end up being accused of terrorism. Aarti, who lives in London with their older son, is visiting for her father-in-law's sixtieth birthday celebration. Aarti's passionate argument in court, in support of her father-in-law, is a loud no to prejudice that brands an entire family, and by implication a whole religious group, with the current favourite word of damnation: anti-national. Aarti (effectively restrained Taapsee Pannu) names the whole herd of elephants in the room.

The entire case is based on prejudice, on Us versus Them, she points out with unerring accuracy. The device of making a practicing Hindu make this argument works well, because it forces us to confront our own prejudice. A devout, bearded, and skullcap-wearing Muslim is as patriotic as the *janev*-wearing,[2] *tilak*-anointed[3] Hindu. Our society does not ask the Hindu to prove he is a patriot. But the Muslim is forever asked to choose between his *quam* (community) and *mulk* (nation): a binary that a Muslim is saddled with. That is the tragedy. Director Anubhav Sinha's entire film silently says a NO that needs to be heard. No can be amplified to go beyond a woman's no to sexual harassment, to speak to the larger bias against minorities. It is significant that it is a Hindu woman's voice that says No.

The No of today needs to be set against the shoddy history of Bollywood when it comes to the portrayal of rape and its devastating effect on the survivor. In 1980, a very respected filmmaker with his own much respected banner made *Insaaf Ka Tarazu* that was ostensibly meant to speak for a rape victim but in overt and covert ways condones the first rape. B.R. Chopra, with a track record of making socially progressive films, adapted the B-grade Hollywood *Lipstick* (1976) that is a capsule definition of sexploitation. The sick film, castigated for its crudity, implied forced fellatio and anal rape. Chopra's Indianized version sanitizes the original as far as the precise nature of crimes goes but keeps the spirit intact. Facile symbolism is his forte. So his heroine is named Bharati but she is presented as a Westernised model who poses in skimpy clothes, mixes easily with men who admire her though she has a fiancé. Zeenat Aman who was the most Westernised actress of that time was aptly cast to underline the evils of reckless Western ways. She lives alone with her school-going sister. Ramesh (Raj Babbar at his sleazy worst) is a rich businessman smitten by her charms and woos her with parties on his yacht. He is presented as a thwarted lover, rejected by a woman who is presumed to be free and easy, not a lecher who will go to any extent to bed the woman he fancies.

Finding her alone at home, Ramesh trusses her up—it is so repulsive from memory that I could not bear to watch it again for getting the details right—and rapes her. The younger sister who happens to come home

---

[2] The sacred thread worn across the torso by a Brahmin
[3] Vermilion mark on the forehead worn by pious Hindus

at some point is manipulated to say that it seemed consensual. Bharati is humiliated during the trial after she had accused Ramesh of rape. His lawyer, played by the veteran Shriram Lagu, says at one point that women like her are a blot on society. I remember the applause in the theatre when I saw the film. Her fiancé Ashok's (Deepak Parashar) parents disown her after this public shaming.

Ramesh is finally shown as depraved monster two years later as he tries to molest the younger sister (Padmini Kolhapure) when she comes for a job interview to his Pune factory. Bharati has shifted from Bombay to Pune. This time, Bharati—who works in a shop selling guns—shoots the rapist dead and stands trial again. She is now dressed in a plain lavender coloured sari, her head covered and confesses that she killed the monster, to avenge the violation of another innocent. In a travesty of our justice system, she is anointed with kumkum by Ashok's repentant parents—they are ready with a kumkum container in court—who are now proud to have such a brave bahu. This wholly manipulative film, high on rhetoric and melodrama, was a success. It speaks of our audience taste for swallowing the progressive claims of a respected filmmaker like B.R. Chopra. Hypocrisy's heyday, in other words. That hypocrisy is being not only addressed but confronted with a rare degree of honesty from the perspective of today's young women, be it an educated Delhi girl working and living away from home, or a small town folk dancer used to being the cynosure of public gaze. Both these women, so different from each other in habitation, profession and experience are as one when it comes to fight for the right to say no.

Pink was widely admired and perhaps not so widely seen. At least, it got a lot of conversation going and initiated some degree of introspection into our double standards and pre-judging women on superficial grounds. Sadly, *Anaarkali of Aarah* (2017) won favourable reviews for its gutsy truth telling and Swara Bhaskar's riveting performance that made the life of a Bhojpuri singer so well grounded in reality. It was not seen by many though the film is essential viewing. Molestation is not just the problem of urban working women. It is even more prevalent in small towns of the hinterland. Even more so if you sing raunchy songs and dance without inhibitions in public. Anaar (Swara Bhaskar) is one such dancer who, as a pre-teen, saw her mother shot dead at a performance during a celebration. Bihar's tradition is to patronize such singers and their troupe of musicians at celebratory events, private ones like weddings, or public shows. A good performer is always in demand and she is a minor celebrity in her hometown and neighbouring areas. If she has a sexy swing to her walk and can dismiss ogling louts with a scornful stare, she is both feared and desired. For her, being stared at is part of her profession. She is aware of the male gaze and cultivates immunity to it. Anaar's career is managed by Rangeela (Pankaj Tripathy) whose job entails keeping the moneyed clients happy, bow and scrape before the important guests who he dare not alienate however badly they behave. The salaaming culture is a necessary part for survival in the small town. Keeping up the *ji hazoori*[4] tradition of servility before the powerful is ingrained in him. But not Anaar. She will sing lewd songs and dance to them with abandon but no one can dare touch her.

The biggest lecher in town is the vice chancellor of a rather grandly named university. Dharmender Chauhan (Sanjay Misra), addressed obsequiously as VC is not only lecherous but also an alcoholic. A bottle by his side during a performance where he is the chief guest, this so-called educationist goes up to the stage and starts touching Anaar inappropriately. She politely asks him to desist but he continues and wrestles her down to the floor while the rest of the audience looks aghast. *Hum bazaaru nahin. Hath mat lagana,*[5] she warns. Freeing herself, still resisting the persistent drunk molester, she slaps him and walks off the stage. Anaar is determined to lodge a police complaint but the local cops try to dissuade her since they don't want to antagonize the powerful VC. Anaar marches into his office and gives him a mouthful while the VC thinks this is the time to conciliate her. She is obdurate and doesn't listen to Rangeela begging her to let things be. The result? When she goes into her bathroom and gets undressed, the cops barge in and pick up a semi-nude man lurking in the bed. Anaar is marched through the streets and charged with prostitution. Out on bail courtesy Rangeela, Anaar is not the kind of girl to take this false charge lying down. She confronts VC in his house and as the cops look on, she takes the cash offered by the VC who calls her a whore. If I am a whore, you are a barking dog, she mutters loudly while walking out. Her bravado doesn't last long … her musicians are missing except

---

[4] Translates as a self-abasing yes, my lord.
[5] I am not for sale. Don't touch me.

for Anwar, the teenaged percussionist who lodges himself in her house, as a devoted fan and friend. Rangeela too is missing since his wife has run away with the milkman, a bystander tells her. '*Yahan Mahabharat chal raha hai, wahan Ramayan shuru*'[6] is her disgruntled comment. Soon, she dodges the louts, set on her by the cops, as they chase her across town. Finally, she has to leave Aarah with the faithful Anwar.

Next stop is Delhi where they find a room at a termagant's house, while Anwar looks for work. At an eatery, where men are staring rudely at her, a Good Samaritan comes to their rescue. He is a fellow Bihari, Hiraman Tiwari (Ishteyak Arif Khan) who has heard and seen her at the infamous incident back home. He works with a small-scale joint churning out Bhojpuri CDs and after much trying and ingenuity, Anaar is finally singing under the name Lal Timatar. The security of fame among fellow Biharis addicted to Bhojpuri songs (Bollywood, beware) doesn't last long. Bihar's cops in mufti come looking for her, with a newspaper cutting carrying the story of prostitution, with the additional charge of kidnapping the minor Anwar. The landlady throws her out and Tiwary shelters them, assuring her that this too shall pass. He has a video of her slapping the VC on his phone.

Das keeps up the suspense of what Anaar will do with this information, though clues are plenty. She decides to surrender to the police, and the vindictive VC and his stooge, the local cop, celebrate. Anaar asks for a performance, to placate him … or lull him into false security. It is a well-attended event, with the higher police officer also in attendance. The VC's wife and daughter are also present, prominent in the first row. Halfway through her raunchy number—its foot-tapping and hip thrusting beat has the VC's daughter tapping her foot in obvious enjoyment—Anaar pauses. At a signal, from the sound system table, the old video starts playing on the backdrop that now doubles up as a large screen, unspooling the sequence of events ending with Anaar slapping the drunken man. There is a brief glimpse of a journalist who had introduced himself in Delhi. The weeping VC is left alone in his seat, utterly humiliated in public as his embarrassed wife and daughter leave in disgust. The police officer calls

---

[6] A play on the theme of the two epics. Mahabharat refers to the great war while Ramayan centres round the abduction of Sita, the hero's chaste wife.

someone higher up and says that the matter is very serious now. It can't be hushed up.

This is not Anaarkali's revenge. It is a matter of justice, of restoring her honour. From the stage, Anaar says: touch any woman, even if it is your wife, only after she consents. It is a message that is not rammed through rhetoric but the raw courage of a dancer who claims the dignity owed her. Avinash Das, the debutant director, opts for a straight, dramatic narrative, always keeping the focus on Anaar and her journey to vindicate her dignity. From a journalist turned filmmaker, the narrative has the feel of a well-researched feature that is topical and hard-hitting without ever sentimentalizing his protagonist or her turbulent life. The film is true to its milieu—the *mise en scène* is authentic in detailing, use of dialect, and casting. Das is right in not sanitizing the double entendre of the songs. He recounted the true incidents that inspired his film.

'Many years ago on YouTube, I happened to see the music video of an erotic song, *Hare Hare Nebuaa*, sung by the Bhojpuri folk artist Tarabano Faizabadi. It intrigued me that visuals of Tarabano singing expressionless in a studio were mixed with a sequence in which a woman is trying to seduce a man. Then in 2011, a very well-known Bhojpuri singer, Devi, pressed charges of molestation against vice chancellor DP Sinha of Jai Prakash Narayan University in Chhapra after he misbehaved with her at a concert. These two threads began to form into a script about a street singer who sings erotically-charged songs but has the integrity to challenge the powers when she is mistreated.'

Speaking of Swara Bhaskar's preparation, he goes on to say: 'She travelled to Aarah to understand the milieu in which such folk singers perform. She spent time meeting and talking to the local Munni Orchestra Group of female singers to familiarize herself with their songs and dialect. She stayed at the cheapest hotel in Aarah and shopped, ate and mingled with the locals. She did her own thorough research to play the part.'[7]

These two films show us the distance we have come from *Insaaf Ka Tarazu* or the other favourite trope, of raising the victim-avenger to the status of a devi. *Angaarey* (1986), written by Salim Khan, deified Smita Patil, as the daughter of an army officer who died in battle. Raped by her lecherous boss and rejected by her would-be in laws and society at large,

---

[7] Interview–Bangalore Mirror.

she is totally alone after her kid brother dies as yet another victim of this melodrama. Smita Patil's Aarti snatches the rifle from a Muslim security guard (for the secular touch) and shoots down the car of the villain setting off a conflagration. She is dressed in a red sari and temple bells clang in chorus. She is the divine executioner, not a normal woman.

Contemporary cinema has left behind these tropes that have no resonance now. French anthropologist Claude Levi-Strauss's division, of 'cold' and 'hot' societies, could be a tentative speculative means to understand this change. Cold was repetitive, holding on to traditions. Society was conceived as cyclic. Hot societies are aware of changes, of the process that are part of the inevitable march of history. Thus, this society is not cyclic but 'evolutionary'. This is a simplified way to understand the concepts. Do we dare pose the question: are we moving, excruciatingly slowly in terms of history, from a cold to hot society? Are we now caught in the flux of this change?

There are two exceptional films from the past that said a resounding NO. *Duniya Na Mane* (1937) is a feminist manifesto much before feminism was a movement. Nirmala (Shanta Apte) is an orphan tricked by her uncle and aunt to make her believe that she was marrying a young man. Her husband turns out to be a widower with two children older than her. Kakasaheb (Keshavrao Date) is supposedly a progressive lawyer. Nirmala is aghast but not defeated. She rebels. She will not accept him as her husband though the household and the milieu is orthodox. Eminent director Shantaram conveys her ambivalent feelings of putting kumkum on her forehead. She pauses, hand lifted, with the kumkum in her finger and looks at her face in the mirror ... she wears it finally, after hesitation. Nirmala will observe the outward trappings of wifehood but will not accept Kakasaheb physically or emotionally as her husband. He is decent enough not to force himself on her but thinks she will finally come around.

The son tries to flirt with Nirmala for which she soundly chastises him. Kakasaheb's daughter is a progressive leader working for women's rights. Shantaram's casting coup was to make Shakuntala Paranjpye (filmmaker Sai Paranjpye's illustrious mother), a prominent figure fighting for liberal causes, play the daughter. She upbraids her father for his actions. Nirmala's continuing rebellion and self-doubts about his own masculinity lead to Kakasaheb's suicide. Shantaram uses a walking stick—a phallic symbol—and a clock ticking, to remind Kakasaheb of the inexorable passage of time. The famous scene when he sees distorted images of his own face in the fragments of a shattered mirror uses German expressionist imagery to underline the psychological fragmentation of a man's ego. He leaves a letter, apologizing to Nirmala and setting her free.

Duniya Na Mane is very much a part of the reform movement that swept Maharashtra. Women's empowerment through education and abolition of child marriage were high on the agenda of the movement. Nirmala played by Shanta Apte, noted for her assertive and unconventional views, reinforced the power of a woman's No. Shanta Apte was a hero to the young of her generation. The late critic Iqbal Masud spoke glowingly of how star struck they were to receive her at Madras station, as she alighted dressed in trousers and shirt, to preside over their college function. This is an indication of cinema's pervasive influence over decades.

A much later film is of course *Mirch Masala* (1987) with the who's who of parallel cinema defining what ensemble acting means in a multi-layered, robust narrative. Director Ketan Mehta made a flamboyant statement of woman power. The incomparable Smita Patil is the fiery Sonbai who stands resolutely against a tyrannical Subedar's lust. The time is pre-Independent India and the place a vibrant village in Gujarat. She repeatedly says No to the Subedar's obsessive pursuit, who sees it as a challenge to his power and masculinity. Sonbai will not submit to his lust even if she endangers the whole community. Her repeated No leads other women to stand by her for a glorious, if brief, moment of victory.

2
Rom com Revamped

'Like a shy, but eager newly-wed bride, the country is slowly shedding her chastity belt.'

—Ira Trivedi, *India in Love*[1]

India is indeed getting out of her ironclad chastity belt. Not just the men, who have anyway exploited the sexual double standards they have always enjoyed. There is a quiet new revolution going on. These seen and unseen chains have loosened women from centuries old conditioning of denial of desire. Women are now expressing their sexuality without false modesty and a degree of frankness hitherto denied them in life and on screen. It has invited the wrath of righteous vigilante groups but the tide is against moral policing, especially when it makes cinema the target. The rom com is the genre that is quietly enabling this new honesty in an engaging way, without being judgemental. Or polemical. Talk of sex is still taboo at the family dinner table but there are other platforms. A sex advice column by the septuagenarian Dr Watsa in the *Mumbai Mirror* and its sister publications in other metros is not only widely read, after initial gasps of outrage, but a well-received documentary, *Ask the Sexpert*, has been made on him. This is a popular daily tabloid coming from the respectable *Times of India* stable, not a sleazy hole in the wall publication with racy centre-spreads and a topless picture of a well-endowed woman on page 3. Yet it is unreal to assume that the old prudishness has disappeared. The moral injunctions of centuries operate subtly in the subtext of films like *Cocktail*. At the same time, a silent celebration is going on in an inherently exuberant genre. The leap from chick lit to radical chic happened in just over a decade. India—and its cinema—is no longer moving at an elephantine pace. We need to retrace this stimulating journey.

---

[1] Page 8, *India in Love: Marriage and Sexuality in the 21st Century* by Ira Trivedi. Alepph Book Company, 2014

The rom com is a tried and tested genre in all film industries. When inspiration dries up, the chorus goes, let's make a rom com. It is a failsafe formula, at least a sure fire date flick. A fuzzy line blurs our understanding of what separates a rom com or romedy (portmanteau terms used interchangeably for a romance with comic overtones) and simple romance, or a conventional love story. Not just Bollywood, we as a society expect a love story/romance to be an emotional rollercoaster: lovers' struggle against insuperable, entrenched odds like caste, class, religion, etc. There is a love story in every film across genres: family drama, comedy, thriller, fantasy, historical spectacles (the latter often has a lot of fantasy as part of its narrative). If there is no love story, how can we create stars to adore with such passion? And spawn star pairs as icons of love? Thus, the centrality of love in an Indian film is unquestioned. Love is a celebration of life.

Star-crossed lovers were few and far between in our films. It is against the theory and practice of Indian performing arts. We leave the tragedy of lovers to poetry and oral folk tradition. The great legendary lovers, both *Romeo and Juliet* and eastern sagas like *Laila Majnu, Heer Ranjha, Sohni Mahiwal*, are reference points in the rhetoric or woven into the lyrics of modern love stories. *Romeo and Juliet* has been the favourite story to transplant. First, in strife-bound Rajput setting where family honour is above everything else in a squeaky-clean charmer, *Qayamat Se Qyamat Tak* (1988). Next, it gave the Hindu-Muslim edge to warring political clans of a UP small town in *Ishaqzaade* (2012). Then came the spectacular and sensuous *Goliyon Ki Barsat, Ram Leela* (2013) set in a lawless outpost of Gujarat where gunrunning divided a distinct ethnic community into rival families sworn to enmity. Traditionally, love stories are meant for happy endings in a country where honour killings of girls (and her lover first) who marries into the wrong caste or religion are recurring tragedies. The escapism of cinema offers an anodyne.

The mating game comes with a chequered history. Love stories of the past not only endorsed but also celebrated a distorted version of courtship: the reluctant, willing-to-be wooed girl stalked and harassed by the obsessed young man. All set to catchy, hummable songs set in Ooty or Kashmir for the lovers to roll down meadows or snowy slopes. Beaches of Goa were for the sporty look. Bigger budgets took them abroad where certain latitude to physicality was tacitly assumed. The most charismatic of them was Shammi Kapoor who was the Indian Elvis Presley in devising a very physical body language that conveyed passion to the demure girl who was all compliance by the end of a song. This set a template for other actors. *An Evening in Paris* (1967) showcased Shammi Kapoor's exuberance. Switzerland was Yash Chopra territory, as the heroine's fluttering chiffon pallu flirts with the hero's colourful sweaters, never mind the freezing cold. The duet in exotic places—the pyramids were briefly in the background for Karan Johar's *Kabhi Khushi Kabhi Gham* (2001)—was the implicit expression of romance, of love reciprocated and consummated. A progression of sorts from the standard shot of two flowers touching, after swaying to a gentle breeze.

The love story was enclosed in the suffocating embrace of the family melodrama, plus villains and vamps who coveted the heroine/hero driven by various motives. An imperious dowager frowned down her aristocratic nose at the plebeian girl chosen by the hero (*Junglee*, 1961) in a blockbuster that made Shammi Kapoor's exuberant Yahoo a youth anthem. A hitherto indulgent father (in a brocade dressing gown and pipe in hand) turned an intimidating patriarch laying down the law against a poor suitor for his darling daughter. (A stock figure played by many filmy fathers in so many films that we lose count.) The impediments to the marriage of true minds were the same in essence, different in details. Other plot complications/add-ons like a separate comedy track, parallel romances of the friends/hangers-on of the lead pair filled up the required three-hour length. Earlier, the conflict was a replay of the rich/poor divide. A few brave souls ventured into the forbidding caste or religious barrier to flaunt a progressive attitude. The surround sound of tired rhetoric alternated with the musical graph of evolving moods and emotions. The shades and moods of *sringara* (erotic love) are a very important part of Indian aesthetics. *Sringara* is the predominant *rasa* of Indian poetics. In a way, the practitioners of a modern form can lay claim to hallowed aesthetic tradition even if many presented a bastardized version of a legacy invoked as a pious platitude rather than a guide to aesthetics. The compensation was how true musical geniuses bequeathed us so many haunting songs that we remember the song more than the film.

The wait for light-hearted love where the couple was the focus was long. There were two candyfloss rom coms proper, much before their en masse arrival post 2000. *Love in Shimla* (1960) and *Dil Deke Dekho* (1959) notably launched two star-actresses, Sadhna and Asha Parekh.

Parekh was the dancing, flouncing, bouffant-haired heartthrob in a score of fluffy entertainers that blur into each other. Sadhna was more muted and played a variety of roles in a serious mien. She is forever identified with her signature fringe that was branded the Sadhna cut. Whoever the star and particularities of the story, the romantic heroine was the object of desire but was hardly given any agency.

The 90s brought in the game changers riding high on the charisma of new stars. It also brought in acronyms for the long-winded titles *DDLJ* (1995, *Dilwale Dulhania Le Jayenge*) *KKHH* (1998, *Kuch Kuch Hota Hai*) which flagged the 90s landmarks. They defined love for a generation and are now paid homage, quoted and dare say, even parodied with affection. *DDLJ* rewrote Indian style meet-cute with youthful panache. It is now part of Bollywood canon. The lovers meet at a London rail station and end at a dusty small station in Punjab. In both scenes, the man extends a hand to pull up the girl running to catch it. It is attraction at first sight but the travails of young love take them from cosmopolitan London to the mustard fields of Punjab where Simran (Kajol) is betrothed to the son of the authoritarian father's old friend. He disapproves of Western ways and the budding friendship with the insouciant charmer Raj (Shahrukh Khan) she meets on a holiday in Europe. The seemingly Westernized Raj, son of an indulgent wealthy father, wants to marry Simran with her father's blessings. This is the touchstone of Bollywood's reaction (instinctive or calculated to allay the anxiety of a basically conservative audience?) to the threat of globalization. It was a reiteration of traditional family values of parental approval for even the truest of love to find happiness. *KKHH* was more contemporary in the sense that love begins with friendship and the hero is part of the generation of young men who are not aware of the depth of their feelings. Both films involve dramatic plotting by well-wishers to bring the truly in love couple together. *Maine Pyar Kiya* (1989) and *Hum Aapke Hain Kaun* (1994) are part of the quartet that sent the liberalizing 90s to search for a bridge between tradition and modernity.

It was in the new millennium that Bollywood discovered the rom com per se. It did this with urgent curiosity and youthful zest to Indianize a Hollywood genre to meet our own cultural imperatives. The rom com, as the abbreviation plainly suggests, is a love story in a comic tone. It is ironic that Bollywood sought to own a Western genre that had run out of steam after a glorious run at the box office and Oscar wins. The critical consensus is that the classic rom com has reached its sell by date in Hollywood. According to a trade analyst, 'The romantic comedy has a branding problem. En vogue since nearly the beginning of cinema, the '80s and '90s proved to be the genre's heyday: when romantic comedies could not only top the box office but also nab critical praise and Oscar nominations to boot. But the aughts brought with it largely a slew of passable, derivative films that betrayed better, earlier influences, and after more than a handful of high-profile disappointments, the genre remains, at least in the mainstream, on what amounts to genre life support. But to think the genre is dead would be totally incorrect.'[2]

A contemporaneous vibe is essential for any rom com to work, be it Hollywood or Bollywood. The silly/serious/situational reasons that separate the couple meant to be together arise from the characters' personality quirks and societal mores of the particular time. Love is forever (ideally) but it is also very much here and now. Meg Ryan, the star of perennial favourites *Sleepless in Seattle, You Have Got Mail* (among others), says in an interview to David Marchese in *New York Times*: 'Think of Nora Ephron. Her observation about romantic comedies is that they were commenting on their time, but with the intention to delight.' From the screwball comedies of the 40s and 50s, the rom com has reinvented itself for every generation. From Spencer Tracy versus Katherine Hepburn battle of the sexes to Doris Day's many capers, Diane Keaton in Woody Allen send ups of male angst, Meg Ryan as America's sweetheart in a slew of well-loved films are trendsetters. The new millennium seems to have dried up the genre of its inventiveness until filmmakers tackled subjects that could be taboo ... teenage pregnancy and the heroine's disillusionment with adults, *Juno* (2007); *(500) Days of Summer* (2009) which gave a satiric edge to the unlikely story of an introvert and the whimsical charms of a manic pixie; *Five-Year Engagement* (2012) that dwelt on the problems of constant moves in tandem with a partner's career path; *What If* (2013) described as a 'perfectly delightful riff on the rom com formula' cast the now adult Harry Potter (Daniel Radcliffe) as a medical school dropout and his feelings for a savvy animator who is already in a steady relationship; *Obvious Child* (2014) advertised as 'the feel good abortion comedy of the year'; *The Big Sick* (2017) 'destined to be a classic'

---

[2] 13 February 2018, Collider.com, referenced by IMDB.

according to critics for the very contemporary story of an immigrant whose traditional parents want an arranged marriage and he falls in love with a White American girl with a mysterious illness. *Juno* won an Oscar and a couple of nominations, *The Big Sick* too won a nomination. All this speaks of a trend that the genre has to reinvent itself with a dose of the bittersweet and grittier realism to survive and make an impact.

Ironically, in the same period, Bollywood revelled in its discovery of the rom com and has made twenty odd noteworthy films in barely two decades. There is a contagious, sizzling compulsion to rewrite romance for the millennial generation. It seems Bollywood has now come to own a borrowed genre. It has been a giddy ride into a liberating narrative that gives more than equal space to the woman. Central to the rom com is the woman who is at the controls of the relationship most of the time. She is no pushover for old style wooing. An urban educated woman with ambitions that don't begin and end with marriage. She oozes confidence, healthy self-image, and sex appeal that is not generic but specific to the actor. The aim is to show love between equals. It is amazing that in the definitive rom coms of nearly two decades, she is the bigger star—or has gone on to become one. Kareena Kapoor was on the way to superstardom in *Jab We Met*. Saif Ali Khan produced and was the hero of *Love Aaj Kal*, but Deepika Padukone was the bigger draw. Anushka Sharma was launched with Shahrukh Khan first and was a known name in *Band Baaja Baaraat*, the leading trendsetter leaping to peaks of popularity. In all three films, the young men are beset with gnawing insecurities. As a counterpoint, the emotional intelligence of women is rated higher. Love and lovers change because they are of a particular time, their airy nothings must and do have a local habitation and name. Meet-cute followed by culture specific conflicts and personality clashes finally end in the boy–girl embrace, followed by the unsaid: and they lived happily ever after.

Meet-cute is the must to get a rom com rolling. According to the influential American critic, the late Roger Ebert, 'a comic situation contrived entirely for the purpose of bringing a man and a woman together, after which they can work out their destinies for the remainder of the film.' If a film fails the meet-cute test, very rarely can it revive the narrative into a semblance of a love story that makes us chuckle as the lovers survive the merry go round, after getting on to it with insouciance. They ride through the ups and downs of talking at cross-purposes, misreading situations and conversations, suffering the miseries of parting ... till they clutch each other in a passionate/relieved embrace with teary smiles and giggles. That is the standard graph.

How an actor owns a well-set graph and breathes relevance into a generic role is significant. She is no longer an ornamental appendage to a 'heroic' hero. The heroes of this genre admit their flaws, fears of commitment, and emotional vulnerabilities. A surprising fact is that all the notable rom coms are written and directed by men even though never before in Bollywood have so many women director–writers are/were successful in the same timeframe. It is almost as if men are searching for emotional equilibrium in relationships while women directors are engaged in larger concerns, and more complicated relationships that are not just limited to romance. They don't want to be confined to women-centric films either—a possible ghetto-ization of sorts. Alankrita Srivastava's debut attempt when she transplanted Bridget Jones under the Indian skin—the favourite chick lit heroine and her well-chronicled weighty angst, complicated by the dilemma of romantic choice—the entire exercise struck a false note in 2011. Audiences were already familiar with the more plausible and persuasive desi rom com and a patently derivative *Turning Thirty* induced déjà vu. The film tried hard to create identification with a whiny woman who becomes boyfriend-less and jobless on the verge of thirty, until a trusted old college mate conveniently walks back into her life to put things back on even keel. Audiences had by then taken to their hearts feisty women who coped pretty well with all the googlies life throws at them, and this manufactured problem did not strike a sympathetic chord. Srivastava had to wait a few years more to make her mark with the subversive *Lipstick under My Burkha* (2016).

Far more significant is how the prestigious, commercial powerhouse Yash Raj banner lent its weight to the burgeoning genre. Its PR machine ensured that these carefully packaged fresh themes were not only acceptable to a new, young audience but also proved successful at the box office. This established banner turned producer and patron of young filmmakers, entrusting them with new age rom coms with a sexual edge. The newbies worked to a tight schedule and were given a star cast. The new films were different in tone and theme from the classic Yash Chopra love story. Vintage Yash Chopra's school of sumptuous romance operated on a grand scale: the biggest stars, the best music directors, opulent sets alternating with foreign locations. Its forte was suggestive sensuousness, and lyrically shot songs discreetly veiled the sexual simmer on view. The same banner now operates like a well-oiled studio working on adequate budgets. It raised the pitch of romance to match contemporary attitudes to premarital sex and live-in relationships. Yet they started cautiously, adapting a Hollywood hit to suit Indian sensibilities.

First things first. The rom com actually began as a *rom con*, under the aegis of Yash Raj films. *Bunty Aur Babli* (2002) is India's watered-down fun version of the Hollywood classic *Bonnie and Clyde* (1967), sanitized with a touch of Robin Hood do-gooding. Under Aditya Chopra's serious public mien (when the reclusive producer–director–studio head deigns to give *darshan* to the media) is an unsuspected penchant for the larcenous pair of lovable small-time crooks. Based on Chopra's original story, director Shaad Ali is more successful in pulling off this uneven caper than *Saathiya* (2002), a frame-to-frame remake of mentor Mani Ratnam's Tamil hit about the post-marriage adjustments of an eloping couple. In the course of their small and big con jobs across North India, with Bombay as the ultimate destination, two 20-somethings from two small towns create a stir in local papers. Rakesh (Abhishek Bachchan) and Vimmi (Rani Mukherjee) desperately want to escape the boring fate decided by their parents. Rakesh's father (a railway ticket collector) gives him an ultimatum: either appear for the interview for a safe government job or leave home. Similarly, Vimmi's dreams of becoming a supermodel are under the dire threat of an arranged marriage with a suitable (synonymous with boring) groom. Their paths cross in Lucknow. Commiserating with each other, they decide to join forces and thus begin their first con job: a matter of getting back at a man who steals Rakesh's investment plan and pitches it to get the job. As their expertise and exploits grow, they assume new monikers, Bunty and Babli. They leave their signature at the scene of crime: BB with an arrow crossing a heart. It is a given that partnership leads to romance. The irreverent, effervescent film falters halfway and peters out into predictability. Especially, when Bachchan Senior, as a gruff and rather scruffy DCP is determined to nab the notorious pair. Moral judgement is suspended as we are expected to go along on their rollicking journey. The film doesn't detail the various con jobs; you get a collage of them essaying varied avatars. The best is when they sell the idea of a five-year lease of the Taj Mahal to a gullible American and his wife!

Rani Mukherjee zestfully fleshes out the dreams and determination of a small-town girl with ambition (whatever shape it takes) and her act is delightful. She contributes equally to the planning and execution of their schemes. She doesn't have a single conventional bone under that lithe frame, forever eager to dance with and romance her partner in crime. Vimmi/Babli represents a young woman who dreads the prison of an arranged marriage and the subsequent ennui of a housewife's life, making pickles, sans excitement/adventure. It is a new amoral woman presented with an extravagant flourish to an Indian audience used to a virtuous girl. They took her into their hearts. Enjoyment is all: a lesson welcomed by an appreciative audience, grown weary of homilies on what a good girl ought to be.

Hum Tum (2004) is the first successful rom com as such. Director Kunal Kohli credits the all time favourite *When Harry Met Sally* (1989) for inspiration. He comes up with a more self-conscious and finally conventional adaptation without the original's crackling wit. Karan (Saif Ali Khan) is a wisecracking playboy, as befits a cartoonist who distrusts marriage, courtesy his estranged parents. His attempt to flirt with a disdainfully cold Rhea (Rani Mukherjee) on their flight to New York thaws briefly into casual friendship at their Amsterdam stopover but ends in a ringing slap when he tries to kiss her. They keep meeting over nine years in Delhi, New York, and Paris. In the meantime, Rhea has been married (Karan helps his wedding planner mother with Rhea's wedding) and soon widowed. It is in Paris that seriousness enters this rocky relationship. Karan's well-intentioned ploy to introduce Rhea to a staid, trustworthy man leads to a predictable twist. The intended groom falls in love with another girl. It is during the engagement party of this brand new couple that Karan and Rhea consummate their on–off friendship but this only prolongs the story. Misreading of intentions is a handy excuse. Karan proposes marriage 'to right a wrong' and Rhea, in love with him, doesn't want a guilt-induced marriage. A year later, she realizes he loves her too courtesy the release of his book *Hum Tum* based on his successful cartoon strip centred on their own private battle. What saves a rather stretched out narrative and predictable plot is the charm and chemistry between the lead pair. The cartoon characters come alive in animation and used as both punctuation and narrator. The amused tone of the animation is a sly wink to the audience not to take the twists and turns of the love story too seriously since it will all end happily. Not just for Karan and Rhea but also his estranged parents. The departures are the hero's unconventional career that justifies his sardonic attitude. The repeated encounters on foreign soil— superficially platonic but the mutual sexual awareness is a palpable undercurrent—find encouragement from the more 'liberated' norms prevalent there. The scenes set in India are all to do with weddings and engagements, while many shot abroad are outdoors, visually suggestive of greater freedom. Most importantly, the heroine is not a virgin nor is it required of her. A Yash Raj film counts on music as intrinsic part of narrative and a marketing tool. *Hum Tum* uses the inherited trope of songs to build the familiar narrative arc.

In 2005, the studio took their successful hero (Saif Ali Khan won a National Award for Best Actor, for *Hum Tum*) to Melbourne and changed the hero Nick's (Anglicized form of Nikhil) profession from trained architect to chef. A celebrated one, of course. After designing a restaurant, Nick decided to indulge his passion for cooking and goes on to be the head chef of the latest place with the buzz. Ambar (Preity Zinta) is a part-time RJ at *Salaam Namaste*, a radio station targeting the Indian diaspora. She is a chirpy go-getter who wants to interview the hot chef, but Nick with his habit of oversleeping doesn't turn up. Ambar, in her other avatar, is an earnest medical student who has been disowned by her conservative family in India, when she stretches her one-year exchange status to stay on to pursue her dream of being a surgeon. The two meet at a wedding unaware of each other's public face and hit it off. Bare male torsos and bikinis at a beach wedding are guaranteed to fire up sexual chemistry. The film narrates the highs and lows of a yearlong relationship as they move on from platonic roommates to uncommitted lovers. Ambar's unintended pregnancy is the insuperable roadblock to their relationship that is banished to an arctic zone of assumed indifference, though they are forced to share a home. *Salaam Namaste* addresses Nick's commitment phobia and Ambar's reluctance to have an abortion with a degree of seriousness not expected in a frothy rom com. Rest assured. The climax takes the handy generic route to final reconciliation: the now repentant Nick uses the desi radio network to locate the woman he loves—with the twins she is expecting. The engagement comes with its quota of situations misread and finally resolved to everyone's satisfaction. The colourful cast of NRIs, from bizarre to goofy to helpful, is a stand-in for the missing families of the couple. This is a first for a popular Indian film, the total absence of interfering parents/families. The peer group is more important.

Ambar's vacillations reflect her uncertainty over the relationship with Nick that was breezy and fun in the beginning. As a medical student who has chalked out her career path, she is aware of what abortion entails. It is just the sonogram of the tiny life moving in her womb that changes her mind. She longs to give birth to the new life. We automatically equate a woman's sexual right as right to abortion, of control over her fertility. The counter argument, often made by fanatic pro-lifers, is valid too when it is not driven by hatred for the pro-choice believers. *Salaam Namaste* makes it Ambar's choice, minus the polemics that would anyway be toxic at the box office. A woman has the right to go ahead with her pregnancy and have her baby, not for the usual moral reasons where abortion is equated with sin. If she wants to keep her child for strong emotional reasons, that is perfectly justifiable. The choice is hers. Even in an earlier film *Kya Kehna* (2000), Zinta played a sheltered teenager with a supportive loving family, opting to have her child even though she is no longer infatuated with the cad she had fallen for. Coincidentally, Saif Ali Khan played the predator who seduces the gullible girl in a small hill station where everyone knows everyone. Agreed, this is the more acceptable reason in a conservative society but no less valid. Ambar can both be a surgeon and mother who risks being unwed. It is part of who she is.

This attitude is very akin to that of *Paa* (2009) where Amitabh Bachchan played a boy stricken with progeria, the rare genetic disorder of premature ageing: he is not expected to survive past his teens. His fiercely supportive mother Dr. Vidya (Vidya Balan) is an unwed gynaecologist who made no demands on the boyfriend who was not prepared for fatherhood. She chooses to live her life on her own terms. Unwed motherhood is embraced voluntarily and is no longer a cross to bear.

Motherhood without marriage and live-in relationships were, are, and will be anathema to the majority of traditional Indian society. No doubt about that. But change is creeping in. What we see today is acceptance—grudging perhaps, or limiting such behaviour to only certain privileged sections of society—not just in films but its prevalence in society. In this past decade and half, we saw film couples living together openly. Some progressed to marriage, like Kareena Kapoor and Saif Ali Khan. Other live-in affairs fizzled out and the individuals have gone on to newer relationships. All this is in the public glare where the paparazzi are everywhere and gossip about stars is not limited to only the film press. It is part of the media, period. Just go back to the 80s. Neena Gupta's affair with the West Indian cricket legend Vivian Richards was common knowledge and so was her pregnancy. The editor of the *Illustrated Weekly* got his reporter to stalk her, locate the hospital where the baby was born, and published the details with unconcealed glee. He claimed it was in public interest. Today, attitudes are mixed. There is, and it was always there, a consuming prurient interest followed by condemnation/sneering contempt. The judgemental crowd has not melted away into anonymity. There are others who shrug it off as part of celebrity lifestyle: it really doesn't concern us because these people live in a stratosphere where star status insulates them from ordinary reality. Then, the snarky question follows, what else do you expect from film folk? In Neena Gupta's time, a noted feminist journalist wrote in the OP ED pages of a leading daily that ordinary middle-class women did not have the luxury of not caring what society said. This disregard for social norms applied only to those inhabiting the world of films and other media. Post marriage, Deepika Padukone spoke of how live-in was not an option for her. She has been in many relationships since the age of 13, she confessed in her interview to a leading daily.

Now, in the globalized economy, we come across live-in relationships in large metros, with or without the knowledge of their families. Many belong to the middle- class, and are not apologetic about their lifestyle choice. It is almost as if popular cinema validates their choice.

Meanwhile, a new independent writer–director helped shape the contours of the genre over three films. Imtiaz Ali made a quiet start with *Socha Na Tha* in 2005. Dharmendra produced it to launch his nephew Abhay Deol who has gone on to remain 'the different Deol'. The director takes an amused and amusing look at the dictum: Lord, what fools these mortals be! It is chaotic when they get caught in the coils of mistaking infatuation for love and too late in recognizing that friendship has blossomed into love. Viren (Abhay Deol) and Aditi (Ayesha Takia) meet awkwardly at the 'bride seeing' arranged by two wealthy families with overbearing and overprotective brothers hovering over the reluctant boy and girl. Viren doesn't know how to propose to his present crush, and Aditi has an on–off unsuitable boyfriend.

The well-meaning Aditi agrees to help Viren in finding out how his crush feels about him. She fibs her way to join Viren and his love object in Goa. One situation leads to another until the foolish pair realize they love each other while they get engaged to the objects of their first crush. It ends in elopement and the two families who first proposed the alliance forgive them as expected. The touch is feather light and the gentle comedy is unforced. Young love's confusions dealt with equal measure of affection and wry humour has made *Socha Na Tha* almost a cult film though it did not trouble the box office unduly. Even in a launch pad for a new hero with *khandani*[3] credentials, it is Aditi who makes the transition from naivety to maturity believable with endearing charm.

Imtiaz Ali followed this up with *Jab We Met (2007)*, an enduring classic of the genre that has passed the test of time and repeat viewing. Make it viewings for people charmed by the chirpy chatterbox Geet (Kareena Kapoor) and the subdued loner Aditya (Shahid Kapur) and their bonding over a journey of missed trains and a rattling taxi driven at racetrack speed. Only the planes are missing. The Hinglish title became so famous that a leading TV channel uses it for its anchor's encounter with a celebrity. Ali comes up with a meet-cute to beat all others in the new Bollywood genre. The garrulous Geet is unbelievably naive and brave. We are introduced to her as pieces of assorted luggage are handed to someone in the compartment of the running train until she is hauled in. She finds the distracted, uncommunicative Aditya sitting in her seat and naturally takes over his life. Geet calls herself an agony aunt to beat all others and dispenses advice on life and love unasked. It is an extension of her bubbling enthusiasm. Words runneth over any encounter, even with a taciturn stranger who wants to be left alone. This follows disclosure of who and what she is to anyone ready to listen. A joie de vivre that is as irresistible as irritating. The way she seizes every moment to live it fully, getting often lost in details, makes these scenes compelling. That is how the suicidal Aditya, scion of a business house, battling with his inadequacies and trauma of his parents' messy marriage where each is in love with someone else, gets his mojo and motivation back.

Only a stone can be immune to Geet, an effervescent life force packed into a petite frame. Declaring her brown belt karate status, she is all

---

[3] Dynastic.

bravado when a bunch of curious louts surround her at a dark railway station. Geet wears her innocence as shield for all the threatening encounters that waylay her. Her self-love (Geet owns up that she is her most favourite person) makes her confident that no harm can come to her.

Geet has had enough of hostels and boarding schools. This Sikhni from Bhatinda is returning to the boisterous embrace of a huge extended family that engulfs the homecoming daughter and her unexpected friend/escort with overflowing Punjabi hospitality. Geet has come home only to run off to her non-Sikh boyfriend Anshuman and settle into marital bliss. Aditya is forced to take her to the said boyfriend and leaves before the scared young man rejects Geet for her blithe assumptions of marriage and happily ever after. Geet's family assumes she has run away with Aditya who they know only as a singer, not a tycoon in the making. A diffident Aditya blossoms into a successful businessman, mentally checking out how Geet would have handled a particular situation. She is Aditya's catalyst of change—from despair to optimism, courage to take decisions both business and personal, from negative feelings for his mother to an understanding of what love could make people do, like running off with her lover from the family business and an unhappy marriage. He names a new product after Geet, assuming she is happy with her Anshuman. It is an unselfish love that Aditya feels, after his girlfriend had dumped him when we first see him. For all her compulsively impulsive behaviour, Geet is a steady star beaming positivity. She does become more thoughtful after the fiasco of la affair Anshuman, and works quietly as a teacher in Shimla. Until of course, Aditya finds her, restores her to the anxious family, which assumes the two are a couple and plan their belated wedding. It is not without significance that Geet has gone missing for nine months. After the symbolic gestation period, Ali delivers the lesson of how true love can transform individuals: Geet's ebullience now quietened to the necessary self-reflection and Aditya's introversion changes to acceptance of love and trust. Geet proves that trusting someone, even foolishly at times, brings out the inherent goodness.

Geet set the template for heroines for a time—unsuccessfully in films because the original is unique. Half exasperated and half amazed, Aditya says she ought to be in a museum where people will queue for tickets to see her. Geet had greater effect on television. Take Khushi, an impulsive, god-fearing teenager tumbling in and out of trouble when she crashes into an angsty tycoon and talks nineteen to the dozen. She is the much-loved heroine of *Iss Pyar Ko Kya Naam Doon* (a firm favourite on Star Plus with repeat runs even six years after the serial ended). She is definitely a Geet descendent. Bollywood and TV soaps have discovered their synergy.

Imtiaz Ali's love trilogy is complete with a more layered, modern take on romantic relationships in *Love Aaj Kal* (2009). As the title suggests, the film is a study of contrasting ideas of love and commitment between generations. Jai Vardhan Singh (Saif Ali Khan) is an architect based in London and Meera Pandit (Deepika Padukone) is an art restorer specializing in frescos. Complementary professions are a great way to start off. They are in a relationship for nearly two years, content to make out uninhibitedly and have fun but not really ready for total commitment. Jai hankers for a dream job in San Francisco and Meera is all set for a restoration project in Delhi that she covets. They are sensible and decide a long-distance relationship will not work. They part amicably, keeping in touch as friends through emails, chats, and phone. There is a passing suggestion that Meera looks for something more concrete in this rather undefined relationship but she is the one who first speaks of breaking up. Is it a self-preservation ploy to avoid being dumped? The film really gets interesting after they part when the conversation as friends—and not girlfriend/boyfriend that has unwritten rules of not hurting the other's ego—is refreshingly frank. Meera tells him some home truths of what she didn't like about him—from shoes to put on charm to impress. He confides about the new woman he finds in SFO who demands more than he can give. Meera reciprocates with dating questions of her own: should she go out to dinner with the suave boss who shows interest in her? From dinner to marriage is a practical, considered decision with no expectations of mind-blowing romance.

During this very contemporary story that veers between rom com and romantic drama, a love story set in 1965 India is revealed in flashbacks. An elderly Sardar, the avuncular Veer Singh (Rishi Kapoor) tells Jai of his romance with the demure Harleen he loved at first sight. This story is a lovely old-fashioned charmer, a counterpoint to this generation's casual attitude that puts work and ambition above love. Veer Singh talks of soul mates while Jai is looking for easy companionship with benefits. Saif

Ali Khan plays the younger Veer and he brings the necessary intensity to an ethos where the besotted wooer puts everything on line to get the girl he loves. The older Veer Singh sees something special in the couple frequenting his cafe. He tries to caution Jai not to let this chance of happiness slip through when it's within grasp. All Jai needs to do is get his priorities right. Jai bravely attends Meera's wedding but she can sense his vulnerability under the superficial good cheer. Ali has a nuanced ear for conversations that break off midway to reveal what the person tries to hide from himself perhaps? Jai's assurance that he's all right stops to veer into half sentences... of not being able to turn time back... if only Meera had insisted on marriage... the wiser Sardar's soul mates stuff, could it be true? Jai's inchoate feelings are transparent to Meera, standing upright in her bridal finery, impassive and impossibly lovely. *Love Aaj Kal* does something unthinkable for a mainstream Indian film. We see Meera waiting in the court's ante room with her new husband for a quick, uncontested divorce. All very civilized and rancour free as befits modern uber cool professionals. The film ends on the same casual note. Jai saunters into the heritage structure where Meera is perched high on a platform diligently restoring the fresco. He repeats the same pick up line he had tried on the self-possessed young woman sitting alone in a bar: I don't want to pile on, his favourite opening gambit. So don't, was the original riposte. This time, Meera alights from her high perch (horse?) and has no sassy comeback. Away from swinging London, in the calm of this isolated space redolent with history, they find each other. There is a new subtext: making amends for the flirtatious past that took them thus far and no further, to the promise of a deeper commitment now that they are wiser. Meera has the courage to take decisions on both occasions: to part because their relationship is nebulous; to divorce and welcome Jai back in her life now that she knows how both of them feel.

Ali's attempt to capitalize on the same formula with a hot new pair, Sara Ali Khan (Saif Ali Khan's daughter) and Karthik Aryan, is an exercise in ennui. *Love Aaj Kal 2* of 2020 is a laboured copy, only the professions of the lead pair change. The difference is merely superficial.

Bollywood welcomed the second decade of the 2000s with the blast of a blaring wedding band and attendant revelry. It is a debut film that became a path-breaker for reasons other than strictly cinematic merit. Yash Raj banner had preferred the glamorous lives of upper-class Indians when they set out to produce, assembly line fashion, pioneering rom coms for family audiences, the emphasis being on the millennial generation. (*Bunty Aur Babli* was the exception but it had megawatt star power.) The cast of known stars was a safety net. It dawned on them, courtesy the stable of assistant directors who were also writing their own scripts while they got hands-on training, that there is another India that is ripe for exploration. One such assistant director, Maneesh Sharma, got the go ahead to direct a story set in downmarket Delhi where new graduates are driven by the desire to do something on their own. *Band Baaja Baaraat* (2010) is made by a Delhi boy, but one who went to the posh Delhi Public School and studied filmmaking in the US. Delhi is a huge urban sprawl teeming with stories that seep into different strata of society.

The debutant director cast the one-film old Anushka Sharma as Shruti Kakkar who has put into action her ambition to become a wedding planner even before she graduates from college. *Band Baaja Baaraat* gave the desi girl a new identity. Shruti is an ambitious 20 something who has a career path all chartered out: be an apprentice to a local Janakpuri aunty who organizes wedding *sangeets*. She is a volunteer who takes care of things like catering and preventing freeloaders from crashing the dinner buffet. Bittoo Sharma (Ranveer Singh in his first film) does exactly that and tries to pass off as part of the video team when a hawk-eyed Shruti catches him. She is practical, down to earth, thinks on her feet. Street smart with the gift of the gab though his way of saying 'binness' betrays his rural origins, Bittoo is desperate for any excuse not to go back to the sugarcane fields back in Uttar Pradesh. He talks his way into being Shruti's assistant and subsequently partner in the brand new business titled Shadi Mubarak.

She is a total Dilli girl, what if she's from grungy Janakpuri. She shares bread pakoras and business plans with him sitting on the sidewalk while mini skirted college girls sashay past them. The lead pair is comfortable in their middle-class skin, even as Shruti dreams of handling bigger weddings with lavish budgets. The pair is hired to assist a celebrity planner. When the high-flying celebrity wedding planner fires Shruti, blaming the assistant for her own short-changing the client, Bittoo chooses to walk out with her. Shruti lauds his loyalty but makes one thing clear: no *pyar* where there is *vyapaar*. She had snubbed his attempt to hit on her.

Shruti sets her heart on upscale Sainik Farms as she climbs the ladder of incremental success. This is where the rich and famous, as well the simply rich and not famous, celebrate high-powered weddings with distinguished names on the guest list. They are carefully curated, pastel-hued decor dripping good taste. Nobody can accuse Shruti of lack of ambition though she has a job to convince her first client. Uncles and aunts of the family get together and arrange things, remarks the bewildered man to whom Shruti is pitching her budget wedding. She asks for and gets five years to get her venture going from her family who are on the lookout for suitable alliances for her.

The first half narrates at a fair clip the nitty-gritty of putting together a reliable team: caterer, tentwallaha, flowerwallaha, videographer, etc. They also pitch in as dancers to get the family and guests to get on the floor, shake a leg and wiggle a derriere, flex the shoulder and twist the wrist in rhythm to the catchy music. Bittoo is the exuberant catalyst and Shruti joins him. Others get up and prance along to the beat. It is the first success—though a modest one in equally modest Janakpuri. But fashion is a mercurial thing, even in wedding decor. Kitsch catches the eye of the sophisticated couple looking for something different for their do. Shruti's drive and no-nonsense practical attitude is the engine while Bittoo dispenses the smooth talk to placate difficult clients. They are a good team, steadily progressing to bigger things.

Going to bed with the business partner is not part of the plan but when it happens one euphoric night after they move up a notch on the wedding budget scale, she takes it in her stride without making a romantic/emotional fuss but assumes it will go further. When a scared Bittoo draws back, she is easy with that too though heartache does gnaw her at times. The feisty, can-do face she presents the world is appealing and what's more to the point, credible. The second half of the film succumbs to the old malaise of taking too long and going round in circles to reach the final clinch. That is because, the partnership breaks up and they become rivals for the same business, putting their loyal team to avoidable dilemma: they have to choose between Shruti and Bittoo. They would dearly love to bang the heads of the obstinate couple together to drive some sense into them. The plot takes the route of a destination wedding—the ultimate prize—to get them to work together on this dream project. And of course, they realize their folly and all ends well for the wedding planners who need to plan their own wedding. The film runs on enthusiasm and energy of the lead actors, their palpable chemistry, the detailing of the milieu, and the fact that everyone loves a wedding.

Shruti is the blueprint for the middle-class girl with dreams of making it big. The delicious irony of *Band Baja...* is that it makes Janakpuri kitsch the new cool. Cool isn't designer brands and borrowed accents; it's being true to who you are and being proud of it.

Band Baaja Baaraat broke an invisible glass ceiling for Bollywood. The film made the shortlist of best films at the Asia Pacific Screen Awards 2011, one of the very few Bollywood films to achieve this. Perhaps this has to do with how the film makes an important aspect of current Indian society relatable. It recognizes not only the aspirations of lower middle-class young to make it big but also lauds the particular path Shruti chooses. Validating a woman's entrepreneurial spirit and skill is rare in popular cinema. She sees there is an emerging market and seizes the opportunity. The professionalization of what was a family-managed event is a new social and economic reality. Across economic and social strata, Indians splurge on weddings. It is a norm that only few defy. This has created a thriving economy even though the obscene display of wealth by the superrich has made many question this lavishness amidst so much poverty. Both the wedding industry and the rich are oblivious to the relevance of this uncomfortable question.

Weddings are obviously a major preoccupation with Maneesh Sharma. Three years after *Band Baaja Baaraat* proved a sleeper hit, he subverted the theme with delicious wickedness. *Shudh Desi Romance* (2013) is an ironic title because there is nothing *shudh* as understood by the broadest spectrum of desis. For hero, we have Raghu Ram (Sushant Singh Rajput) a tourist guide in Jaipur with a sideline. He is one of the rental *baraatis*[4] in the employ of Goyal (Rishi Kapoor), a world weary wedding planner who has seen it all. But Raghu and Gayatri manage to surprise even this hardened cynic. Raghu meets Gayatri (Parineeti Chopra), a rental *baraati* on the bus taking him to his own arranged wedding. A wedding to be deemed respectable needs a decent entourage to show his status in society. Raghu is immediately impressed—and also strongly attracted—to this feisty young woman who smokes and freely expresses her non-conformist

---

[4] The bridegroom's entourage accompanying him to the wedding.

views. An aside. Hindi film heroines are made to smoke to show they have indeed come a long way, toeing the vintage Virginia Slims Ad: you have come a long way baby. Some clichés are forever.

Already prone to premarital jitters, especially when he is to marry a stranger he hasn't even met, Raghu runs away and ends up at Gayatri's door step two weeks later. Gayatri is a girl with a reputation in her inquisitive, censorious mohalla. She breaks all rules in a society that holds a girl's virginity sacrosanct until she marries. Then it is her duty to be fecund. Gayatri tells Raghu of her live-in boyfriends earlier and he ends up being the latest (though he tells a neighbour that he is Gayatri's brother). They share a searing sexual chemistry that is often playful when not passionate. Gayatri is often the initiator. They decide to get married but Gayatri runs out on him, not prepared to go through with the wedding.

The plot is a merry go round of meetings at weddings and bolting through the bathroom. At yet another wedding, Raghu meets Tara (Vaani Kapoor), the bride he stood up. She comes on strongly, at first as revenge ploy to attract and then dump him. But the two start a steamy affair before Gayatri enters their life once more … where else but a wedding? Tara catches the two reconciled lovers in a clinch, both confess their feelings. She sportingly steps out. The fed up Goyal orders them to get married and they comply … only to run away separately from the wedding, to meet at the gate. So they go back to live happily together minus the wedding.

The idea of preferring a live-in to marriage, more so by a young woman, is revolutionary for popular cinema. The unwritten rule has been that after all the expected hurdles and misunderstandings, the girl will be anointed with sindur and wear the mangalsutra. This distrust of, and God forbid disrespect for, the institution of marriage is desecration. The setting is Jaipur which is still conservative, even if it's a tourist hub exposed to White foreigners and their ways. Gayatri and Tara, too, are today's women whether it is accepting sexual relationships without asking for or giving deeper commitment. The best thing about the film is its fun-filled non-judgemental attitude. Of just letting young women be.

Bollywood has a peculiarly defensive mindset when they set their films in the West. The director wants to ingratiate himself with the Indian Diaspora which is sometimes caught in a time warp. The India they left behind stays the same in nostalgic memory even as contemporary

Indian society has changed. The foreign locale must also serve a double purpose for desi audience: a touristy trip and a showcase for how well Indians have done for themselves in their adopted country and yet, placate the stay at homes that they are the true upholders of Indian culture and its values. It is a strange mixture of envy, approbation and disapproval that they left the homeland for economic gain. It really needs a mind free from these preconceptions and the need to please and flatter such diverse segments of the unpredictable mass audience to make a successful film set in the US.

Debutant Shakun Batra took the title of a much loved song *Ek main aur ekk tu ...* added an extra k to the title (to appease numerology pundits?) and came up with an unexpected charmer, full of verve and wisdom. He has acknowledged Woody Allen as an influence and there can't be a better mentor than the master of self-mocking angst and skewed relationships. *Ek Main Aur Ekk tu* (2012) begins in Las Vegas, comes home to Bombay and then goes back to the sin city for a delightfully ambiguous resolution. Meet-cute doesn't get any insanely cuter. Rahul (Imran Khan) an out of work architect and Riana Braganza (Kareena Kapoor) a hairdresser who can't pay rent find themselves married after a night of post-Christmas drinking to drown their respective troubles. They had earlier run into each other at a psychiatrist's clinic and Riana ends up with his file by mistake. Rahul is a diffident loner, brought up by an authoritarian father (Boman Irani) and a distant socialite mother (Ratna Pathak Shah). Riana comes from a middle-class Roman Catholic family, with loving parents and a boisterous extended family. They are all part of a close knit community—one of the delights to discover in Bombay's old localities. Riana is nothing if not self-confident and helpful. She takes the slightly younger Rahul (another taboo being broken) under her wing as they try to get the unintended marriage annulled over the holiday season.

With her apartment lease ended, Riana decides to visit her family and takes Rahul along. He stays with her welcoming family, gradually loosens his uptight behaviour and doesn't tell his parents that he is in Bombay. They live in a snooty part of the city. But he is discovered as he must, and passes off the visit as a research project, and Riana as an assistant. The comedy of manners at the exquisitely set dinner table of the parents is sharp and finally sparks Rahul's rebellion. He comes out with the truth to his disbelieving parents, goes back to Riana's informal home and tries to mend his relationship with her. He has fallen in love with Riana and tries to kiss her while she has nothing but friendship in mind. Both head back to the US. Rahul finds another job. Riana is back on her feet, a good friend and a dependable shoulder for the newly confident Rahul to lean on when he craves support. He is determined to change their relationship status and waits in hope. Riana is in no hurry to make such a commitment. The film ends on the brink, poised between hope and disappointment. This honesty in dealing with modern relationships between people from different backgrounds on a neutral territory is refreshing for mainstream Bollywood where the compulsion is to rush a tentative couple into an embrace. Batra's writing and direction bring sensitivity and understanding to male vulnerability and a woman's reluctance to commit. Riana comes across as carefree, fun loving girl and foolishly spontaneous to begin with. But she is not the flaky ditz (a Rom com favourite), for all her impulsiveness. Slowly we see the layers under the exterior. Her empathy comes from the wisdom of experience and openness. It is a singularly new take on the Rom com without the mandatory happy ever after ending, where the woman is left free to make her choice.

Other taboos and box office rules are being broken. Though body shaming is politically incorrect, Hindi cinema has used the fat girl as a figure of fun, from the comedienne Tuntun to the plump, pretty girl as part of the heroine's gang of girlfriends. That was in the 60s and 70s sappy love stories. Things have changed now that Bollywood has gone to the Hindi heartland to set its stories in. It became trendy—and paying—to leave the big city and find authentic locations to tell real stories about real people: the unwritten proviso being that real did not mean gritty documentary style of narration. Characters became more important than plot twists, so that they could engage us emotionally. Here, the woman is as important as the man, for these films basically centre around marriage, adjustment, and contentment. Ecstatic romance of the filmi kind was thrown out of the small barred windows of cramped houses lining narrow streets. Bhumi Pednekar as Sandhya, the overweight heroine of *Dum Laga Ke Haisha* (2015), took everyone by surprise. Even greater surprise is how heart-warming this character was and is while she broke every stereotype of what a Bollywood heroine should look like. She is part of an almost paradigm shift seen from the 2015 onwards.

Stories shifted base, to small towns where homey middle-class girls nurture dreams that are not unachievable. They have to battle against tradition and age-old stereotypes of demure submissiveness to fulfil these dreams. Bhumi Pednekar is an unobtrusive trailblazer. She is really the most unlikely actor to have reeled off three successful films: *Dum Laga Ke Haisha*, *Toilet* and *Shubh Mangal Savadhan*. All within the span of less than three years. That takes some doing—and daring, on the part of directors who cast her in de-glamorized yet endearingly earthy roles. She anchored stories rooted in the soil. Pednekar exudes a refreshing mix of healthy sensuousness and sensible level-headedness. She is the attractive girl next door, vulnerable at times yet with a practical streak that makes her a go-getter who will do it with self-respect intact. She takes on the man in her life without simpering coyness. Instead, her shrewd intelligence helps her to come off better in the small and big battles of love cum-arranged-love marriage. This new social practice and its evolution in many parts of neo-urban India is a stark contrast to the metros where the young are into speed dating and Tinder, swiping right or left to gamble for mating stakes. This new reality comes with the cache of novelty. If the small town ethos is a familiar reality to people in the hinterland, it is novel for blasé metro audience.

Bhumi Pednekar's Sandhya in *Dum Laga Ke Haisha* carried off her weight issue without apology. There are no euphemisms, like pleasantly plump, or the typically Panjabi term 'healthy' to hide her pounds. She is a graduate to her husband Prem Prakash Tiwari's (Ayushmann Khurrana) school drop-out. Set in 1995, the cassette shop he runs in Haridwar acts as musical commentary. Soaked in the romance of Bollywood songs, his favourite crooner being Kumar Sanu, Prem dreams of a Juhi Chawla-esque girl for a wife. Straitened family circumstances lead his hard-headed father to get Prem married off to an overweight educated girl looking for a teacher's job. Even the ceremony is part of a mass wedding. Director Sharad Katariya gets the locale and idiom with perfectly dovetailed details. The extended family and intrusive neighbours add to the aural and visual authenticity as Prem stubbornly refuses to consummate the marriage even as Sandhya signals her willingness—even eagerness—without false modesty. She wears a new shiny nightie as a come-hither sign. Couples in an arranged marriage often go through an awkward period before consummation. Just because a girl doesn't meet the slim and sexy requirements, it doesn't mean she has no sexual desire or the right to express it.

Sandhya is willing to wait for Prem to accept her but can't stomach the public insult at his friend's wedding and slaps him. She walks out and demands a divorce. Indian families will not let an arranged marriage end in divorce and their combined efforts, plus the judge's decree of asking them to live together for six months, sets off the thaw in their former coldness as friendship burgeons. English has been Prem's bugbear and Sandhya's meticulous tutoring helps him overcome his fear, to finally clear the exam. If only the film had followed the simple logic of friendship turning into conjugal affection! The director had to be literal. He manipulates the script to include a race where husbands carry wives on their back and no guesses who wins. This is followed by a song and dance number complete with back up dancers—all in garish colours—as the end credits roll. It betrays a slavish capitulation to formulaic expectations, as if the talented director did not have confidence in his story and the ensemble cast who perform brilliantly.

What saves *DLKH* is the comfortable—not crackling, mind you—chemistry that Khurrana and Pednekar share to make the end acceptable. It is remarkable how Pednekar makes us root for her dominant character without in any way lessening our understanding of Prem's dilemma. She is strong but not intimidating and that is part of her appeal. *DLKH* gratifyingly was chosen Best Hindi Film by the National Film Awards jury. And Pednekar deservedly won a couple of movie magazine awards for best female debut.

The same comfort between the lead pair makes *Shubh Mangal Savadhan* (2017) work, in its humour that never goes over the top and yet has us chortling at the right place with understanding and even empathy. Without that comfort level, this pair could not have pulled off the tricky subject of the hero's erectile dysfunction without dressing it up in euphemisms or recourse to vulgar double entendre. As Sugandha, Pednekar brings the working girl of non-posh Delhi to nuanced life, who does not want to chicken out of marriage to a non-performing groom, since it is the first decision she made on her own in life. Director

Prasanna is able to transplant his Tamil film *Kalyana Samayal Saadham* (2013) in the environs of lower middle-class Delhi of DDA flats with thin walls. Much of the credit goes to Hitesh Kewalya for dialogue and screenplay that catches the particulars of Dilli Hindi, its idiom and intonation. For a Maharashtrian, Pednekar displays, with natural flourish, tone perfect mastery of nuanced Hindi in all her three films.

Sugandha's parents are suffocatingly protective. And intrusive. She has an overbearing uncle from Haridwar always quick to take umbrage if his seniority in the family hierarchy is not respected. For perhaps the first time, a heroine is given the introductory voice over to describe her situation and thumbnail sketches of the family and wittily recount her first brush with the hero Mudit (Ayushmann Khurrana). Her voiceover sets the tone. She is amused, flattered and attracted. The object of these mixed emotions—and signals to the clumsy suitor—is Mudit, a diploma holder doing a marketing job and happily mispronouncing resume and onion like a native Dilliwala. She plays hard to get, sending the importunate Mudit into a nervous tizzy. No wonder, he can't perform when the newly engaged couple find themselves conveniently alone in her thin-walled flat and she has to understand his 'gents problem.' It is funny and affectionate. Prasanna doesn't descend to graphic details but uses a limp sodden biscuit to describe Mudit's plight. You have to give it to Sugandha to be both understanding and forbearing most of the time till the interfering family jumps wholesale into the bridegroom's non-performance with glee, dispensing free advice, all sorts of remedies including Mudit's marriage to a tree.

As happens all too often, the second half runs out of ideas and comic steam. What keeps *SMS* (the non-sexual acronym could become the code for ED) going is the unflagging spirit of the lead couple and the superb ensemble cast. Sugandha takes charge: when she runs away, distraught at Mudit's persistent ex-girlfriend or how to face this impasse. Finally, her matter of fact attitude to non-happening sex in her marriage is believable. It will happen when it happens, is her uncomplaining attitude.

It is not sex—which is pretty satisfactory—but the need for the privacy of a toilet that is the basic problem in *Toilet: Ek Prem Katha* (2017). Jaya (Bhumi Pednekar) holds her own against what is primarily an Akshay Kumar vehicle. She is dismissive, flirtatious, sarcastic, mulish, and adjusts to being a head-covering bahu to placate a cussedly conservative father-in-law even though she comes from a more modern family. She is tech savvy, determined and resourceful—all with taken-for-granted casualness. Sadly, Jaya is reduced to a token presence, to make a statement than the engaging individual she has been in the first half. The press reported the case of a woman divorcing her husband for the lack of a toilet, much before the film was made. *Toilet: Ek Prem Katha* carries enough heft with its theme to be featured in the *New York Times*. Jaya is the catalyst for change in this message-oriented love story. The political agenda soon takes over; there is a media circus, courtroom drama while Jaya's reasons get swamped under the hero/producer Akshay Kumar's endorsement of Modi's Swachh Bharat Abhiyan. Incidentally, Bhumi Pednekar gained considerable weight for her debut film and then lost it to play the attractive heroine of the next two films in her nascent but noteworthy career.

To update Pednekar's impressive career, she played the second female lead, as the dark complexioned lawyer, comfortable in her skin, in *Bala* (2019) where the story revolved round a young man's premature baldness. Pednekar is Latika, the eponymous hero's (Ayushman Khurrana) school classmate. The narrative tries rather clumsily to equate male baldness and female dark complexions as barriers to self and social acceptance. Latika is a capable lawyer who defends Bala in court—for deceiving a pretty fair model into marriage—and has the self-confidence to reject the chastened hero's proposal. She opts to remain his friend.

The more traditional kind of rom com centred round the travails of young love survives in a slew of passable to indifferent films. Alia Bhatt, the brightest and most talented of the young brigade, brought her acting nous and sparkling charm as the mettlesome bride in the *Dulhania* franchise... *Humpty Sharma Ki Dulhania* (2014) and *BadrinathKi Dulhaniya* (2017) with the same co-star Varun Dhawan.

India's multi-lingual, multi-ethnic society offers enough obstacles in the path of true love that struggles to run smoothly. What's surprising is how few films use this inherent conflict. *Vicky Donor* (2012) framed the marriage of the sperm donor and bank officer against the cultural war between the uncouth Punjabi and the refined Bengali. That was just a minor part of an unconventional hero's struggle for acceptance.

The culture war raging between a similar uncouth Punjabi hero and the sassy Tam Brahm heroine is the issue to be resolved in *2 States* (2014), a campus story—IIM Ahmedabad no less—based on bestselling writer Chetan Bhagat's novel that is purported to be autobiographical. He claims that *2 States* is not so much a love story of a Punjabi boy and Tam Brahm girl but an introspective look at troubled relationship between an authoritarian father and rebellious son. According to him, all his novels are an exploration of this theme some way or other. He also admits that *2 States* ends on a reconciliatory note—between angry son and distant father as well as the hero's estranged parents—unlike what happened in his real life. Even an autobiographical novel about the troubled path of love in the face of parental opposition needs a happy ending for the feel good factor. That's honest.

The confessional tone continues in the film. A morose Krish Malhotra (Arjun Kapoor) tells his unseen psychiatrist that he contemplated suicide. These confessions on the couch punctuate the narrative without establishing an identifiable time frame but you get the general drift of why the IIT-IIM-A graduate wears a habitual hangdog expression—Arjun Kapoor's version of angst and wry self-deprecation. Many troubles bear down upon the shoulders of a strapping Punjabi young man: his cold war with an angry father Vikram (Ronit Roy), the ambition of wanting to be a writer warring with the security of a bank job, and the course of true love not running smoothly.

Naturally, opposites attract. The feisty pocket-sized Ananya Swaminathan (Alia Bhatt, pert and pretty), a beer guzzling, tandoori chicken eating Tam Brahm from Chennai with clear cut career goals, takes the lead in the campus affair. She has the grouse of an Economics major (she was a topper) against IITians who have an unfair advantage when it comes to Maths. Her ego taking a minor hit, she initiates joint studies with Krish who too has no friends. She is a firecracker, who argues with the server at the dining room about bad food and portion size even as others keep quiet. Right away, the film establishes that Ananya is not a girl who will take things lying down. From studying together to sleeping with each other is a natural progression and director Abhishek Varman films it with casual candour and without prurience. A refreshing first followed by an equally honest outburst from Ananya. Wondering where the relationship is headed after college, she says: it doesn't take five minutes for a guy to jump into bed but he wants more time to think about commitment. Her honesty is matched by Krish's sotto voiced cautionary wisdom: there is nothing more *khatarnak*[5] than a Punjabi mother-in-law.

The brash Punjabi mother Kavita (Amrita Singh's overbearing manner is protective mechanism for her insecurities of a bad marriage and fear of losing her only child) meets the snooty Swaminathans at the convocation. Radha (Revathy) is voluble in her condemnation of Kavita as uncultured and Shiv (Shiv Subramaniam) is a genius at radiating disapproval with dour silence. The real battle is on now. The young lovers don't want to elope (why use the word elope for a court wedding?) but decide to win over each other's parents. So, at heart, *2 States* is also about loving your family and wanting their blessings to tie the knot. Things haven't changed from the time of *Dilwale Dulhania Le Jayenge*. Ananya is determined to win both sets of parents over but not at the cost of her and her family's dignity. She is more resilient than Krish. But she is also adamant about cutting off all contact with him when things are bleak. Of course she thaws when he comes to Chennai to woo her back.

Krish's battles are on many fronts: with his own mother and her extended family by implication and the thinly veiled hostility of the Swaminathans when he opts for Chennai for his posting. In one of the best lines in the film, Krish describes the minimally furnished traditional house as one which was robbed by thieves who left the sofa behind because they didn't like it. Binod Pradhan shoots the two interiors—the cluttered Delhi flat and the space around the central courtyard with carved wooden pillars in Mylapore—to visually encapsulate the different sensibilities and life styles. But having the Swaminathans eat off banana leaves every day—festive days are different—stretches credibility. Melamine plates versus stainless steel *thalis* would be a more plausible lifestyle contrast.

There is rather efficient economy of comic observation in an otherwise sprawling script. Events unfold at the level of daily tedium but that is how it happens in real life. For drama, Krish takes Ananya to Delhi for the big fat Punjabi wedding of his cousin. The *len-den*[6] fracas is solved by Ananya's fiery feminist intervention. The point gets drowned out by the

---

[5] Dangerous.
[6] Dowry demands.

obligatory big ensemble dance where Ananya prefers Bhangra *thumkas*[7] to Bharatanatyam *mudras*.[8]

More to the point are the mutual racist barbs shot by the inimical mothers. Kavita accuses Ananya of trying to *patao* a *gori-chitti* Punjabi *munda*[9] as all dark-skinned South Indians are wont to do. Krish points out that Ananya is much fairer than he is but for Kavita, the exception only proves the rule. Radha's riposte is that 90% of Tamilians—she insists on the Tamil tag, not generic South Indian–are highly educated. Finally, begrudgingly, both sets bless the couple at a visually stunning ceremony. The pillared courtyard of a temple, silhouetted against a mellow setting sun, acknowledges Tamil aesthetics submerging Punjabi *Show Sha*.[10]

The spirit of the revamped rom com wafts up to the older generation X too. *Qarib Qarib Singlle* (2017) is the only rom com of note to be made by a woman. Tanuja Chandra returned to filmmaking after a longish sabbatical with this quirky romance cum road movie that depends on the acting chops of the always dependable Irfan (challenge him in any kind of role) and the talented Malayalam actor Parvathy. Parvathy is an articulate, outspoken feminist who analysed on a TV interview (Off Centre, CNN 18) how Indian women internalize patriarchal norms in the wake of Me Too movement. Parvathy lets her feminist beliefs lie dormant when we meet Jaya: the sober 30 something Malayali widow is tired of being the single-window support system for all and sundry—colleagues at work, neighbours, and friends of friends—always ready to oblige. She is the self-described 'stepney aunty' to her friend's children. Goaded by friends that she will turn back into a virgin if she doesn't meet any men, Jaya uploads her profile on a dating site. The first date is a recipe for disaster: Yogi, short for a name running into a sentence, is scruffy, laidback, spouts his own *shairi* (published and unpublished), is not only late but somewhat creepy in the way he gets Jaya's phone number. She is already regretting coming to the coffee shop out of boredom with her un-happening life. Her only emotional connection is talking with a younger brother studying abroad.

This North–South first meet is seemingly destined to be the last ... but destiny works according to the scriptwriter's diktat. Piqued by the man's

---

[7] Hipswing.
[8] Hand gestures.
[9] Hook a fair and handsome Punjabi boy.
[10] Slang for Punjabi showy revelry.

self-assurance that his three ex-girlfriends are still pining for him, and his eccentric charm, Jaya gives in to a whim. With nothing interesting to do, Jaya takes up the casual challenge of going on a trip that is something like Bharat Darshan to check if indeed the exes are carrying a torch for this unpredictable man who is winsome in a weird way. An odder couple, you wouldn't meet in a rom com. But the point of this particular form of storytelling is how it brings together the most unlikely man and woman and gets a conversation going ... that's leading somewhere.

Conversation is the high point of this loosely structured narrative, a journey that stops to smell the roses and inhale coffee flavours with delightfully impromptu diversions. Missed trains become an occasion for an insanely hilarious road trip with a character (who merits a capital C) for driver. The conversations are real and reveal Jaya's insecurities under the show of confidence and Yogi's real strengths under the eccentricities. The film is also a daughter's tribute, by updating her mother's radio play. Tanuja Chandra's mother Kamna Chandra (she was scriptwriter for a couple of Yash Chopra's films) wrote a play that is so eminently adaptable to contemporary times. Gazal Dhaliwal collaborated on the script and wrote the dialogues that drive the film with wit and insights into human nature. Jaya and Yogi have experienced life's highs and lows. They now realize that there is more to life than mere closure ... something valuable could be theirs after the tendentious beginning. It is a road movie that rises above the cliché that all journeys are both internal and external. It lets us into this process with delightful spontaneity. A few small glitches can be overlooked for this enjoyable trip. QQS emphatically underlines that life doesn't end for a widow and she has a second chance at romance, courtesy an unlikely friendship.

The genre generates its quota of mediocre and outright bad films. That is inevitable given the popularity of the rom com. It is easy to fall into the bad habit of stereotypes. In *Bareilly Ki Barfi* (2017), the heroine Bitti (Kriti Sanon) has to choose between two men in a Cyrano de Bergerac scenario. Bitti who works in the local electricity board stalls her mother's constant effort to get her married to a nice suitable man. She wants a husband who will understand and love her for who she is ... including sneaking cigarettes from her father's pack. Smoking is equated with modernity. More effort is expended on the two men who are ostensibly her suitors and their compulsions. It is basically

Rajkumarr Rao's triumph for donning the rude, arrogant egotist avatar of the author of the book that Bitti admires when he is really a nice, timid sari salesman.

There is not much comprehension of what draws an art house filmmaker determined to tread the 'bold' path to depict a young woman's sexual obsession. Sachin Kundalkar is a fine director with the unusual triptych *Gandh* (2009) to his credit. *Gandh* linked three Marathi short stories through the sense of smell. His experiment in *Aiyya* (2012) takes the olfactory sense to bizarre lengths, making it the most potent part of a young woman's sexual yearning. Rani Mukherjee's Meenakshi is a librarian who seeks escape from her crazy family through her fantasies. She falls in love at first sight with Surya (Malayalam star Prithviraj), a Tamilian art student and stalks him, following his scent. Instead of a whacky sexual comedy, the film is a cringe-inducing, if brave, effort on the actor's part to essay a sexually 'bold' role. A middle-class Marathi young woman in conservative Pune lusts after this elusive stranger. In her fantasies, they dance with wild abandon as if they are a mobile illustration for the *Kamasutra*. It is embarrassing to see an actress of Mukherjee's calibre succumbing to this misdirected expenditure of energy. It is unintentionally risible when meant to be sensuous. It does take all sorts to make Bollywood's bouquet of romance.

The NRI fixated filmmaker is a hardy specimen in the Bollywood landscape. Now, there is even more desperation to be different. We had to suffer an *Anjaana Anjaani* and *Break Ke Baad* both in 2010. The implausible coming together of two desi New Yorkers to live out a last wish before committing suicide—a most puerile bucket list imaginable—turned into a road movie that went nowhere. We just didn't care about what happened to Akash (Ranbir Kapoor) and Kiara (Priyanka Chopra) and wished they would get it over and done with, one way or the other. Priyanka plays the confused hottie who is seductive and standoffish by turns, with no clue to what is going on in her pretty head. Not that we want to strain our exhausted brains to figure that one out however hard director Siddharth Anand tried.

Then came *Break Ke Baad* where Aaliya (Deepika Padukone) naturally wanted a break from the clingy, besotted boyfriend-cum-childhood buddy Abhay (Imran Khan). She hotfoots off to Australia's Gold Coast and its laidback ways. Apparently well-to-do Dilliwallas like Imran Khan have an Australian visa all ready for romantic contingencies and he is there the next morning after he hears a man's voice on the girl's phone. We get the point within 15 minutes but the film labours over it for two hours: a modern, independent girl needs her space. Commitment phobia is not just for men. Metrosexual women—if the buzzword past its sell by date is gender neutral—are not easy to pin down. A similar affliction of trying too hard to be different at any cost infected the suave and market savvy R. Balki. He attempted a marital rom com, spinning it on the axis of role reversal. *Ki & Ka* (2016) presents us a heroine, a corporate tigress prowling her way up career ladder, her sights set on the CEO's post ultimately. Instead of applauding a career woman's ambition, the film reduces Kia (Kareena Kapoor) to a heartless, conniving player. She finds a compliant boyfriend in Kabir (Arjun Kapoor) who happily settles into being a househusband even though he has an MBA with a tycoon for an estranged father. Being a househusband leaves Kabir a lot of free time that he fills with playing physical trainer for the neighbourhood homemakers and soon, becomes a media celebrity handing out life choices *gyaan*. He is so persuasive that even Jaya Bachchan invites him home to her visibly disgruntled husband's chagrin … an in joke that doesn't raise more than a polite smile. The point of this lacklustre rom com is that the man is the ultimate winner in this unequal fight. Its feminism is fake and limited to glamorous power dressing. As for entertainment, the romance is lukewarm and comedy cold—not chilled out as envisaged by Ad man turned filmmaker. It left the audience cold too, as they were not primed to accept a CEO wife and housebound husband.

A really corny film validates rom com 2.0 circa 2000 by converting a Hollywood-weaned NRI succumb to the power of Bollywood's hybrid romance. *I Hate Love Stories* (2010) ostensibly spoofs Bollywood's filmmaking ethos. It is strewn with tributes and send-ups of classic Bollywood to take a true fan to spot-the-reference heaven. The send up of a syrupy, song, and melodrama driven film is flaccid because the writing sheaths its claws that were not sharp to begin with. The homecoming, wannabe director NRI Jay Dhingra (Imran Khan) is a sneering assistant director to love story specialist Veer Kapoor (a complacent Samir Soni) who is oblivious to the newbie's jibes. The hit-maker's ego is stroked by his new art director Simran's (Sonam Kapoor) dewy-eyed adoration. Piquantly, Jay has to report to Simran. That's when the sparks fly.

Simran also has the perfect boyfriend who is fated to be dumped for no fault of his. While she finds Jay's professed loathing of love stories obnoxious, she also feels the vibe between them. Punit Malhotra who wrote and directed the soppy film loses out—by design and intent—the chance to parody classic Bollywood romance by repeating the same clichés in his own film. Simran is the breathless spokesperson for the sentimental appeal of standard Bollywood romance. Naturally, Jay and Simran go through the preordained cycle of verbal war, friendship peaking to true love—all in the space (varied locations including scenic New Zealand) and time for the film-within-film to be completed. Jay's sarcasm withers and vanishes as does his permanent smirk of superiority. Love triumphs. Bollywood, old and its new refurbished avatar, is not just validated but celebrated by the foreign-bred sceptic. *I Hate Love Stories* became a box-office hit even while critics panned its sell out to the formula despite protestations of critiquing it. Refurbished formula's poetic revenge? Not really because the non-conformists were also winning accolades and box-office success at the same time.

There is a postscript to the rom com story. Luv Ranjan is the successful director who has created a franchise for the anti-rom com snarky laugh riot. *Pyar Ka Punchnama* (2011) did conduct a post-mortem on the dominating genre and did a surgical job on how shallow modern love is. Girls exploit their besotted boyfriends and date exes with no qualms of conscience. This film and its sequel depend on group dynamics because the leads are three bachelors who share an apartment and are also privy to each other's love lives. Bromance triumphs over romance. Ranjan followed it up with *Pyar Ka Punchnama 2* (2015) repeating most of the cast from the original and the doubts about their girlfriends' loyalty are doubly reinforced and once again, the trio of young men conclude that only their mothers love them truly. This antidote to contemporary love continued the laugh riot with *Sonu Ke Titu Ke Sweety* (2018) where the lead actor Kartik Aryan this time rescues his friend from a scheming fiancée who is out to cheat him and his family while posing as the ideal bahu material. These antidotes were successful as near cult films for deluded men—and enjoyed by women too for the wit and energy of the narratives—but the rom com is a hardy specimen immune to these subversive versions. It has become the staple: wholesome *dal chawal* spiced up into flavourful *biryani*.

3
Non-conformists Are the New Cool

Non-conformists are not cut from the same cloth and come in one size fits all. The daughters down the decades of the original rebel Nirmala of *Duniya Na Mane* (the first film to advocate female empowerment in 1937) are individuals who choose their battles—sometimes they are chosen—and fight them in their own way. If choice and acting upon it is the overall definition of post-feminism, *Queen, The Dirty Picture, Ishqiya, Margarita with a Straw, Manmarziyan, Piku, Cocktail,* and the latest addition, *Thappad* presents different facets of non-conformism. We need these rebels—with and without a cause—to make mainstream cinema meaningful even though it operates under commercial constraints.

Non-conformists are born. One cannot carry out genetic engineering on their DNA however diligently one works to whittle away the core of their personality. Circumstances can make a person conform to some extent but the suppressed gene, waiting for chance, pops up to get back to non-conformist freedom; or chaos according to conservative critics. Non-conformism can also be a fake attitude, donned like the latest designer label. However, the pose dissembles quickly enough for those whose sensibility and self-preservation instinct makes them follow all rules—reasonable and unreasonable, irrational and prejudiced that a basically conservative society imposes as the unwritten law. One cannot pour an instinctive non-conformist, comfortable under her skin, into a saleable, non-threatening mould. Make no mistake. The non-conformist is perceived as dangerous to the establishment that upholds the status quo for its own safety.

There are more non-conformist male actors than actresses. Roles for actors with unconventional looks and attitude are written, depending on how their films fare commercially. Producers took a chance with Irrfan and it paid off handsomely at home and internationally. Now they are willing to gamble on Nawazuddin Siddiqui, not just as a prominent character actor, but as romantic lead. It is still a man's world even in the mainstream-meets-Indie cinema. Fewer actresses who don't conform to the given 'look' and accommodative attitude, go past the first few films that many not set the box-office blazing. It is almost impossible for an unconventional actress—in demeanour and attitude—to get past the casting director if she has with no *khandani*[1] connections to the industry. Alternatively, she finds an Indie godfather to promote her. But a few brave women with grit in their bones and resolve in their blood have leaped over these hurdles to become iconic disruptors of conventional expectations. Kangana Ranaut, Vidya Balan, Kalki Koechlin, Taapsee Pannu have all broken mouldering stereotypes. Their track record is remarkable. The women they bring to life on screen all come with a certain élan of unpredictability. Even if the genre—they are not well-defined in our film industry—is a familiar one with its own narrative tropes and conventions, the characters these actors portray surprise, if not shock the audience. But one distinction needs to be kept in mind. These films and these roles are not the equivalent of parallel cinema's path-breaking portrayals.

The contrast with the iconoclastic days of parallel cinema is striking. Parallel cinema made non-conformism a virtue and celebrated it. It was the satisfaction of succeeding against the norm, the sense of accomplishment in backing such actors in significant films. It vindicated the filmmaker's creative instinct and faith in casting unknowns. In the process, these auteurs created new stars that rank among the pantheon of greats. You just have to look at Shyam Benegal's repertory performing brilliantly in film after film (not only his but other auteurs as well), while minting shining stars of the Other Cinema—Smita Patil, Shabana Azmi, Deepti Naval, Naseeruddin Shah, Om Puri being the most famous—who went on to light up mainstream films with their artistry. Smita Patil and Shabana Azmi did not conform to the popular definitions of prettiness. Smita was dark-skinned and not curvy. She was also not a trained actor but depended on intuition and instinct. Smita scorched the screen with her intensity. Shabana negotiated the divide between mainstream and parallel almost from the beginning of her career more adroitly. A trained actor, Shabana caught the *sur*[2] of whatever film she

---

[1] Family or dynastic.
[2] Pitch, in the musical sense.

acted in. The deglamorized, no make-up look was the norm for many parallel films. Smita's fiery Bindu, suspicious of city folk purporting to help poor villagers in *Manthan* (1976); Shabana, as the pregnant Rama, a shunned *musahar* (scheduled caste) herding pigs across the swollen river in *Paar* (1984) are incomparable. For both, stardom and enduring critical acclaim came for their epoch-making work in the Other Cinema This school of film-making is impossible now—for commercial and creative reasons. Now non-conformism is a carefully calibrated experiment where finding the right actress is absolutely crucial because the narrative adheres to mainstream format, at least most of the time. Within these constraints, she should spark off a certain sizzle, a frisson of excitement about the particular film she is in. It is another matter that the sizzle can fizzle out and it does happen to both fake and far out non-conformists. To reiterate how crucial the right actress is for a landmark film that runs counter to the prevailing norm, the careers of Kangana Ranaut and Vidya Balan offer different graphs. Now Taapsee Pannu joins their illustrious ranks. Their off screen personality finds a way to infiltrate the narrative. After the success—of *Queen* and *The Dirty Picture*—this coalescence of the role and persona spills over into subsequent films.

Kangana Ranaut is a true trailblazer who has won three National Awards—twice for best actress and once for best supporting actress—and flaunts a reputation for taking on Bollywood bigwigs head on, publicly accusing them of blatant nepotism so prevalent in the industry. This is an ongoing battle in which claws are unsheathed, rumours and gossip recycled to cater to a public that is divided in its support. It has now reached a plateau of indifference. That plateau can suddenly peak with excitement. Ranaut has declared she is making a film on her life and she will direct it—who better?—post the lukewarm reception of her mega project *Manikarnika* (2019) that sacrificed content for spectacle. Her journey into Bollywood writes itself as a riveting screenplay. She was a total outlier, from a hill town in remote Himachal Pradesh come to claw her way into this exclusive men's only club. Entry is by invitation only to star kids and those without connections survive by sheer determination, sustained purely by the passion to act. But over the past two years and more, Ranaut's shrill partisan avatar on social media and her fervent endorsement of Hindutva contradicts her early image: the gutsy actor who thumbed her pert nose at Bollywood establishment. Her credibility is severely damaged. But that cannot detract from the impact of her early films.

It is to the early Ranaut we need to look at, to understand what set her apart from a host of newcomers struggling to get a foothold. With no background of modelling, TV, or theatre, this waif with a halo of curls, delicate features, and an indomitable spirit started out in small films as a neurotic woman poised on the edge of breakdown—*Gangster* and *Woh Lamhe* both in 2006. These were the almost assembly line films rolling off under Vishesh Films banner—heavily sexualised, edged with crime/supernatural/horror—casting comparative newcomers entrusted to directors unfurling their storytelling skill sets. Sometimes Mahesh Bhatt took a particular interest in a film close to his heart like *Woh Lamhe*. This was Mahesh Bhatt's story, fictionalizing his relationship with the glamorous diva Parveen Babi whose mental illness drove her to tragedy. Ranaut played the suicidal, schizophrenic star Sana Azmi, exploited by a boyfriend who was more an abusive pimp. Aditya, a filmmaker who first scorned and then challenged the passionate actor in Sana, tries to take care of her when she is on the road to self-destruction. Ranaut brought both the necessary vulnerability and mercurial mood swings with a kind of abandon uncommon to mainstream films of the time. She was foul-mouthed and flagrantly exhibitionistic to portray a Bollywood star whose screamathons and outrageous public conduct made her scandalmongers' darling. Bollywood hardly made films about itself or its stars and when it did venture gingerly into this mine-strewn territory, the starry characters being portrayed were either shown as pitiable birds in a golden cage or goddesses worthy of fan adoration. *Rangeela* (1995) and *Mast* (1999) with Urmila Matondkar by Ram Gopal Varma; *Filmstar* (2005) with Mahima Chowdhury directed by Tanuja Chandra; *Heroine* (2005) with Kareena Kapoor by Madhur Bhandarkar; *Fan* (2016) with Shah Rukh Khan by Maneesh Sharma; and all those decades ago, *Sone Ki Chidiya* (1958) with Nutan by Saheed Latif, to name only the more prominent films.

In that sense, Ranaut and director Mohit Suri were rule breakers, blending pathos and romantic drama to get good reviews but commercially, it was an average success. *Woh Lamhe* established Ranaut as 'different', willing to walk on the wild side. And enact 'bold' scenes as an added cachet. Then came *Life in a … Metro* (2007) directed by Anurag Basu which told a quartet of interconnected stories of couples out of love, others searching for love and the narrator/hero as outsider in search of a good job. The ostensible stance was amoral and non-judgemental but as one probes the not so deep subtext, conventional morality triumphs. The woman on the brink of leaving her unfaithful husband for an actor who could become a soul mate steps back to save her marriage. The modern working woman Neha (Kangana Ranaut) is shown finally repenting for sleeping with her married boss to get additional, out of turn perks. Predictably, she attempts suicide and is saved by the narrator/hero Rahul (Sharman Joshi) who had a yen for her. Ranaut is pert, dismissive, and finally remorseful as the narrative dictates.

An early high point in the careers of two actors confirmed our perceptions of the fashion world and its highly ambitious models. It fetched Ranaut her first National Award for Best Supporting Actress and Priyanka Chopra her only Award for the Best Actress. The film was Madhur Bhandarkar's *Fashion* (2008), one of his better films that capitalized on our almost prurient interest in the lives of fashion models and our unspoken moral judgements of their choices. Success extracts a price: compromises, sexual favours demanded and given, the insane insecurities, dependence on drink and drugs to cope with these insecurities, and bitter rivalries that do not let friendships survive. Shonali (Ranaut) is the reigning supermodel, arrogant and disdainful of newcomers, hardly ever acknowledging their existence. Even at her peak, Shonali is gnawed by insecurities and emotional hollowness. Meghna (Priyanka Chopra) a fresh-faced girl from Chandigarh persuades her parents to let her try her luck in big bad glamorous Bombay. It is the classic story of a star is born, with the crucial difference that Shonali is not the mentor whose decline runs parallel to Meghna's rise. Shonali's self-destructive path is a cautionary tale as she ends up a wreck of the super cool, supermodel who had swept her imperious way to the crown. There can only be one supermodel at a given time. It is shaky ladder, the one at top conscious of usurpers climbing steadily up to dethrone her.

Meghna is resourceful and hardworking. She models for a lingerie ad to pay a top photographer for her portfolio. Working her way up, she gets into a live-in relationship with an aspiring male model. That is, until the powerful head of the modelling agency offers to make her the face of Panache if she becomes his mistress. He is married but Meghna agrees. Her face is on the huge billboard displacing Shonali's. Bhandarkar's films plough along set tracks and he is prone to sensationalism in the name of realism—a self-proclaimed 'experimental' filmmaker. Shonali is not just distraught. She is destroyed, a junkie clamouring for her next fix. Meghna throws up a steadily rising career when she aborts an unwanted pregnancy and in a reckless moment tells the truth to the boss' wife who all along is aware of his affairs. Her new arrogance has alienated the two good friends she had made in a cutthroat business. The final shock comes when she wakes up next to a stranger after a party where alcohol flows like water. Self-worth low, career in doldrums, she goes back to her parents who nurture her self-esteem. A father who had wanted her to be an accountant encourages Meghna to go back and begin anew. Healed and resolute once again, a few good friends help to revive a career. Meghna lands the coveted showstopper slot and though frozen momentarily, she strides onto the catwalk and a new future.

The director inserts an arbitrary twist to redeem Meghna with dollops of compassion for the haughty woman who had ignored her. She brings home Shonali who is living like a waif on the streets and tries to help her recover. Broken and grateful, Shonali does try but the rot has seeped deep into her fragile bones. She is so brittle that one is afraid a touch would shatter her. The police find her dead on a murky, dingy street. The director is adept at drawing attention to something that happens in real life, incidents torn from tabloids, to reinforce his claims of authenticity even while his narrative trudges along the beaten path. He did have real models play themselves for the right ambience. Bhandarkar was true to his tabloid instincts. He based Shonali Gujral on Geetanjali Nagpal, daughter of a naval officer who was educated in good schools and went on to be a top model. Later, after a turbulent life, she was found on the streets of Delhi begging for food and liquor. Ranaut admitted that her character was based on Gitanjali, causing an uproar. Affronted women's organizations tried without success to stop the screening of *Fashion*. Nagpal was eventually helped by The Delhi Commission for Women.

Ranaut's capricious ways in *Tanu Weds Manu* (2011) saves the film from a rom com that does not know whether it wants to stick to the genre rules or take the route of satire. It veers into screwball comedy territory for the chaotic ending. There has not been a more vain, changeable, and whimsical heroine than Tanu bored out of her skull in Kanpur's sprawling family home crammed with the extended family. A confused Tanu is on the way to shaping an acceptably non-conformist image of the new heroine: spunky and spicy but not unacceptably naughty. Post-feminist critiques of media representations of women have become conformist as well as inaccessibly arcane. The debate has moved on from flag-bearing 60s feminism. The emphasis now is on individual nuance in a comfortable middle-class setting, exploring the mindset of millennial women.

It is all right for Tanu, the Kanpur girl whose head is turned by a few years in a Delhi college, to be a rebel without a cause until she finds the nice, undemanding NRI who will comply with her freakish ways and try to fulfil her whimsical demands. *Tanu Weds Manu* takes on the Rajshri formula of arranged marriages for docile, biddable girls and manages to turn it on its head without malice but lots of good humour. In a nice, likeable way, it subverts the spoilt NRI groom and the virtuous desi bride formula. Manu (Madhavan) the London-based doctor goes on the girl-seeing junket with the resigned attitude of fulfilling one more family obligation, with not a romantic bone in his rather stodgy but quietly appealing body. He is part-engineer part-doctor, working with pacemakers, as he confesses rather apologetically. He is definitely not the sort to set a girl's heart racing. Even the staid doctor falls in love at first sight of the reluctant girl who falls asleep when the bride-seeing interview is going on at its awkward pace. So smitten is Manu by the wayward Tanu who demands that he reject her that the good man goes to great lengths to unite her with the man she thinks she wants to marry. Raja (Jimmy Sheirgill) is a handsome hunk full of macho bluster. He is not exactly a Mafiosi, part of a criminal gang but a tough man for hire to politicos. And a decent brother who wants his slightly handicapped sister to marry a caring man like Manu. No wonder Tanu has his name tattooed on her chest, as she coyly confesses to Manu. At the same time, she wants to needle the reserved doctor into reaction. She just can't bear it when men aren't in love with her.

Ranaut's Tanu is perky and impertinent but not petulant. She smokes, maybe she had done drugs too, and changes boyfriends at will. She strongly fancies Raja for husband, much against her long-suffering family's wishes. This family, tucked away among the narrow Kanpur backstreets, spills over with aunts, uncles, cousins including a little tot running around naked while he welcomes the groom's party with a courteous *aayiye, aayiye.*[3] The father of the bride sits on the terrace listening to Vividh Bharathi while the women bustle around the old-fashioned kitchen. All the families we meet are believable while the narrative meanders to trigger multiple mini climaxes, then lets in some calm passages before haring off to yet another crisis and its resolution. The supporting cast of groom's buddy and the girl's best friend are bracingly practical. The hero gets stodgier while he tries to fulfil Tanu's wish to wed her Raja and reconcile her parents to the wedding. Where is the thrill in that? Why a boring wedding that everyone blesses? Tanu keeps changing her mind as whom to marry at predictable intervals and she does wear out our patience. Aanand L. Rai is a director more comfortable with people than the frenetic action he has chosen.

In hindsight, we can understand why *Tanu Weds Manu* was successful, because it is surprisingly low key in its humour. You understand why the small-town girl wants to escape the preordained fate of a dutiful daughter, docile daughter-in-law, and biddable wife but doesn't really know how and what this imagined freedom is. This reassertion of the small-town girl's aspirations reflects the social and economic reality that was first noticed in the success of cricketers, boxers, and athletes emerging out of the hinterland. A profound change that escaped the national radar, which was so firmly focused on the metropolises, is now part of the discourse—be it our cinema, politics, and economics. A discussion on NDTV had Anupama Chopra grill Karan Johar, Habib Faisal, and Vikramaditya Motwane on the waning power of the NRI formula and the emergence of small-town North India. Karan Johar cried mea culpa for triggering the herd mentality that equated designer brands and NRI stories with blockbusters. Now is the time of the small-town ethos and desi girls who are unafraid to be quirky. And let down their hair.

From the image of the capricious, sometimes promiscuous, given to smoking and drinking, emotionally unstable young woman Ranaut was slotted into, evolved non-conformism of a totally unexpected kind. *Queen* (2014) is the anti-rom com film when rom coms were ruling the box office. Bollywood coronations, which by their very speculative nature are tentative, usually reserve the honour of Shahenshah and Badshah for hot male stars. An exception occurred with Kangana Ranaut being

---

[3] Come in, do come.

crowned the new Queen of a hesitant anti-rom com trend. Vikas Bahl seems to know exactly how to spice up the journey of self-discovery by a diffident, protected girl from Delhi's proudly Punjabi enclave of Rajouri. Rani remains a quintessential, sheltered Indian girl with a limited worldview whose two weeks in Paris and Amsterdam have made her accepting and non-judgemental of other people, mores, cultures, and ways of thinking. She returns to the welcoming warmth of her loving family with enough steel in her spine and a tongue in her mouth.

Rani Mehra is the girl next door, sweet as the jalebis at her father's mithai shop, doted upon by her over-protective parents. Shy and obedient, she is to marry Vijay (Rajkumarr Rao playing the smarmy cad without sugar-coating his sense of entitlement) who had courted the timid student of Domestic Science (what else?), waylaying her outside her college to the giggling amusement of her friends.

Rani's rosy world collapses, as she is practically left at the *Mandap*[4] (two days before the wedding) by Vijay, who after a brief London posting, finds that Rani no longer suits his upscale status. She meets him at a cafe, escorted by her younger brother when she is shell-shocked by the rejection. She is abject, stammering, and pleading with an unfeeling man who feels superior to her. She shuts herself up in her room for a day. Her decision when she comes out takes everyone aback. Rani will go on her prepaid honeymoon all by herself. Is it a face-saving ploy to get away from the scene of her humiliation? Or is it something intangible that urges her to fly the coop for a short while? The parents cannot refuse her anything and Rani flies off to Paris. Thus begins her journey into self-confidence, wide-eyed awareness of the world outside her safe cocoon.

Rani's education begins with Vijayalakshmi (Lisa Haydon, impressive in the way she carries off her brand of chutzpah with assumed Gallic élan), the insouciant half-Indian single mother, part of the housekeeping staff at the small hotel. Rani comes out of her bewildered disbelief at the carefree attitude to sex and relationships she encounters. The writing and Bahl's direction, along with Ranaut's improvised dialogues (for which she is credited), unpeels the layers of reserve to bring out the fun-loving 24-year-old who is ready to cope with anything. She tackles a bag snatcher,

---

[4] Decorated wedding altar.

sheds her inhibitions to dance with abandon at a nightclub with her new friend and guide.

We root for a reticent Rani who overcomes her humiliation and we laugh with her—rarely at her—as she encounters a series of culture shocks. The change is both gradual and radical. She accepts three young men of different nationalities as roommates in an Amsterdam hostel and makes friends with them; then wins a cookout competition under the nose of an affronted, stereotypically condescending Italian chef. The plot is episodic but with a strong linear thread. It is a story of quiet self-assertion, minus a flag-waving feminist manifesto. The drama is muted and told with persuasive, if calculated, charm. A mis-sent photo to Vijay's phone by Vijayalakshmi reveals the ex-fiancée's hip new avatar and he chases her to Amsterdam but finally gets his comeuppance for being such a total jerk. Rani has come a long way from *behenji* to modish young woman but she still retains her sweetness. After all, how could she not be sweet, since everyone describes her as being dunked in *chashni* (sugar syrup)?

Bahl is playing with stereotypes here. He reveals the inherent racism of Rani's fear of the African while reinforcing the other stereotypes we have inherited: Vijayalakshmi's dangerously inviting dusky sexuality versus Rani's fair-skinned virtuousness. Ranaut proves that sweetness doesn't have to be cloyingly saccharine because she retains her faith in people and trusts her new experiences, willing to learn from them. Getting worldly wise to the ways of men and fashion tips from the feisty Vijaylakshmi is along predictable lines. What is most appealing is her interaction with her roommates and overcoming both fears and prejudices: the comical Japanese who hides the tragedy of losing his family in the tsunami with his perpetual clowning, the rangy Russian Oleksander who wears a permanent expression of Slavic melancholy and finally gives up trying to correct Rani's pronunciation of his name, and the big built African who is so unexpectedly gentle. Bahl confronts our stereotypical perceptions with humour. Rani's middle-aged father tucks in his paunch while the overweight younger brother gapes at Vijayalakshmi's breasts as she bends into the frame while Rani Skypes with the family. Both lose interest when she exits the screen. The self-explanatory scene punctures our hypocrisy with sly candour. These touches, plus the strict avoidance of any romantic dalliance—even with the dishy Italian who persists in calling Rani pretty lady—makes *Queen* the trendsetter of fun feminism. Rani is not scandalized by the sex worker in Amsterdam's famous district and finds pole dancing great entertainment. She still remains an innocent, buying sex toys with no clue to what they are for and finding other uses for it, to the amusement of her new roommates.

Yet she remains virginal through her education on her European holiday. Her innocence has been insular, because of non-exposure to other modes and mores of existence. Rani comes back with a sexier wardrobe, no longer the dowdy *behenji*. Vijay and his mother are now begging her to resume the engagement but Rani has the last confident laugh. She gives the ring back, and walks away with a bit of swag and a pleased half-smile. Is *Queen* the counterpart of 80s *Arth* (1982) minus the angst and bitterness? Shabana Azmi's Pooja, an orphan, is emotionally and financially dependent on her filmmaker husband who is having an affair with the clingy, schizophrenic actress Kavita (Smita Patil). *Arth* is less about Mahesh Bhatt's involvement with Parveen Babi but more about doing justice to Pooja. She finally stands on her own feet, and doesn't need a man in her life. Most definitely, not the husband who has wearied of schizophrenic Kavita's emotional demands. Pooja will not take him back. *Arth* is Hindi cinema's *Unmarried Woman* (1978), the influential Paul Mazursky's film starring Jill Clayburgh. *Queen* is the dis-engaged new Indian girl, enjoying her freedom. Bahl takes care not to ruffle middle-class audience expectations by linking Rani's coming of age with an affair. Conservative families can celebrate a daughter's right to reject a fiancé but not if it comes with the tag of sexual experience. Marriage is not the be all and end all of a girl's life even when the film started with a loud family preparing for a big fat Punjabi wedding. Ranaut won the National Award for Best Actress for her portrayal of a sweet-natured naïf's discovery of self-worth.

There is an ironical footnote to the film's success. There were murmurs of Bahl's tendency to sexually harass women. They were overlooked. With Me Too came charges by an assistant of constant harassment by the director and Kangana Ranaut seconded the charge. The cohort of producers Anurag Kashyap, Vikramaditya Motwane, and Madhu Mantena disassociated themselves from Bahl who was part of this informal group. According to trade news, Bahl has been partially reinstated by his erstwhile producers.

Ranaut's consecutive National Award for Best Actress was for the sequel *Tanu Weds Manu Returns* (2015) directed by Aanand L. Rai with the same cast. There is a piquant addition, Ranaut's double role: Tanu a bored, vengeful harridan after four years of contentious marriage, and Kusum AKA Datto, a down to earth Haryanvi athlete studying in Delhi on a sports scholarship. They can pass for each other at first sight. Tanu is shrill, discontented, and a clothes horse while sporting a veneer of London glamour and haughty attitude. Datto leaves an impression of muscular athleticism matched by her practical commonsense. Tanu is fair and dainty; Datto couple of shades darker, sturdy, with a hint of buck teeth. The opening sequence is an unbelievably crude farce, of Tanu getting Manu put away for mental illness and domestic abuse when they are at a mental health facility in England. Tanu becomes a caricature of her own capricious self. The nice and acceptably naughty waywardness of the original Tanu is unrecognizable in the conscienceless bored woman who will do anything for a lark. She is now pathologically vain, can't let any man within vicinity not crush on her. Her shenanigans are calculated to shock the socks off the prospective groom who has come to see her cousin. Tanu saunters into the courtyard, wrapped in a bath towel and outrageous attitude. Leering appreciatively is the new law student ensconced in the house as a non-rent paying tenant. Tanu takes the tag of *bindas*[5] to a level never seen before.

Manu comes back to Delhi, thanks to Tanu's parting kindness of ringing up his best friend Pappi (Deepak Dobriyal) to come and free the incarcerated doctor. Manu chances upon Kusum alias Datto when he goes to Delhi university campus to deliver a lecture. Her resemblance to Tanu makes a stalker of him and he tries to further the acquaintance. Aanand L. Rai is content to skim the surface of emotions. The only creative expenditure is to make Datto a girl to remember. Simple, yet outspoken, she values her scholarship above everything else, because sport is her only chance at getting a good education. Her patriarchal Haryanvi family would not let a girl go to Delhi even though she would be living with her brother and *bhabhi*. The circus chase starts once again, from Kanpur to Delhi to Haryana. It is raucous, with only scattered humour to relieve the predictability of coincidences galore. Tanu's old and new

---

[5] Wilfully carefree, given to breaking rules.

flame add to the combustible mix until she realises that Manu (to whom the law student has sent a divorce notice) is about to get married to a good girl who deserves him. Tanu lands up at the start of wedding festivities tossing Manu on the horns of an old dilemma. The familiar woes and few thrills of remarrying a known harridan finally trump the wholesome appeal of the athlete who, he is sure, will bounce back on her feet. Datto is the saving grace of a comic caper gone off the rails.

Datto represents the spunky, resilient new breed of girls from Haryana who have broken the shackles of Khap Panchayats ruled by dictatorial patriarchs. Ranaut is tone and nuance perfect as Datto while she lets Tanu veer off the course of credibility. Was it by design to highlight the differences between the two? Buoyed up by her third National Award, Ranaut was in a combative mood. 'Success is the best revenge ... women should answer back with either sarcasm or success. That really kills.' This was Ranaut on national TV to Barkha Dutt, India's best known woman journalist, when the knives were out for her public slanging match with Hrithik Roshan, Bollywood's Greek god and golden boy. He denied the affair Ranaut claimed had happened between them. This wrangling turned ugly with bizarre allegations but Ranaut retained her sangfroid all through the very public spat.

Ranaut's overconfidence is evident in *Simran* (2017), the much talked about film about an Indian woman Sandeep Kaur's bank robbing spree in the US. Directed by Hansal Mehta, the film gives shared writing credits to Ranaut and Apurva Asrani. Mehta is a National Award-winning director for *Shahid* (2013), an uncompromising political film about a Muslim lawyer shot dead for advocating the rights of young Muslim men charged with terrorism on the flimsiest grounds. Ranaut plays baccarat-addicted Praful Patel—a divorcee who stays with her disapproving father and Bollywood- diehard fan mother: her futile wringing of hands doesn't help the situation. Praful works in the housekeeping department of an Atlanta five star hotel. She wants to move out to an apartment of her own but her loan application doesn't pass muster. Ranaut plays Praful with oodles of chutzpah and insolence—only occasionally allowing chinks in the armour to reveal her hurt and exasperation with her conservative parents. She has beginner's luck at the baccarat table in Las Vegas and the addiction spirals out of control—losing her savings, borrowing from a loan shark, and finally a life of larceny. After robbing a gas station, Praful graduates to banks and gives her name as Simran when almost caught. Simran the Lipstick Bandit (she leaves a message with red lipstick) becomes notorious in and around Atlanta.

Desperate to shake off the threatening loan collector, she seeks her father's help who makes it conditional on her meeting a prospective groom. Praful does like the non-judgemental Sameer (Sohum Shah) but not enough to give up her career of crime. Sameer is in love with her and helps out on occasion but neither he nor her family is willing to stand by her when cops take Praful away. The film is notable for Ranaut's performance—it shows Praful as a vulnerable young woman whom circumstances make a criminal, without apologizing for her sex life where a one-night stand is all right if it buys her the sexy red dress she covets. It is convincing but not extraordinarily enough to win the audience over. Two factors are responsible for this. First, it is a one-woman show all the way, with no one to play with or against. All other characters are glorified cameos. Is it an example of hubris from a non-conformist nonpareil? Even more importantly, Indian audiences are not ready to accept a convicted criminal for heroine, however well played by an acclaimed actress. A lark like *Bunty Aur Babli* is well-received but not a woman who chooses robbery to pay off self-incurred gambling debts. The morality metre ticks faster when the audience finds no emotional connect with an unrepentant criminal.

There are other kinds of non-conformists who cause disruption that is more persuasive, by making the woman a strong centre of emotional identification. '*Filme teen cheezo se banti hai. Entertainment. Entertainment. Entertainment. Aur mai entertainment hoon*'. (Films are made of three things: entertainment, entertainment, and entertainment. And I am entertainment.) The self-assertion is followed by a knowing wink. Vidya Balan proved that *She* is entertainment. And the industry took this pithy pronouncement as the new mantra. After *The Dirty Picture* (2011), Balan minted a new image of the non-conformist as a self-confident entertainer who writes her own destiny.

It needed a dirty picture to celebrate—perhaps even liberate?—female sexuality without apology or pious pretensions. It is not as if our films discovered the female form and its power to seduce only with Vidya Balan essaying the factionalized story of the 80s South siren Silk Smitha. The female body was, is and will be prominently present in cinema everywhere.

How and to what degree it is displayed, exploited, or celebrated depends on the shifting cultural mores of a basically male dominated film industry. So let us not delude ourselves that heaving breasts and gyrating hips are new. What is different is the intent and impact of Vidya Balan in *The Dirty Picture*. But a brief history of the changing image of the woman in our popular cinema is in order.

Conventional wisdom according to feminist texts is that the woman's body was calculated to cater to the male gaze and so basically, it was voyeuristic. Whether the actor thus on display was a willing participant or a victim, or if she was even aware of exploitation by male directors and producers has been a subject of heated polemics. Even more pertinent is to ask this problematic question: is the actor even conscious of being reduced to a sex object without being allowed to express her sexual desire? The debate that was part of the feminist discourse of the 70s and 80s seems academic today. Now is the post-feminist age. It legitimizes the conscious use of her body and sexuality as a means of not only achieving power but also a form of self-definition. We are no longer caught in the puritan trap that condemned female sexual expression as contrary to the good Bharatiya Nari ideal. She was deified as the supremely self-sacrificing asexual being with no claim to autonomy. Hypocrisy subtly eroticized the woman's image to cater to the male gaze, stretching permissible depiction in step with social changes that followed globalization. A brief look at the past sets the context.

Mumtaz, Zeenat Aman, Parveen Babi, Hema Malini, Rekha were the precursors—in varied degrees of artful exposure of the desired female sexual form (Zeenat Aman was certainly made to expose skin beyond contemporary standard by Raj Kapoor) —to the erotically charged images of Sridevi and Madhuri. Whether it was Sridevi cavorting in rain in her transparent blue chiffon sari in *Mr. India* (1987) or Madhuri heaving her bosom in *Beta* (1992) and *Khalnayak* (1998) to gain the *dhak dhak girl*[6] title, the male gaze was still predominant. Just think back to Sanjay Dutt's eye patch while Madhuri coyly hints at what is under her choli. It emphatically draws attention to the focused male gaze. The point to remember is that the enticing woman is virtuous if her sexuality is reserved

---

[6] The first line of a famous song translates as my heart is beating, and the visuals are of her heaving bosom.

for the one man in her life—even as she fuels collective fantasies of millions of men out there in the dark secrecy of the theatre.

With the globalized 90s came the assembly line bodies to fit into the mandatory minis and midriff baring tank tops. International fashion houses made the voluptuous female figures of Khajuraho and Konarak déclassé. And then came the size zero obsession and with it the loss of *desi tadka*.[7]

Things were different down South. Well-endowed women were what the filmmakers and audience wanted. Along with avoirdupois, she also had to bear the burden of unbesmirched virtue: the ideal was the epic heroine, the chaste Kannagi conjoined with the Sita-Savitri dyad. Into this hothouse world of ubiquitous hypocrisy sashayed Silukku/Silk Smitha—dusky, she of the inviting bedroom eyes, orgasmically parted fleshy lips, and an attitude that gloried in the power of her cleavage and undulating hips. Even when Silk Smitha was demurely covered up in a sari, with a mangalsutra nestling on her chest, her eyes suggested wanton desire. Or take the scene most Hindi audiences are familiar with. In *Sadma* (1983), she is the sex-starved wife of the older man who suggests naughty things to the patently uncomfortable Kamalhaasan, as she waters the plants with a hose, dressed in mini shorts and skimpy top.

Vidya Balan overcomes the handicap of her Tambrahm looks, and scores as she owns and revels in the power of her sexuality. Even with her oily hair in a tight braid and dressed in the traditional half-sari, she confronts leering louts and tells off a man for not having a functioning *pichkari*.[8] She is sassy as the runaway Reshma, living with a distant aunt in Chennai and desperate to make it in the movies. She is persistent as a buzzing mosquito. When she finally gets a chance to be part of the chorus, Reshma brazenly makes love to the whip, which is her prop. The canny producer knows how to save a film from being a flop by putting back the song the aspiring highbrow director had cut. The high-minded new director doesn't want to sell his film through suggestive sleaze.

Reshma morphs into Silk, the woman who will sell desire to men lusting after her body. What is refreshing about Reshma/Silk is her total honesty and awareness of her own power in a male-dominated industry.

---

[7] Spicy garnish, indigenous style.
[8] Spray pump.

Rajat Arora's sharp, earthy lines spice up her double entendre and ability to seduce the reigning superstar Suryakant (Naseeruddin Shah) to get ahead in her career. The original Silk Smitha spoke in a husky, breathy tone while Balan's mellow mezzo has music built into it. The actor who was cast as the plain Jane, disheartened Sabrina Lal in *No One Killed Jessica* (2011) oozes oomph with the chutzpah one associates with Salman Khan taking his shirt off.

Reshma is her own woman, living on her own terms, taking on the establishment—the star gossip columnist who reluctantly comes to admire Reshma's gutsy honesty, the petulant wife of her married lover, the scorn of the disdainful director Abraham (Emran Hashmi) who falls helplessly in love with her. She dares the world at large whose opinion she doesn't care as long as her fans fill the cinema halls.

The first press interview is a power statement of who she is. Reshma has nothing in the modest house to impress the journalist who has come for an interview after the dance becomes a hit. She talks to him while immersed in a hastily procured bathtub placed squarely in the middle of the room with the aplomb and amusement befitting a screen diva. Unfortunately, Milan Luthria's direction cannot achieve an ironic distance from the film world he is depicting as crude, stereotypical, and exploitative. When a film is about the world of films, a director has to be able to subtly shade the two narratives through texture and tone. Reshma's life outside the studios of Chennai is treated exactly in the same way as the awful films she makes—the title song *Ooh La La* is both a parody of 80s kitsch and some kind of tortured homage.

That is why Balan's performance doesn't have the nuances and richness of *Bhumika* (1977). Shyam Benegal's classic was based on the memoirs of a rebellious Marathi star, Hansa Wadkar. Smita Patil played Usha, the heroine of the 40s and 50s, acting in all the popular genres of the time. Success is hers but happiness is elusive. Hers is the ironic dilemma of an actress searching for her true role in life. Unhappily married to the cold, determined, control freak Damle (Amol Palekar) who initiated her film career (as a child), Usha has a series of affairs. First, with a co-star in love with her but lacking the courage to own it publicly. Then follows the pretentious intellectual, a director (Naseeruddin Shah) who thinks he is too good for the industry. He tricks her into a so-called suicide pact that he has no intention of carrying through. She leaves home to stay in a hotel where she meets an older man, a rich landlord who gives her the status and respect due to a wife (his first wife is an invalid) but she is not allowed to step out of the feudal estate. Usha escapes, back to the familiar environs of Bombay. Her daughter is now married and expecting her first child. Usha is gratified that at last a woman of the family tarred with the brush of 'singing class women' has gained respectability. Usha accepts that she must learn to live on her own terms, draw on her own strength. Benegal's script is complex, where a *lavani*[9] that Usha is performing for a film is a recurring punctuation mark, to narrate chapters of her troubled, dramatic life. It draws the emotional arc, connecting the films, changing genres, and her search for meaningful relationships. It was an astonishingly bravura performance by a 22-year-old of an older woman's turbulent journey to mature self-acceptance. It had gravitas.

If Reshma does not have even half of Usha's complex inner life, it is not her fault. The fault lies with the writing and direction. Balan gives a totally honest and courageous performance, where she mirrors the character written for her. She wears no disguises, no veils that mask the honesty of what she feels but the problem is that the film doesn't give her more. We share her rage, disappointment, fear and cheer her when she takes on the establishment. Balan's real triumph is the shedding of vanity. She lets us see her paunchy belly when she can't button her jeans, the dark circles under distressed eyes, and skin sagging on sallow cheeks while she sinks deeper into drink and despair as her career dives south. She is even inveigled into the sets of a soft porn film from where she runs out into the street, distraught and filled with self-disgust.

The final flourish is predictable. She smears on red lipstick, sticks on a red bindi, and wears a red bridal sari before taking an overdose of sleeping pills. It is an outworn cliché. It hints at her concealed desire for the societal sanction of marriage. For all her rage and rebellion, she too craves for respectability. Or emotional stability at the end of journey: newcomers have displaced her; she is in debt and the only chance of working is in the surreptitious porn industry. From being the goddess of desire, she can't reduce herself to cheap porn.

The Dirty Picture begins with a quote from Nietzsche: 'You must have chaos within you to give birth to a dancing star.' The chaos the script gives

---

[9] Maharashtra's vigorous, sensuous folk dance.

Reshma is one whipped up by a studio fan. It does not come from the churning deep within. If the writing had more depth than mere superficial cleverness, *The Dirty Picture* could have been a radical restatement of the unfettered female—sexually and in deeper aspirational terms. It does resurrect the voluptuous woman in our anorexic times and this seemed to work at the box-office. After all, it was the time for Southern spice. Balan was both brazen and vulnerable, a self-confident over-reacher who gloried in the power of her sexuality and used it with cunning self-awareness and spontaneity. Chutzpah was her middle name.

Reshma/Silk won Balan a National Award—plus every other made-for-TV popular award—in a film where her performance towered over a cleverly punchy script and conventional direction that aimed to titillate rather than explore the protagonist's world in any depth. The film demanded a fearless non-conformist to play Reshma/Silk.

Balan is the quietly assertive non-conformist who will not fit into the stereotype of size zero tyranny, a mannequin on and off stage for designer wear, content with a few songs, glamorous locations, and semblance of stories of the conventional kind. Except for the mishap *Heyy Baby* (2007), Balan's work has been commendable, catching our attention in the multi-track multi-starrer *Salaam-E-Ishq* (2007) as the lively TV reporter stricken with memory loss. The love story of Tehzeeb Hussain married to a Hindu cameraman was the only one that worked in the multiple love-stories marathon. Balan looks Indian and obviously loves it—curves, flowing saris, jhumkas, bindis, etc. It is so refreshing to see a Bollywood star dare the fashion police who had pilloried her mercilessly. Balan doesn't look a clone of her contemporaries. She has found herself, the actor and public persona.

Except for a few missteps on the way, there was always something about Vidya Balan. The signs were all there in *Parineeta* (2005). Pradeep Sarkar's sepia tinted updating of a popular Sarat Chandra story to 60s Calcutta vowed us with a demurely delightful Lalitha who broke the constraints of domestic drama as the *bhadralok*[10] Bangla girl with steel in her spine and unexpected fulfilment of discreetly hinted erotic promise. It might sound like blasphemy to uncritical aficionados of vintage classics but Balan was better than a very young Meena Kumari, a heartbreakingly vulnerable

---

[10] Prosperous, well-educated class.

teenager who considers herself married to the much older, spineless Shekhar. There was beguiling innocence in Bimal Roy's *Parineeta* (1953) that stayed close to the text, as was his wont (minus the kiss mentioned in the novel that supposedly took a thoroughly scandalized Bengal by storm when it was published). But the old *Parineeta* is pretty dated. Except for the ridiculous climax with Saif Ali Khan battering the dividing wall between adjoining houses with a heavy marble pedestal, Sarkar's *Parineeta* did the near impossible with neat perfection: infuse nostalgia for the 60s with contemporary relevance. Balan personified this fusion with grace, dignity, and convincing flashes of passion. Even in her first make or break film, she was never coy. Lalitha considers herself married to the vacillating Shekhar not because she garlanded him at an auspicious time but because the impulsive, unthinking action naturally leads to sex. Even before *The Dirty Picture* cashed in on her sexuality, it is remarkable how comfortable and spontaneous Balan is in her tastefully filmed intimate scenes. She is both decorous and sensuous, imbuing Lalitha with shades of emotional expressiveness. Balan's non-conformism is respectful to the spirit of the original (Bimal Roy's film and Sarat Chandra's novella) and yet she breaks the mould of a de-sexualized Lalitha to reflect contemporary concepts of a woman's sexuality.

Balan's non-conformism misfired in *Bobby Jasoos* (2014) where she played a Hyderabadi Muslim detective (amateur hoping to become a professional) solving small cases and stumbling upon a major crime. She mastered the Deccani patois and ways of the old city. Balan teamed her salwar kameez with clunky trainers and had her hair in two braids while she carried on her work with ingenuity. She not only wants to combat crime but win her disapproving father's affection. Balan donned disguises every other scene and brought in enormous enthusiasm but the unconventional story sans a love interest and expected thrills of the genre did not find favour with the audience.

Balan proves that non-conformism is ageless. A suburban middle-class homemaker can also break conventions of the set rules for a stay-at-home wife and mother. She is not a graduate to begin with. Nor is she working in a bank like her carping older sisters. Hence, a conventional job for a middle-class woman is ruled out. So what if she has people skills (excluding her disapproving sisters, their spouses, and her taciturn father) that can establish warm connections in situations that could otherwise be forbidding? Balan's endearing Sulu in *Tumhari Sulu* (2017) has these qualities and more: enormous enthusiasm and drive to barge into a radio station to demand a chance to host a late night chat show. It sounds sleazy for a respectably married woman with a young son living the suburban life even to contemplate talking in a sexy siren's voice to an audience of predominantly male listeners. Not only does she convince her hesitant husband—who might be losing his job—to let her take up the challenge but makes a huge success of her sexy, breathy *Hellooo*. Sulu has an instinctive knack of empathizing with the lonely callers and that makes the show a surprise hit. Discreetly sexy and warmly caring is a winsome advantage for an unseen woman behind the mike. The film also breaks the stereotype of the female boss who comes down even more heavily on her women subordinates. Neha Dhupia as Maria is not only encouraging but is also Sulu's cheerleader- in- chief. Of course there are inevitable glitches and family misunderstandings but humour and understanding solve them all. Her show *Tumhari Sulu* goes on to be a huge success. No wonder Jitesh Pillaai, editor of *Filmfare* writes about Vidya Balan in Editor's Choice, February 2019 issue: 'It won't be an exaggeration to say she is our Meryl Streep.' The tribute is titled, *40 is the new sexy*. Balan's sexuality is voluptuous and lit with homely warmth when a film needs it.

The non-conformist inhabits the hinterland too. Balan also brought off a daring coup in *Ishqiya*: a merry widow using her sex appeal to lure a pair of con men, an uncle and nephew, to do her dubious bidding in rural India. A caste-driven, male dominated Hindi heartland where private armies and criminal gangs are playing double-crossing games. *Ishqiya* (2010) directed by Abhishek Chaubey is deliciously wicked and veers between suspense and black humour. Khalujan (Naseeruddin Shah) and his nephew Babban (Arshad Warsi) are bumbling petty crooks on the run from a vengeful boss. They seek shelter with Verma another gangster but find his widow Krishna (Vidya Balan) who houses them for her own devious purpose. Krishna spells seduction in a domestic setting as she goes about her chores with a swing in her walk and allure in her eyes and invitation in her voice. Both the men fall for her and she cleverly plays off one against the other. She wants them to kidnap a small-time businessman who was her husband's partner. She promises much to the uncle but goes to bed with the younger man. There is an unbelievably erotic scene where Krishna sucks Babban's finger, her eyes boldly locked with his hinting at more pleasures in store. Krishna is convinced her husband is alive and hiding. The unravelling plot, of betrayal and faked death, ends up in a conflagration with the trio escaping into the jungle. It is a twisted tale told with engaging wit and earthy humour. The verbal transitions from courtly Urdu to rustic Hindi dialect are delightful. Balan makes a scheming woman who finally stages a gas explosion to kill her husband (who was planning to kill her earlier) incredibly sexy and convinces us why she is justified in doing what she does. The ambiguous ending is deliberate to accommodate a sequel.

Talking of *Ishqiya*, his first film, director Chaubey recollects: 'I built her up to be what you'd call a femme fatale in cinematic terms. Quiet, introverted Krishna with her sharp tongue was different from the outgoing Vidya whose laugh rings out on the set ... The look and feel came from the women I had met in small towns who looked beautiful in inexpensive synthetic saris and were not shy of wearing bright colours. I couldn't understand why we'd doll up our heroines in western wear when they looked so sensual in the six yards.... Almost a decade has passed since I shot my first film, but people still talk about Krishna's frank sexuality, completely fresh at that time. They rave about how alluring Vidya looked and how she managed to hold her own against two macho, domineering men.'[11]

Not all non-conformists are flamboyant. She can quietly defy centuries old sanctions that patriarchy endows a man with: violence, overt and covert, that he can unleash on his wife. *Thappad* (2020) empowers Amu (Taapsee Pannu) with calm determination and serene courage that can withstand family pressure—from both natal and marital—and society at large that blames a woman for the breakup of a marriage for what it considers *just* a slap, to which an otherwise good husband is entitled. Taapsee Pannu, who has grown from strength to strength after the landmark *Pink*, makes a resounding statement in *Thappad*. A single slap can rouse a contented homemaker to demand the respect due to her, when her ambitious, stressed out husband does the unthinkable at a party, before family, friends, and his colleagues. Amu not only has to battle well-meaning advice to just let it go and move on. This is a family matter after all is the reason her mother-in-law (who lives away from her affluent husband with the younger son, with no explanation as to why) offers, wilfully

---

[11] *Bangalore Mirror*, February 27, 2019.

blind to the unreasonableness of her advice. Even Amu's mother thinks she must not make too much of an issue out of a non-issue. Both these older women have imbibed these lessons from their mothers and grandmothers. A chain that now must be broken, and Amu dares to snap these unseen iron shackles.

Amu has to overcome generations of advice fed with breast milk to the girl child: it is her duty to sacrifice self for the family. She must adjust to the small and big demands made on her and learn to compromise, even at the cost of self-respect. Men are born entitled; Vikram (Pavail Gulati makes an impressive debut) doesn't even think it is necessary to say sorry. He was slightly drunk, the expected promotion as the head honcho in London does not come through, and he is angry that corporate politics denied him his due. It does not occur to him that his humiliated wife is deeply hurt and silently resentful. He expects she will get him bed tea as usual, then serve breakfast and see him off handing his lunch, wallet, etc. as he leaves home. Amu silently does her routine work, hinting at the churning within; teaches kathak to the neighbour's teenaged daughter, takes care of her diabetic mother-in-law... all with no overt expression of anger. But one senses a resolve crystallizing within her.

Everything seems normal—if rather quiet—until she decides to go and stay with her parents, with no word of returning when a bewildered Vikram goes to his in-laws expecting her to come back with him. When Amu stays put, even her brother thinks she is 'over-reacting'. Her mother Sandhya (Ratna Pathak Shah) thinks it's a wife's duty to subdue her own dreams and get on with life. There is a telling scene when she tells her husband (the sensitive Kumud Misra) that she too had to kill her heart's desires—the untranslatable phrase is *man marna padta hai*—and this supportive man was not even aware of what she went through by giving up her music. Amu's doting father is the only person who supports her. He had thought she could have gone far as a kathak dancer but Amu chose to be a homemaker.

In just three years, Anubhav Sinha has carved an enviable niche for himself as a director with a social conscience who asks uncomfortable questions. *Mulk* (2018) exposes the Hindu majoritarian view that unthinkingly brands patriotic Muslims terrorists, and in *Article 15* (2019), he crafts a taut thriller where a city-bred police officer confronts the miasma of caste politics and deep-rooted prejudice in the hinterland where he is posted. Along with his writer Mrunmayee Lagu, Sinha demands us—men and women—to ask uncomfortable questions of ourselves. How aware are we of subtle putdowns (often disguised as a joke) women are subjected to even in educated, affluent families? Are we prepared to support a young woman like Amu who will not live in a marriage where she is denied respect? She wants a divorce by mutual consent and makes no monetary demands on Vikram. Lagu, basking in the critical appreciation of her writing that has sparked serious conversation, says: 'The only questions I had were about how are we going to achieve this absolutely simple story with such a huge message. How are we going to write it in a way that it comes across—it has that impact, it resonates with people, doesn't feel preachy.'[12]

Thappad weaves in stories of two other couples—Anu's brother Karan and his fiancée Shweta, a legal assistant; sophisticated Netra, a successful lawyer and her high-profile husband who attributes her success to his family connections—to convey different shades of men's sense of superiority and condescension when it comes to women's work. An attitude they are not even aware. Such scripts necessarily add the working-class woman, to broaden its ambit to accommodate a cross-sectional view of society. Sunita, the domestic help accepts being beaten up by the husband as a fact of life but she too gives it back to him when her threshold of tolerance breaks. Sinha weaves all these strands around Amu's steely resolve, to add texture and layers to the theme that is narrated without high decibel drama. It is deliberately underplayed, to avoid sermonizing from creeping in. So much is revealed in the quiet conversations that are organic to the situation. It gets ugly when rival lawyers enter the plot, raising the stakes, calculating that it can lead to an out of court settlement. Through all this, Amu remains committed to her decision. She is not bitter and warmly accepts her mother-in-law's celebratory puja: the occasion is Amu's pregnancy. She belies everyone's assumption and Vikram's hope that pregnancy will lead to reconciliation. Amu is conciliatory only to the extent that Vikram has a right to co-parent the child but she will have custody. Sinha refuses to take the easy, feel good way out. He stands by his admirably courageous Amu. Pannu brings measured poise and hidden depth to Amu, speaking as much through her silence and body

---

[12] *Bangalore Mirror*, 3 March 2020.

language as the well-crafted lines that reveal her intrinsically decent and generous personality. Her core values will not forgive the loss of respect and she can't love the man who doesn't respect her. She will not be in a marriage without love. It is a simple logical progression that has as much emotional validity as ethical integrity.

It is interesting that men have reacted more positively (in print and on TV) to the message of *Thappad*; it seems to have sent them on an introspective path. Women critics, while lauding the strong message of standing up to men's unthinking denigration of their wives, find the script lacking in strong motivation and rather schematic. The few unsatisfactory aspects are outweighed by the powerful theme and Pannu's restrained performance. One act of violence or repeated slighting of a woman's professional achievements may not count as violations of a woman's dignity and selfhood but the very ordinariness of the act can impel a woman like Amu (and Netra, or Sunita) to assert her right and not submit to the conformist stereotype of the forgiving, accommodative wife. Amu does it with grace and dignity.

Anurag Kashyap's forte of edgy black humour and sexual frankness makes *Manmarziyan* (2018) an important contemporary film: it centres on a rebellious young woman's dilemma of choosing her life partner. Is it better to opt for a rollicking sex life with a man not ready for marriage or choose the stability of an older non-judgemental man who lives in London? He has created a kickass young woman who does what she wants and doesn't apologize for her choices. It is set in the heartland of Punjabiyat with a nod to Amrita Pritam in the credits.

Kashyap and his preferred actor Taapsee Pannu make the iconoclastic woman acceptable. On her own terms, breaking from a cliché-ridden Bollywood tradition that permanently marked a woman with sindur once she is married and denied sexual choice even when the first love came back into her life. No respectable woman could sully the sanctity of marriage is the assumption. Kashyap validates marriage but on the woman's terms. It is like tasting forbidden fruit and keeping it too. All this without a strident feminist sermon but creating a woman we can understand and feel for. He also breaks the mould of the love triangle that had calcified over the decades. *Manmarziyan* sets off an interesting speculation: do filmmakers who had hitherto gloried in the violent excesses of unbridled machismo make persuasive feminists?

Rumi (Taapsee Pannu) is in her late 20s, an orphan living with her uncle's family, complete with a doddering Dadaji who is mostly napping on the terrace while her lover leaps over adjoining roofs for an assignation in the rooftop room. She is besotted with a wannabe rock singer Vicky (Vicky Kaushal) who dresses and behaves like one—tattoos, skintight Tees and jeans, swag and strut in place. But not a commitment bone in his wiry body: he doesn't know what it means or entails. Rumi's family wants her to marry and settle down. She wants to marry Vicky but he runs away at the word marriage after agreeing to come and meet the family. Though she loves Vicky and shares great sexual chemistry with him, Rumi is fed up. She agrees to meet an NRI banker who has come to Punjab, ready for an arranged marriage. Rumi's reputation has preceded her in the mohalla like milieu of Amritsar. They get married and Rumi's sulky withdrawn behaviour on the honeymoon sends its own message to Robbie (Abhishek Bachchan). Sex when it finally happens is awkward and cold on her part.

Her determination to be faithful to the quietly understanding Robbie weakens when Vicky comes back, begging and pleading to be forgiven. The many pre-marital romps now turn to post-marital sex. Even if it happened only once, Rumi confesses to her husband and they mutually agree to get the marriage annulled. Other more suitable girls had been suggested to Robbie but he develops a yen for the hockey-playing, don't-give-a-damn individuality that is so intrinsic to Rumi. He also appreciates her honesty about her past. What we see unfold is a tentative friendship and mutual respect grow between the newly annulled couple. Rumi has now realized that Vicky will never settle down and who knows where this new bond based on honesty is headed. The door is left ajar on this ... leaving room for ambiguity to crystallize into something concrete. Rumi's flaws are not hidden: she is headstrong, not above manipulating her orphan status to get her way. She is passionate—not only about Vicky—also other things she believes in: complete honesty about her past and one time lapse. Rumi is in the line of parallel cinema heroines of *Ankur* (1974), *Bhumika* (1977), *Chakra* (1981). She does not suffer their social and economic constraints but believes in sexual autonomy.

Could anyone imagine the glamorous Deepika Padukone, Bollywood's highest paid actress, venturing into non-conformist terrain that is deemed box-office poison by industry pundits? But she did, and splendidly at that in *Cocktail* (2012) and *Piku* (2015). *Cocktail*'s Veronica is perhaps the most complex and under-appreciated role in recent times. The film is a triangle that does not fit the frothy rom com formula. How can the star actor who plays the female lead not end up with the man and her mousy best friend is the preferred choice for marriage? Under the glitz of a frenetic lifestyle that looks dazzling, the subtext makes desi virtues win over Western glamour and its assumed moral laxity. But, and this is a serious but, the narrative does not pose morality in stark black and white terms. There is subtle celebration of the essentially nice and generous heart under the bright party girl veneer that camouflages Veronica's loneliness. The writing and direction are invested so deeply in Veronica that it invites a similar deep engagement with her—her life, the choices she makes, rejection she suffers as not an ideal Indian daughter-in-law and wife and thus punished for not adhering to Indian values. Veronica wins for her emotional intelligence and large heart, trumping the obvious, superficial conclusion that she is the loser. It is Veronica, the flawed and engaging woman who emerges the winner, upending the rom com formula in the process. She takes us into the working of her mind and heart and the involved viewer shares her emotional turmoil.

Cocktail has Imtiaz Ali's writing stamped on it while the director Homi Adajania infuses unexpected irony into the familiar comedy of a new age triangle. Veronica is the poor little rich girl, in her own self-mocking words, a rich bitch. Her London flat is home for human strays Veronica picks up on a whim—so she pretends, but it is really her compassion for Meera (Diana Penty) a stranded Indian girl thrown out by a husband who had married her for money back home. Soon, it becomes a non-sexual kind of ménage a trios with Gautam (Saif Ali Khan) moving in with Veronica after a one-night stand following a club encounter. It is a casual, no strings relationship and Meera overcomes her initial dislike of the congenital playboy who had hit on her at the airport on arrival. This convivial threesome splits soon after Gautam's typical Punjabi mother lands up from India to check if her darling son has found a suitable bride with traditional values. Her first sight of the son let loose in licentious London is enough to send her reeling in shock: Gautam is in drag, lips painted a smudgy red, garishly made up eyes, prancing to *Sheila Ki Jawani*. To heighten the shock, Veronica saunters around in just a shirt and no bottoms. Gautam tries to save the day by pretending that he has fallen for Meera, who is modestly dressed and prays regularly. Ironically, the pretence turns real. Meera tries to be noble and stay out of the scene when she discovers that under the party girl vivacity, best friend Veronica too is in love with the rather unworthy Gautam. Good cheer gives way to bitter outburst: you test drive with me and choose Meera for marriage, Veronica accuses Gautam who has now discovered his serious, committed side. He nurses Veronica when she is hit by a car. Misreading his concern, Veronica tries to convince him that she can be a good Indian wife, like cook biryani and raita. She abjectly suggests even a real ménage a trois: Meera the wife and she, the mistress. At one point, Gautam complains that the two girls are playing snatch the toy game.

Veronica has finally found true friends, compensating her sense of being abandoned by a rich father who regularly sends a fat cheque in lieu of parental presence. Veronica, once she realizes how deeply her two good friends love each other, tracks down Meera in India and unites them. The real winner in terms of emotional growth and maturity is Veronica—gallant and truly generous in feeling happy for the couple. Of course, *Cocktail* can be read as yet another validation of traditional Indian virtues a man seeks in a wife and rejection of Veronica's Western ways that also include casual sexual relationships. The subtext of Veronica's generous nature and graceful acceptance of reality enriches her character, rather than make her a willing sacrificial lamb. Despite her insecurities, Veronica has enough self-worth and genuine goodness to move on. Yes, she is weepy and angry initially but gets over it and convinces us that she has. She is in no way apologetic about her choices, of her lifestyle. She accepts herself and makes us accept her for the complex, genuine young woman who has no regrets in life. She will remain the non-conformist desi, not submitting to the usual compulsion of the diasporic Indian to declare adherence—orally if not in practice—to Indian cultural values. Hypocrisy is not for Veronica. Imtiaz Ali brings a rare honesty to the tangled relationships and conflicted feelings of desire, love, and coping with rejection.

The magic of Juhi Chaturvedi's writing lies in making what polite society considers vulgar—even more acutely given our puritanical mindset—central to her witty and insightful observation of relationships in *Piku* (2015). Chaturvedi has her pulse on what this generation feels, thinks, and wants. She does it with uninhibited yet intelligent humour, understanding and a capacity to make the unmentionable so acceptable and common place that we can laugh with and at the situation: an independent, unmarried career woman's life and work is dependent on whether her cantankerous Baba had a satisfactory motion that morning. Piku (Deepika Padukone) is no forbearing martyr as Bhaskor Banerjee (Amitabh Bachchan who insists spelling his name with *o* to underline the correct pronunciation of his Bengali name) plays the domestic tyrant without any compunction of conscience. He demands it as his right. He is widowed and she is his only child. Piku is inured to his hypochondriac ways and can call his bluff and yet, the two share a genuine bond that runs the gamut from exasperation to affection with such ease that it carries us along, chortling and guffawing with glee. Piku can complain that he is a most unnatural father who announces at a party that she is no virgin, financially independent, and in no need of a permanent man in her life— except, her frustratingly irksome Baba. Yet, she puts up with his tantrums and high-handed ways that drive a maid away and can drive others batty. To sum up this impossible man: impossible to live with and difficult to live without. She reprimands his so-called feminism when he speaks of his late wife's low IQ at a family dinner in honour of her birthday. Her feisty aunt endorses Piku's reprimand with her usual gusto. Feistiness is inherited through the maternal DNA in this unconventional family.

The film underlines a new urban truth: daughters have become caregivers, contrary to the assumption that sons are duty bound to care for their parents. Married and unmarried daughters have proved to be more caring and responsible, breaking many traditional rules of not being dependent on a daughter. She was considered *paraya dhan* (wealth given away and belonging to her marital home) on whose time and resources parents, more so the father, had no claim. Piku's filial duty does not mean she can't reprimand her Baba for unreasonable demands but she will accommodate his wishes as best as she can. Shoojit Sircar brings such an assured touch to this brilliant writing, creating the right ambience for strongly individuated characters to inhabit a tale of two cities and the defining journey from one to the other. The Banerjees' Chittaranjan Park home in Delhi's Bengali enclave is cheerfully crowded and the Bengaliness is subtly underlined, not just through a sprinkling of Bangla in the fluid mix of Hindi and English. You catch a fleeting glimpse of Satyajit Ray's portrait on the wall. Piku when set up for a lunch date by her partner Syed (they run a graphics and design outfit) dismisses the man as someone who has not seen a single Ray film! This comes after a graphic conversation with her father regarding the colour and consistency of his stool as her date is about to order. Naturally, he loses his appetite and Piku (who is so used to such embarrassments at home and work) just shrugs it off her shapely shoulders. She shares a demanding relationship with her father as an equal, even if he exasperates her beyond bearing at times.

Piku is equally difficult and imperious too, in her own way. She can drive—as we see on the trip to Calcutta—but refuses to face Delhi's traffic and has a daily altercation with the driver of the private taxi she takes to work. Here comes the interventionist Rana *non-Bengali* Choudhury (Irrfan), the owner of the taxi fleet. He is driven to the end of his tether by an unrepentant Piku for a client plus a grasping sister and virago of a mother to contend with at home. Baba has to travel to Calcutta to decide on what to do with the ancestral home there. He refuses to fly (the most important place, the toilet makes him claustrophobic), the train is out because it agitates his innards beyond bearing and so Rana ends up driving the infuriatingly eccentric duo and their faithful retainer to their city of birth. The road movie part of the film fulfils all that is expected of it—the understanding of each other, gradual appreciation of quirks, vulnerabilities, and strengths. We see Piku the woman, beyond the daughter and businesswoman, handling difficult situations with careless grace. The drama is laced with humour interspersed with quiet reflective moments. Rana plays a no-nonsense peacemaker and dispenser of home remedies. Bhaskor blooms from domestic tyrant to nostalgic son and older brother when they reach the lived-in magnificence of the ancestral home with its huge courtyard overlooked by galleries running around the first floor. You see another side of the self-centred Bhaskor in his interactions with the timid brother, his discontented wife and bearing up well when the effervescent, much-married, highly critical sister (a delightful Moushumi Chatterjee) of his late wife turns up with her full entourage on her way from Delhi to Darjeeling. The city of his youth seems to liberate him in a profound way and he liberates his daughter too—dying peacefully in his sleep after cycling through the city, eating desi junk food, and having the best motion in his life.

The aftermath is tentatively contemplative. The mood engulfs a subdued yet spirited memorial meeting for the deceased man where affection prevails. Piku says at one point, parents become children and need to be cared for with the same patience and love you give a child. Simple words but so profoundly true, as we experience it in our lives in our own way—beyond duty, with just affection. Irrfan plays the catalyst with cool, incisive charm. Though Amitabh Bachchan commands attention for the bravado with which he carries off a role that could be a caricature at times, Deepika Padukone is blindingly brilliant, conveying a range of emotions with panache. Piku does not fit the dutiful daughter template. She is the contemporary working woman running a business, treating her father as an equal to whom she calls tell some necessary home truths. To conclude with an irrelevant fancy ... Susan Sontag, in her seminal essay *Illness as Metaphor*, describes how geniuses like Keats, the Brontes, and Kafka dominate the popular imagination with associated illnesses. Could Bhaskor Banerjee be the defining fictional character for the miseries of constipation? And Piku the non-conformist daughter best able to deal with such an eccentric father?

In a staunchly patriarchal society, the impact a nurturing father can have on a daughter is effectively underlined in two salient films of this decade. In *Thappad*, Amu's strongest and consistent support is her father. He is not perfect but the tenderness and understanding he so matter of factly lavishes on her, leaving Amu to make her decision, is deeply touching. Kumud Misra is so adept at understatement that he makes it all the more affecting.

Irrfan, in his comeback *Angrezi Medium* (2020) after the break due to his rare illness, is a heart-warming winner all the way. This small town mithaiwala is willing to stake everything he has—and he does not have much materially but his heart is enormous—so that his beloved daughter can have the education in England she craves. Nothing is too much for his girl, he reckons. The film blends comedy—brilliant as is expected with Irrfan and Deepak Dobriyal together—and sheer, overflowing affection to stay entrenched in our hearts. Fathers who empower daughters are a rare breed. They are to be cherished.

Another set-in-concrete stereotype was waiting to be broken. The Muslim young woman and her relationship with her immediate society that lays down rules for her: head scarf when she sets out from home, her time after college strictly accounted for and no social life of her own as such. Meet fiery Safeena (Alia Bhatt, the most talented of the clutch of young actors) of *Gully Boy* (2019). Zoya Akhtar has created a young woman who has the courage to defy the constraints her family imposes on her. She is studying medicine, aiming to be a surgeon and committed to her school sweetheart Murad (Ranveer Singh). They both live in Dharavi, but their homes could not be more different. His is a cramped shanty, now expected to house his father's new wife along with his mother, younger brother, and grumbling grandmother. Safeena's house in the same locality is a larger, proper construction as befits a doctor's home. She sets out for college head fully covered in a scarf and once in college, her hair is flowing freely. Her bathroom is the place for assignations, from where she can call him. When her cover is finally blown and the fact that she not only meets Murad regularly but also attended his act at the Rap competition is known, Safeena is slapped by her orthodox and dominating mother—anointed the custodian and enforcer of rules set by patriarchy.

Her father gives her patient hearing. Safeena finally vents her pent up grievances. She doesn't want to hide things from them; not lie to attend a college function or a Rap gig. I want to be *normal* is her heartfelt cry. She is forbidden to meet Murad who will soon be crowned Bombay/India's new Rap sensation, hailed as the gritty urban poet. Safeena is nothing if not clever and ingenious when she is not being violently possessive about her man. Twice she attacks girls who she thinks are poaching on her territory even if it leads to a police complaint. The second time she breaks a bottle on the other girl's head. This fierce possessiveness is part of her equally deep commitment. Safeena is so radically different from the demure, decorous, *shairi* spouting girls showcased in those old-fashioned Muslim Socials (an extinct genre now). She knows what she wants and will get it at any cost. Safeena redefines what a young contemporary Muslim woman wants in this age of identity politics—frankly and without any apology for what she believes is her right.

Not just Bollywood, but Indian cinema as a whole, has had a most shameful history of portraying people with handicaps, physical and mental. The assumption is that a physically challenged person, more so a woman, cannot possibly have sexual feelings and desires. *Margarita with a Straw* (2014) is set to shatter this false and demeaning assumption. Shonali Bose's film is able to create a warm, fuzzy, feel good ethos that overcomes the film's tragic end. Bose, writer, director, and activist, treads Indian territory from the insider-outsider's perspective, having spent most of her adult life in the US. The basic premise of *Margarita with a Straw* is the belated recognition and celebration of a teenaged girl's right to explore and enjoy her sexuality even if society at large does not even consider that someone with cerebral palsy has a sexual self. Laila (Kalki Koechlin) is a bright Delhi University student who writes songs for her college band. Her family, more so her Aai (Revathy) fiercely fights for her daughter's right to not only good education—driving her to college in a Matador fitted with a ramp to enable the wheelchair bound girl to move freely—but almost thrusts her to take up a scholarship for a creative writing semester at NYU. The Sardar father and pesky younger brother all treat Laila as a normal individual—her disability is not insurmountable in their view.

It is a cheerful family, the Punjabi and Maharashtrian sides amicably squabbling over food preferences and other such differences with good humour. What nobody, not even the mother who is so close—emotionally and physically—recognizes is Laila's need for sexual expression. It is as if society and even those closest to a differently abled person is in denial of this. Laila's overture to the lead singer of the group ends in rejection and the humiliated Laila welcomes New York's open ethos to find her true self. Yes, the need to go abroad (Paris and New York are favoured destinations) to find yourself is a cliché but the challenge is in how the director uses it. Bose casually brings out the differences in the facilities provided—the public transport in NY has handicap access and the university provides a caregiver and a writer to the new student—without being either judgemental or apologetic. Laila not only discovers a margarita's potency but is also seduced by the feisty, attractive Khanum (a blind Pakistani-Bangladeshi activist) to sample the pleasures of a gay relationship. Aai who had accompanied Laila to settle her in thinks of Khanum as a welcome new best friend for her daughter. Laila is now emboldened enough to initiate hetero sex with the cute young man who is assigned to her as a writer. She has now flowered into a confident young woman. Bose limits Laila's blossoming only to her sexuality and takes just a passing interest in her writing. A little more attention to Laila the writer would have rounded off the character.

The script that has settled into a cool plateau now needs a push to reach an emotional denouement. Aai's cancer provides the emotional sucker punch though Bose deals with it in a restrained manner. Both Laila and Khanum are in Delhi for the vacation. It is time for a double whammy. Along with Khanum finding out her lover's hetero experiment, Laila has to cope with her Aai's terminal cancer. She is now the caregiver to a woman who has cared for her all her life. There is poignancy in this role reversal without it ever getting maudlin. Both Revathy and Koechlin are too strong and self-willed—as actors and the roles written for them—for easy sentimentality. Yet, we still see an element of manipulation to take Laila's journey to a desired destination. We admire the film for its complete absence of self-pity and making Laila a remarkably well-rounded personality who is sensitive, brave, and intelligent. Koechlin's obvious hard work to get under Laila's skin, and aim for nuance perfection—the difficulty of articulation, slurred speech, physical coordination of limbs that refuse to obey—is remarkable and award worthy. Even as we applaud the courage of the maker and the cast, the niggling dissatisfaction of manipulative storytelling remains. The colours are all warm and tasteful, the locations and interiors are authentic. Bose won the Netpac prize (given to an Asian film by a select jury) at Toronto.

The sexual needs of a much older disabled woman are not only recognized but also fulfilled with motherhood in a film that we can't take seriously except for who made it. The film is the bizarre *Zero* (2018). Shah Rukh Khan, the producer and star playing a cheeky, manipulative dwarf, and director Aanand L. Rai have tried to tell a story that is half allegory, half satire and ambitiously futuristic. It is a ridiculous mess. Bauua Singh (Shah Rukh Khan) is a vertically challenged son of a Meerut businessman, desperate to get married and finally have sex with a willing woman if marriage does not happen. He is brash, insulting, and repulsively insensitive when he meets Aafia Bhinder (Anushka Sharma) an eminent rocket scientist with a fictional space research organization planning to send a human to Mars. Aafia has cerebral palsy and she too yearns for a relationship that is both emotional and sexual. Sharma's effort to portray cerebral palsy is pathetic, to be kind. We can't just accept why she agrees to marry an irresponsible jerk like Bauua Singh. In an attempt to be different and have a brilliant woman with cerebral palsy for heroine and reducing it to caricature, Rai fails to respect her. This is unforgivable. Please spare the disabled from such misdirected attempts to 'normalize' them all in the name of some half-baked surreal entertainment.

4
Woman the Hero

Neither Bollywood nor our pulp fiction has created superheroes of Marvel and DC Comics genre. Our heroes and superheroes are mined from our rich mythology. Hero as the righteous (and at times troubled) warrior usually draws upon Arjun for his focused battle/quest/journey. Epics and mythology are the ready reckoners for deeper impact. That is why, when woman is the hero—or shero preferred by some current feminists though the word can be traced back to 1836—she comes trailing clouds of mythological glory. Direct references to Shakti and Devi are often invoked, as the avenging divinity, counterpart to the idealized Sita-Savitri dyad. Woman the contemporary hero still draws from the concept of Shakti but there is also something universal at the subliminal level of characterization and mythical association.

For that, we need to look to the fascinating work of Joseph Campbell. This influential American mythologist in his seminal book *The Hero with a Thousand Faces* finds that the basic structure of the hero's quest is essentially the same in all cultures. Campbell calls it the monomyth. The book explores and explains the similarities between ancient myths of the world. What is so wonderful about the monomyth is that it can deconstruct and describe modern myths too, like the cult *Star Wars* series spread over four decades (from 1977 to the last one in 2017) and going back all the way to the much-loved *Wizard of Oz (1939)*, if we apply it to Hollywood. Lucas admits that his path breaking series was inspired by Campbell's work. *The Lord of the Rings* trilogy (2001, 2002, and 2003) is an immersive recreation and annotative text of Campbell's expansive exploration of interconnected myths. Something revolutionary happened both in Hollywood and on a smaller scale in Hindi cinema a few years ago.

Today, the hero's One Thousandth One face is female. Post the clamour for women's empowerment and meaningful representation in cinema, the brand new mythology of woman the hero across popular culture is born.

Gal Gadot's Diana, in *Wonder Woman* (2017), of DC Comics became the superhero on par with male superheroes, triumphing over their machismo by her genuine curiosity and compassion for humans. Patty Jenkins the director layered the film with a feminist narrative that is engaging, empowering, and enduring. Take the totally different and edgy mind space of the TV series *Homeland*. The protagonist Carrie Mathison is the volatile and bipolar CIA officer whose out of the box thinking sometimes lands her in a series of misadventures, only to emerge a winner—even if battered and bruised, wearing her scars as badges of honour.

Hero is actually gender neutral and it describes a person who sets out on a significant and perilous quest, overcoming many obstacles to emerge triumphant for the greater good of humanity. The trailblazer of woman the hero in India is Vidya Balan in *Kahani* (2012). There is an association with Indian mythology, of Durga, as well as universal elements of the monomyth. Vidya, as her name signifies, comes armed with the knowledge of technology. She has something else intangible but strongly felt: a mind churning with ideas and possibilities, quick to act and think on her feet and yet so endearingly warm with kids and teasingly affectionate with Satyoki 'Rana' Sinha (Parambrata Chatterjee), the rookie cop who helps her. It is revealed in the end that she along with her husband Arup Das and another colleague Milan Damji who crossed over to the bad side are specially trained agents of the Intelligence Bureau. A retired senior officer had trained them and kept their existence secret from the IB and their files are not available at the National Data Centre in Kolkata. Vidya, sporting Bagchi as her surname, is ostensibly the Tamilian wife of Arnab Bagchi who she claims was sent to Kolkata for a job and did not return to London where both were working as software engineers. When woman is the hero, it means hers is not a parallel or equal role with the male hero. She is the engine of action, driving the narrative. In *Kahaani*, she is the mystery in search of another unsolved mystery.

Balan followed up her award worthy performance in *The Dirty Picture* with yet another outstanding portrayal that is stunning. From the sleaze of South's B grade cinema to Kolkata caught up in Puja fervour is a daring leap of imagination that Balan pulls off with the ungainly gait and innate grace of a heavily pregnant young woman. *Kahaani* is the kind of thriller you want to see again, if only to find the loopholes and marvel anew at the engaging fusion of story, style, casting, and the sting in the tail. The last time I wanted to go back and savour the seamless narrative was when I first saw *The Sixth Sense* (1999). Sujoy Ghosh has made an excellent thriller by Indian standards–never mind the inevitable minor holes we spot on reflection. It is even more pleasing because we seem constitutionally incapable of making thrillers for the sheer fun of it, or even enjoying it without the usual padding of songs, romance, action for its own dubious sake and even a dash of melodrama to satisfy our craving for the *nava rasas*.[1]

To complement Balan's bravura performance where she waddles along grimy back streets in maternity gowns that all have the same cut, Ghosh conjures up an edgy ode to Kolkata, a city guaranteed to grow on you. One of the criteria laid down by Campbell is that the new world the hero is forced into should be different from the old familiar one she left behind. He describes this new world as 'fateful region of both treasure and danger ... a distant land'. Handheld camera goes into crowds that are seemingly unaware of its presence (most of the time, at least) and we feel the ebb and flow of anonymous humanity going about life's daily grind. The city is all around, imprinting itself on us with immediacy. The dingy corridors of a rundown guest house, the curious faces of men gawking at the pregnant woman demanding to see the guest records from an overwhelmed clerk, the winning smile on the bright face of a young lad running errands, the muted lights of the city framed by grimy window bars, loud voices clamouring to be heard in the typically bare-boned police station, gloomy stairwells, dust-laden offices, shadowy interiors of a late night tram ... Ghosh creates subtle shifts of mood and menace, loneliness and sudden new friendships with a fine blending of sound and sights. Like the monomyth's hero on a quest, the journey takes Vidya Bagchi to the mandatory unfamiliar terrain where danger bides unseen but felt in her cells and sinews.

The shifts from normalcy to uncertainty keep us on tenterhooks. Balan bestrides this teeming urban landscape, pregnant with unspoken threats and lurking dangers, impatience battling with fierce determination, intelligence aided by ingenuity, transforming herself into Vidya Bagchi in search of her mysteriously missing husband, Arnab Bagchi. Balan is

---

[1] The nine emotions essential to a complete work of art as laid down by Natyasastra, the ancient text of poetics.

marvellous in complementing her public persona of determined young woman pursuing truth with a doggedness that both exasperates and endears her to the people she meets, with private moments of overwhelming despair. Rana, helplessly drawn to her vibrant personality, is half in love with this intriguing woman as he accompanies her to distant parts of the sprawling city and chivalrously shepherds her through its winding gullies. Vidya Bagchi's persistence antagonizes officials; prime example is A. Khan (Nawazuddin Siddiqui), sent down by Intelligence Bureau in Delhi to head her off. His brusque arrogance and undisguised rudeness do not deter Vidya Bagchi from getting to the root of her *kahani*.

Ghosh uses motherhood as a linking symbol—from Vidya's pregnancy that makes her utterly vulnerable and venerable, to a nurturing Durga who can transform into Kali; to the young mother with a crying baby in the prelude where a baby's feeding bottle triggers the poison gas attack in the Metro. That was two years ago. Ghosh is not afraid to be obvious. In the process, he insinuates an intriguing subtext, which could have gone deeper to lend *Kahaani* ambiguity, but he stops just short of it. In Vidya Balan's splendidly virtuoso performance, he finds both protagonist and subtext. The supporting cast—even cameos—translates into solidly believable characters. Another requirement laid down by Campbell is the talisman—in classical myths this is a magical object with supernatural powers. In *Kahaani*, it is the prosthetic belly used to create the appearance of pregnancy that acts as Vidya's shield and weapon too. Afterwards, mission accomplished of destroying evil, she merges into the swarm of festive women, all in white saris with red border and faces smeared with sindur. Into this anonymity of the crowd of celebratory married women, she, a widow, escapes the two cops who are using her to help them and she has used them instead. This realization dawns on their bewildered faces tinged with reluctant admiration. She has left evidence to nail the person within IB who has been helping the man who disappeared after the Metro poison gas tragedy. Vidya Bagchi has melted into the crowd and they are left clueless to her real identity. The play with a projected public persona and hidden identity is part of the hero myth in its modern superhero avatar. Tagore's famous song, *Ekla chalo re*,[2] in Amitabh Bachchan's

---

[2] Walk alone even if no one else marches with you.

signature voice blends inspiration and admiration. It underlines the essential loneliness of the hero who risks everything for a mission.

Unfortunately *Kahaani 2: Durga Rani Singh*, (2016) not exactly a sequel, does not live up to the expectations raised by the first film which bestowed on Balan the title of the female Khan—a name that could sell a film and propel it to success. Here, Balan is the hunted, not the hunter. Her screen name is once again Vidya, fusing the character with the actor. (It also reminds us of Amitabh Bachchan's screen name Vijay in films where he is the angst-ridden avenger.) Vidya Sinha (Vidya Balan) is a single mother and teacher in moffusil Chandan Nagar, sepia tinted and smelling of seedy old-world decay. Her daughter is Minnie, a wheelchair bound cheerful girl paralysed from waist down. Vidya is working hard to save enough money to take Minnie abroad for an operation that might make her walk. All of a sudden, Minnie is kidnapped and a frantic Vidya, searching for her daughter, is hit by a taxi. She is taken to a not very efficiently maintained clinic and is in coma. The local Inspector Inderjit Singh (Arjun Rampal) searches her house for clues and stumbles upon a diary that reveals Vidya's real identity: she is Durga Rani Singh who earlier worked as a clerk in a Kalimpong school, accused of kidnapping Minnie and murdering her grandmother. There was also a young man who was interested in her but he too had vanished from the scene.

The theme is child sexual abuse. Minnie, an orphan, is being abused by her uncle Rahul Dewan and Durga is concerned for the reticent child who falls asleep in class. Her efforts to help, first by posing as a teacher from the school, prove futile. The police complaint she lodges absolves the uncle. Yet, Durga persists. The hostile grandmother (proud chatelaine of a beautiful old house) is in denial and accidentally killed. Somehow, Durga, herself a child abuse survivor, manages to escape with the girl who is injured when she jumps from the terrace in desperation. Now, after years, Rahul has traced them. He kidnaps Minnie and holds her hostage for ransom. The complicated plot takes Durga, desperate to rescue Minnie, to Kolkata just before she could be taken into custody. The cat and mouse game between Durga and Rahul unfolds with the Kolkata cops and Inderjit Singh hot on her heels.

Yet another twist from the past surfaces. Durga was once married to Inderjit and he helps her escape with Minnie to the US even as his ancestral house—which is surrounded by cops—is set on fire and Durga is presumed dead. The smokescreen really does not help to convince us of the past being mixed up with the present; or sustain suspense as the game of feints and falsehoods, decoy and hunter, is played out. Well intentioned, it focuses on the subject of child sexual abuse that is hardly acknowledged by cinema, following the lead set by a wary society in denial. What makes Vidya/Durga a hero is her determined fight for a cause that is tragically unaddressed.

It is intriguing that Vidya's fake pregnancy in the first film is in a way fruitful as she becomes surrogate mother to an abused young girl. Here, the hero needs help from others to accomplish her goal. That makes Vidya/Durga a minor hero with a laudable cause.

Anushka Sharma, with many hits behind her, turned producer to make the kind of gritty film she had in mind. No production house would back a film like *NH10* (2015) that posits a modern working woman as an action hero who confronts the entrenched patriarchal forces edging Delhi's border. Meera (Anushka Sharma) finds unsuspected strength to survive her husband's brutal death and avenge him in the implacably anti-woman Haryana badlands. The other India we see is frightening. Yet, the film celebrates a courageous woman's fight against a male dominated power structure. It breaks the rules to give physical and dramatic space for the heroine to emerge a real hero. The thriller is taut as a bowstring. Navdeep Singh brings to *NH10* the same dark, brooding look of his debut film *Manorama Six Feet Under* (2007). The opening shots of a car speeding on Gurgaon's broad, bustling road create a paradox of intimacy within and threat without. You hear the easy banter between Meera (Anushka Sharma) and Arjun (Neil Bhoopalam) while the car shoots like an arrow on the straight, dark asphalt road past islands of glass and concrete high rises, squares of lit windows casting eerie non-reflecting light, where danger could hide under the flyover to pounce suddenly like an urban beast on wheels. The very much in love Dink couple are on the way to a party that Meera is not enthusiastic about while Arjun cajoles her, with promise of leaving early to do more interesting things. The director builds up a nice rhythm of long and short scenes before zapping us with the first shock. Meera leaves the party after an emergency work call and when she stops on the road to change music channels, a speeding bike takes a calculated look at a lone young woman, and ambushes her with accomplices summoned for the assault. Meera's car blocked by goons makes you recall the many horror stories of women attacked on Delhi roads even when they are driving their own cars. Meera's quick thinking helps her get away with a broken windshield and shattered confidence. The cops advise her to get a gun and thanks to Arjun's high level contacts, she reluctantly carries a gun in her handbag. The modern working woman in what has come to be known as India's rape capital needs something more lethal than pepper spray to defend herself.

This prelude to the heart of the story is dramatic, scenes written with economy that effectively establishes the couple's North-South marriage (she speaks in Tamil code for wild lovemaking, to tease Arjun), with busy professional lives that do not give them much time together. Finally, they are getting away for a short vacation at some resort in Haryana. The ride is the usual mix of petty squabbles and making up. The danger that will soon overtake them once they leave the highway to stop at a dhaba simmers in a slow build up ... to the sudden eruption at the dhaba where a young couple is thrashed and loaded into an SUV like cattle to be slaughtered. Arjun intervenes to stop the violence while others are mute bystanders. He is beaten up and a shaken, angry Meera is helpless when Arjun decides to follow the goons. The first intervention is understandable. You cannot just look on when a young girl is being slapped and kicked senseless by her enraged brother, egged on by three other men. What is not so plausible is Arjun following them in this unknown territory, confident that Meera's handgun is enough protection. It is essential to the story but the screenplay could have fleshed out Arjun's character to give this rescue mission enough motivation. Both Arjun and Meera are typical of their class, who would not get involved in this kind of violent family feud, more so when they are on the way to a well-earned vacation to celebrate Meera's birthday. Violence builds up to spine-chilling brutality and the city couple is aghast, witness to the killing of the eloping young girl and her lover. The leader of this honour killing group is the brother Satbir (Darshan Kumar) and his next target is Arjun.

Navdeep Singh is now on full throttle thriller mode as afternoon darkens into night ... a black night where Arjun and Meera are on the run in a terrain of stunted bushes and hollows that does not offer much cover. Arvind Kannabiran's mood enhancing lighting and prowling cinematography complemented by Jabeen Merchant's fluid editing give *NH10* its edgy sophistication that sets it apart from the generic slasher film

(*NH10 is* supposed to be based on one such British potboiler). Singh had Indianized elements of *Chinatown* (1974) in *Manorama Six Feet Under* while paying homage to the noir classic. In this latest thriller, two Indias collide to cataclysmic effect in a ruthlessly regressive ethos where women barely survive as an endangered species. It takes a gutsy Meera to tap deep within to find the raw courage to overcome the odds so heavily stacked against her.

Meera's survival instincts kick in once Arjun is shot in the leg and she has to lead them both to safety—sans phones, their car, and that crucial gun. She manages to drag the badly wounded Arjun under the railway bridge and sets out to find the police. Her education, and ours, begins. This is the land where the Khap Panchayat rules and the police are in collusion with locals who carry out honour killings with impunity. The inspector whose help Meera seeks with a city person's instinctive trust disabuses her of her faith in law. The Constitution ends with Gurgaon's last mall, he tells her. Here, what prevails is the rule of Manu, the ancient lawgiver of Hindu patriarchy, which forbids *sagotra* marriages.[3] The pitying tone in which he talks to Meera is scary, precisely because it seems kind and yet mocking her alien modern ways. She cannot even tell him her husband's caste and *gotra*. Inter-caste marriage, he deduces patronizingly even as he calls her Madam with mocking courtesy. Meera is now alert to the unsaid. Her antennae are up. She manages to escape in the dark, only to find Arjun's lifeless body. She is a woman on a mission now. Limping, battered, she digs deep into herself and finds long buried animal cunning to keep going. Luck helps. She seeks the Panchayat head in a village de-populated by people gathered at a gaudy public performance.

Now for the sucker punch. Dipti Naval turns in a brilliant cameo as Ammaji, matriarch of the family that ordered the killing of the eloping couple. Within the conventions of a thriller, where the hero has to play a constant cat and mouse game, Meera comes into her own. She is locked in along with the long-suffering meek wife of Satbir. Her anger makes her seize even half an opportunity, to not only survive and escape but turn into a cold, implacable avenger. The way she drags an iron rod with deadly determination recalls a soldier hunting down the enemy. In a conventional Hindi film, this would be accompanied by invoking Kali

---

[3] Marriage of people deemed to be of same clan (traced to an ancient seer) is forbidden.

through some kind of associative symbolism. The director is more sophisticated. This Meera is a modern woman who has seen such unspeakable brutality in the course of a day that she simply has to kill the enemy with equal ferocity … to avenge the death of her husband, her own harrowing experience, and the death of the innocents she has seen. The irony is that it is a woman, a powerful matriarch who upholds oppressive patriarchal laws without compunction. There is only personal vengeance of the jungle as Meera limps away into the dark night. This is catharsis without cleansing of the soul. It is a bleak conclusion where a woman can live only by executing the male killers. The final point is, only women survive: Meera, Ammaji, and Satbir's wife who really does not grieve for her sadistic husband.

The crucial point of the film comes when one of the older men confronts Meera crumpled on the floor. *Aankhe neeche*,[4] he commands repeatedly. Meera does not lower her eyes and defiantly looks him in the eye. She is bruised but not broken. That is what makes her a hero. She is able to live through excruciating suffering and emerge a winner in a world inimical to independent women. Women like Ammaji proliferated for a while in TV soaps set in rural North India. Ammaji also calls for comparison with Radha of *Mother India*. Both are matriarchs who uphold Dharma that is inherently patriarchal. Radha is idealistic and her actions flow from concern for the honour of a girl from the village—even if she is the villainous moneylender's daughter. She shoots down her son, the rebellious Birju, who, in her heart of hearts, she loves more than the obedient good son. Birju had always spoken up for her even as a child. In Ammaji's case, idealism evaporated long ago. She values only the lives of sons. Daughters and daughters-in-law are expendable. It is a comment on the extent agrarian society has devalued women that she is valued only as the mother of sons. And now that she has attained that status, and internalized the values of patriarchy, she is evil and conscienceless in holding on to that position. *NH10* makes it a battle that a modern educated Meera has to fight on her own and reclaim the right of a woman to exist. On her own terms, in Meera's case.

Akira (2016), even with an action-expert A.R. Murugadoss of Tamil cinema for director, fails as a narrative with substance beyond mere

---

[4] Lower your eyes.

action that is often idiotically inserted for no logical reason. Murugadoss, who butchered the definitive psychological noir landmark *Memento* (2000) into a messy *Ghajini* (2008), does no better with the original Tamil film *Mouna Guru* (2011). He merely changes the protagonist's gender to proclaim his commitment to woman empowerment. Audiences ought to be spared such a convoluted story that believes in repetition and plentiful coincidences. We have Akira, trying very hard to be a shero, a misunderstood protagonist. Akira, we are told by the narrator, means 'graceful strength'. Nothing to do with any intended tribute to Kurosawa. This girl, destined to be heroic, was taught karate instead of kathak by her well-meaning father in a Rajasthan small town. For foiling an acid attack by local goons against whom she had earlier given evidence, schoolgirl Akira ends up in juvenile detention for three years. When she comes out, Akira is told her beloved father had died and soon, mother and daughter are frisked away to Bombay by the son who had distanced himself all these days. The parents had not accepted the girl he chose for wife but now, he needs Mamma-not-so-dearest to look after the baby. Akira chooses to live in a hostel closer to her college.

Akira may want to keep out of trouble's way but big trouble ambushes her at every conceivable turn. Her nemesis is the corrupt ACP Rane (ace director Anurag Kashyap relishing his villainous avatar). He and his incompetent subordinates end up with a huge cache of money after they have killed a speeding motorist on a lonely road. Rane's mistress (who has waited to retaliate for his abusive behaviour) records his conversation about the crime and pays for it with her life. A chain of predictable incidents implicates Akira in their plot. When the plan to kill her goes awry— this truly stupid sequence ought to be on a loop for unintended comic incompetence—Akira is shut up in a mental hospital. She is administered electric shocks and potent drugs to certify her as a delusional psychotic. Even her family believes it, hinting that that her childhood incarceration in a juvenile institution was perhaps justified. No wonder Akira is so uncommunicative with her family.

Enter the incorruptible SP, Rabiya Khan (Konkona Sen Sharma) who is entrusted with the apparent suicide of Rane's girlfriend. She thinks it is murder and soon stumbles upon Akira's unwitting entanglement with the case. A very pregnant Rabiya is sympathetic and soon nails Rane and his accomplices but her attempt to force Rane into clearing Akira's reputation fails. Political expediency, of probable riots if Rane's involvement in another killing of a North Indian politician's kin is revealed, hammers the final nail on police corruption at large. Akira turns executioner of her tormentors, and serves a minimal term, thanks to Rabiya's conscience. She comes out, and follows her idealistic father's calling: teaching children in a pastoral setting. In a way, Akira has to be de-feminized to reach hero-hood. *Akira* the film is particularly disappointing after the hype, heralding Sonakshi Sinha as action star. Akira is a girl at the mercy of fate and she is strangely inert most of the time, except when it comes to dealing out karate kicks. It is hard to get into her mind, to sense what she feels. We are clueless to her growth, if there is any.

Heroes are not always defined by aggressive public action. There are quiet heroes, seemingly ordinary women achieving extraordinary feats of public valour that overcomes private insecurities. 2020 ushered two heroes of a different kind played by two top stars: Deepika Padukone and Kangana Ranaut. Padukone was in the limelight for her support to the beleaguered JNU students just on the eve of *Chhapaak's* (2020) release, a film she not only acted in but also produced. For her first production, Padukone chose Meghna Gulzar to direct the film based on a real-life acid attack survivor, Laxmi Agarwal. Gulzar's métier has been her sensitive, non-sensational narratives that subtly fictionalized real-life characters with empathy and an admirable degree of objectivity. Malti (Padukone) is introduced with her scarred face, as she goes through a futile round of job interviews only to be rejected on flimsy grounds. A girl from the working class, she is beholden to her father's kindly employer for the multiple surgeries that lessen the deep scars left on her face and torso by a man who was hitherto considered a family friend.

Laxmi Agarwal was barely 14 when she became an acid attack victim. The film makes Malti a 19-year-old 12th standard student. The attacker is a Muslim, older by more than a decade. He becomes aware of Malti's beauty and dislikes her friendship with a classmate on the verge of becoming her boyfriend. Padukone's support for the left-wing JNU students' union resulted in the canard that the film changed the religion of the attacker into a Hindu man. The rumour-mongers were left with egg on their face, since Gulzar is known for adherence to truth. She is not one to timidly succumb to notions of political correctness in our polarized times. Padukone the star and producer risked the possible adverse reaction of the Right's troll army. Her conviction won the day, and possibly posterity's admiration too.

The narrative cuts between courts where the accused gets repeated adjournments and Malti's PIL[5] to ban the sale of acid that is so freely available. Malti's apathy and total withdrawal from the world outside needs the forceful urging of her determined lawyer and the benefactor's constant encouragement to get out and keep the fight going. Her animal scream of anguish the first time she sees her reflection in the mirror—all mirrors in the small home are papered over—is gut-wrenching. The process of Malti coming to terms with her appearance and determination to help the family economically—her father has died and younger brother has tuberculosis—is imbued with an underlying sense of purpose and optimism. She meets Amol (Vikrant Massey) who runs an NGO that helps acid attack survivors and Malti finds her vocation. And also love, for the serious man so deeply committed to a cause that he has no time to celebrate the small joys and hardwon victories of life. Malti finds the grit and resilience to pursue the long hard grind of the judicial process. She rediscovers a latent spontaneous courage to declare her love for Amol. It is up to him to accept. Acknowledging their mutual love is the joy that has finally lit Malti's life with optimism. Laxmi Agarwal too found love in her life.

Gulzar's narrative presents Malti's scarred face to us throughout the film and it speaks volumes of Padukone's lack of vanity. It is the final coda when she is describing how the attack happened that you see Padukone in all her beauty, minus the glamour associated with her. She is a simple Delhi girl from the working class. What *Chhapaak* celebrates is the growth from victim to activist who embraces other such victims as soul sisters. The film embodies the human spirit that can transcend agonising pain and society's rejection that only sees her external being. Padukone gets under Malti's scarred, pitted skin and makes us aware of every step of her growth, from fearful seclusion to an active public life with confidence.

Ashwini Iyer Tiwari's *Panga* (2020) is a warm, feel-good family drama starring Kangana Rananut as an ex-kabaddi player re-discovering her undying love for the game and a successful comeback to the national team at 32. We meet Jaya Nigam as a wife and doting mother of a six-year-old

---

[5] Public interest litigation.

son. She plods through her work as a ticketing clerk of the railways in Bhopal—far from even a thought of the kabaddi arena. That is the only job offered to an ex-India captain. It is when friend and old teammate Meenu (Richa Chadha, bracingly acerbic) comes as coach of the local girls' team that she begins to miss her playing days of glory. Jaya was made the captain of Indian women's kabaddi team when she delivers a premature son and motherhood becomes her primary concern. It is the adorable son Adi (Yagya Bhasin, a natural scene stealer) who is determined to send his mother back to the sport that had brought her so much joy and fame. Adi cites Serena Williams as an example and monitors her training. Jaya's husband Prashant (Jassie Gill) is a staunch supporter and takes over the house and Adi's care when Jaya has to go to Kolkata to try her chance at selection into the eastern railway team.

Jaya's biggest hurdle is to acknowledge her right to her own dreams. A mother has no right to dream, she had declared with the kind of self-righteousness that she is slowly encouraged to overcome—by Meenu, the straight shooter who tells unpalatable truths, and her own family that rises magnificently to the occasion. It is as much the family as Jaya's determined hardwork that must be credited for her selection to the national team. The final segment faithfully follows the arc of lows and the ultimate high, typical of sports drama. We can see the contribution of the director's writer-director husband Nitesh Tiwari of *Dangal* fame in the predictable finale. Ranaut lives the emotions, hesitations, and triumph of Jaya with supreme ease.

Single mothers are finding their voice and space in Bollywood. It is also a salute to the dream of upward mobility of a working-class mother who wants better for her daughter than to cook and clean for others. Only education can help realize this dream that reflects Indian society's aspirations: to be the district collector is the acme of achievement. This person is the visible symbol of the government that is an abstraction to most of us. *Nil Battey Sannata* (2015) gives us the working-class woman as hero. Ashwiny Iyer Tiwari sets her heart-warming film in Agra and one of the delights is the local inflections given to Hindi. Chanda (Swara Bhaskar finally in a lead role) is a single mother slaving at multiple jobs so that her 15-year-old daughter gets an education. Maths is the bugbear for daughter Apu and you see how Chanda cajoles, scolds the teenager more interested in watching TV and reading Bollywood gossip. When even threats don't work, Chanda finally enrolls in the same government school to Apu's acute embarrassment. Soon, the mother's progress motivates Apu to take a classmate's help to understand the basics of maths. The film's message is: schools must challenge the reluctant learner. Tiwari doesn't make it a preachy tract by infusing fun, credible characters, and situations to weave the completely uplifting tale into an engaging narrative. Chanda is not the treacly, teary mother familiar through the ages. She is gutsy and fierce, eager to learn so she can challenge Apu to do better. Ratna Pathak Shah is wholly in character as the doctor for whom Chanda cooks; not just helpful by taking on obdurate school authorities with her breezy nonchalance but really motivating the maid to disprove the adage that a Bai's daughter will be a Bai. Chanda proves to herself and society that a Bai's daughter can dare to dream of being a collector. Tiwari's casting of major and minor characters is spot on and her humour—though forced on occasion—hits the right key most of the time. Chanda is not actually living vicariously through her daughter but motivating her to pursue the impossible. I must include a personal note. The film is not just a cheery fable. My domestic help who worked for 20 years with me put her only daughter through college and made her a chartered accountant. Such ambitions do come true.

A cheer goes up for the youngest hero Bollywood has ever seen. *Secret Superstar* (2017) celebrates many things: the mother-daughter bond, a stubborn 15-year-old's passion for music, and the democratic platform that internet offers to rank outsiders to display their talent. The last phenomenon is the new reality. YouTube enables talent to be seen when the person has no access to conventional platforms. Debutant director Advait Chandan follows the dream of a Muslim girl living in Baroda. Insia Malik (Zaira Wasim in her second film after *Dangal*) is passionate about music, a gifted songwriter and singer, desperate to take part in a local music competition. Her orthodox father Farook (Raj Arjun) might send her to a co-ed school and not insist on a headscarf but is adamant, about not letting Insia sing in public. A domestic dictator, he abuses his meek wife Najma (Meher Vij) whenever he is home on the weekend. He is away during the week, and the small family is happy in his absence—including his mother. The only person he showers affection on is the younger child—a son, naturally. Insia constantly asks her mother to walk out of this travesty of marriage and is disgusted when her mother refuses. With a teenager's impatient arrogance, she calls her mother a coward: perhaps unable to see how an economically dependent wife can't afford to divorce her husband.

Najma pampers the children, Insia and her younger brother Guddu. She gives her daughter a laptop, the prize offered at the competition, by selling her gold necklace. The laptop enables Insia to record her song and put it on YouTube. She is the anonymous secret superstar since she hides her identity under a burkha at her mother's suggestion. Identity politics with a purpose and not as part of an ideological standoff between Islam and Hindutva. Insia's Muslim identity is treated as normal, and she is like any other Indian girl who can't bear to see her mother abused. It is also an integral part of the plot, to explain the father's unbending rigidity and his plans to get Insia married off to a friend's son once the family shifts to Riyadh where he has found a better job. Insia's YouTube postings of soulful ballads in her unique voice make her a sensation. The euphoria is short lived, because Farooq forbids anymore singing and makes her throw the laptop from the terrace. He finds out that Najma sold her necklace to buy it.

Meanwhile, Insia has accepted the Bombay-based music director Shakti Kumar (Aamir Khan in a self-mocking parody) who comes with a rather sleazy reputation. Insia's condition for recording a song with him is to meet the divorce lawyer who had successfully represented Kumar's wife. Kumar is not as obnoxious as his reputation makes him out to be. Insia's secret day trip to Bombay is courtesy the help of her classmate Chintan who has a crush on her and knows her identity as the mysterious singer who has taken YouTube by storm. This is a rather sweet story of teenage crushes, told with charm and delicacy. Events hurtle towards the Malik family's departure to Riyadh. The sullen family is lined up for check in and when it is pointed out that they have excess baggage, Farooq picks up Insia's guitar bag and smashes it. This is the last straw. Najma signs the divorce papers Insia has been carrying. She and the children march out. The ending is in line with the wish-fulfilling euphoric climax. Insia is nominated for an award but she had decided not to attend. Now the happy family is at the function and though Insia doesn't win, the winner wants to give it to Insia: the more deserving nominee according to her. It's time for unmasking. Insia reveals herself as the secret superstar but announces that the real superstar, the true hero is her mother.

Secret Superstar sticks to a predictable narrative but there is a lot of heart in the story. The casting is perfect. Farooq's threatening anger and simmering violence is conveyed very often through his eyes and taut body language. When the outburst comes, the shock sends the family into cowering retreat. During the build up to the climax, Insia's grandmother reveals how Najma fought to save the baby she was carrying, against her husband's wish that she abort the female foetus. Insia is overwhelmed and that is why she hails her mother as the true hero. The narrative demands a feel-good end to a story that has carried us through tears and triumph, teen angst and journey to maturity. Insia emerges hero because she is not willing to give up her dream. The spine of the story is the mutually empowering bond that Insia finally recognizes with pride and salutes her hero mother. The first step in feminism is realizing the mother's contribution, to see the woman behind the mother, what made her who she is. For an adolescent, the mother could be a role model or the converse: of what she doesn't want to be. Either way, understanding the centrality of this relationship is crucial to her growth—as an individual and a woman.

We also have a story and predictable conditions manufactured to create a hero. *Hichki* (2018) is a vehicle for Rani Mukherjee to display her acting chops as a woman suffering from Tourette syndrome. Naina Mathur is a bright young woman, bent upon a teacher's career though her father, even if he has separated from the family, uses his contacts to get her a bank job. One of the reasons for the parents' separation is his acute embarrassment when in public with Naina. Her mother and younger brother, a chef who runs a gourmet restaurant, are Naina's pillars. They support her to do what she wants, rather than merge into the background to evade others from noticing her condition. She will not let her disability—it makes her suffer facial tics and inability to control her vocal chords from breaking out into incomprehensible sounds—come in the way of teaching which is her vocation. It is a neuropsychiatric condition that Naina has to accept and learn to live with. Sidharth Malhotra adapts Brad Cohen's autobiography *Front of the Class: How Tourette Syndrome Made Me the Teacher I Never Had*, to fit an elitist private school that has been forced to accommodate kids from a slum nearby. St. Notker's had demolished the slum school in its expansion drive and creates a special division for these unruly, 'unteachable' children (according to the obvious villain, the science teacher

Mr. Wadia). The school finally calls Naina Mathur (Rani Mukherjee) to take up a mid-term position. She had unsuccessfully applied to her alma mater and rejected though her academic credentials are excellent.

The narrative works on a sure fire premise: underdogs against the privileged. Cheering the underdogs—though they are reluctant learners at first and mock her disability—is the cheerful, never say die Naina. She swallows the mocking mimicry and discomfiting stares from students and staff, never giving in to either self-pity or dejection at the immense challenge she has taken on. She tells the sceptical principal that her class of 9F will pass the annual exam. 9A is the other division of achievers who are expected to become prefects. It is given that the two are locked in mutual hostility. The underprivileged children are truculent, not amenable to any kind of discipline. They are aware they are in the school by sufferance. They are merciless when Naina comes to their class. They don't recognize their champion, who will plead for their cause. This follows the predetermined curve set for this kind of story. Soon, her non-judgemental attitude, and innovative teaching methods that make concepts easier to understand, succeed in awakening their curiosity, the first prerequisite to learning. She eventually wins them over, except for the lone resistor. There is an attempt to differentiate the children as individuals but they come across as a group sharing common disadvantages of slum life and the demands made on their time to help at home.

Naina's optimism is not a put-on attitude. Children can see through fakes. She is an innate optimist because she had struggled as a child, humiliated in class, and shunned by other children. Till one exceptional teacher infused confidence in her and changed her life. She wants to transfer it to these children and the plot is designed to make it happen after of course strewing the path with inevitable obstacles and even more facile solutions. The film gets both sentimental and predictable. Mere good intentions and a professional performance by the protagonist are not enough to make the kind of inspirational film the director and actor aim for. The script glosses over the basic class divide and the fundamental issue: the slum children's struggle against great odds to be able to learn. The rosy optimism that the elite will embrace the poor after they prove their mettle is to take a blinkered view. *Hichki* doesn't really have a larger vision of the enormous problems facing our education system. It is not *Taare Zameen Par* (2007) or *Hindi Medium* (2017) that had a genuinely egalitarian view of how to redress inequalities of opportunity. Naina is a contrived hero who succeeds despite the many hiccups that impede her way. We see her 25 years later, retiring as principal of St. Notkers, as teary students bid her goodbye. Yes, the slum children have all made good.

A rash of biopics has erupted in Bollywood in the 2000s. There seems to be a collective yearning to remember and honour our sports heroes and the trend was set; it started including other achievers. *Paan Singh Tomar* (2012) is a notable departure from the usual celebratory narrative. It turns bleak, indicting the establishment that drove a soldier, an athlete who represented India internationally, into becoming an outlaw. *Bhaag Milkha Bhaag* (2013) and *M.S. Dhoni, the Untold Story* (2016) blend the personal and social factors that shaped their destiny. *Bhaag Milkha Bhaag* is the better film while the one on the much loved and admired Dhoni remains a hagiography. How could filmmakers ignore the achievements of women in sports that began with Magnificent Mary and now continues to the victories on the badminton court? The other women athletes outperformed men at the last summer Olympics and other international meets.

It is most appropriate that this valorization of Indian women's heroic exploits began with *Mary Kom* (2014). It is not easy to remember everything this celebrated boxer achieved in a career that had all the classic elements of the journey from an unknown to an icon. So a brief recap is necessary because the film does not include all of them. Chungneijang Mary Kom Hmangte (born 1 March 1983), better known as Mary Kom, is the Indian Olympic boxer from Manipur. She is the only woman to become World Amateur Boxing champion for a record six times, and the only woman boxer to have won a medal in each one of the seven world championships. Nicknamed *Magnificent Mary*, she is the only Indian woman boxer to have qualified for the 2012 Summer Olympics, competing in the flyweight (51 kg) category and winning the bronze medal. She was also ranked No.1 in AIBA World Women's Ranking, Light Flyweight category. Mary Kom became the first Indian woman boxer to get a Gold Medal in the Asian Games in 2014 at Incheon, South Korea and is the first Indian woman boxer to win gold at the 2018 Commonwealth Games.

Casting Priyanka Chopra to essay the inspirational journey from Mangte Chungeijang Kom to Magnificent Mary was a commercially canny choice than having a Manipuri girl play the champion boxer as some critics suggested. A big star would attract an all-India audience because even Mary Kom became a public figure only after she won a bronze at 2012 Summer Olympics. This reflects an unfortunate reality: the North-East remains outside mainstream media focus, whether it is the problem of insurgency in many parts or the sporting triumphs of athletes from the region. Mary Kom has spoken of it in anger and sorrow. Then there is the perception—even in our metros—that they are 'outsiders' and the women (students and working girls) are often targets of sexual harassment. It is an attitude that we can't bury under our patriotic soil in ostrich fashion.

The star cast and big banner, though the director Omung Kumar was something of an unknown quantity, succeeded in making the film widely seen, including a premier opening slot at Toronto Film Festival in 2014. It was a first for a Hindi film. The narrative starts with the pregnant Mary in labour and her husband Onler Kom (Darshan Kumar) walking to the hospital because they can't find transport. Onler is beaten up, being mistaken for an insurgent. A bandh has been declared by the insurgency. The year is 2007. Then follows the flashback to her childhood when Mangte Chungeijang finds boxing gloves at the site of a plane crash. She has always been a fighter, this daughter of a poor rice farmer. She lets her fists fly at boys, some bigger than her. Chasing a boy after a scuffle, she runs into a gym. Thus begins the association between a legendary coach Narjit Singh (Sunil Thapa) and the future champion. Like a guru of old, he will watch her for a month and only then accept her as his student. It is he who christens her anew: Mary Kom. Mary tells her mother about this but hides it from the disapproving father who later goes on to say, who will marry a girl with a black eye from boxing? She has already met the footballer Onler Kom who will go on to be the most supportive husband any aspiring boxer could wish for. It is when she wins the state championship that her father learns the truth and pushes her into a dilemma: choose between boxing and him. She chooses her passion and zooms to her incredible career. Mary wins the Women's World Amateur Boxing Championship in 2002 and 2006. That is when she accepts Onler's proposal. He promises to never ask her to quit boxing. In fact, he urges her to go back to training after Mary has twin boys and she is resigned to obscurity: pasting press cuttings of her triumphs in a scrapbook and one of the babies wets the newspapers she has yet to cut a clipping from. With a wry smile, she balls up the papers and throws it away.

When she applies for a government job as a world champion, she is given the post of a police constable. Incensed, Mary refuses to take the insult. It really hits her when a little girl in the bus, who wants to be a boxer and get Mary Kom's autograph, doesn't recognize her idol sitting opposite her. The return to National championship, after renewed vigorous training under her mentor, is not happy. Mary feels the authorities have ganged up against her and withhold points to make the opponent win. Mary protested—even threw a chair, for she is a woman with a temper—and this got her a ban that is lifted only after her apology. The boxer is miffed that the film glosses over this whole incident. Omung Kumar obviously wanted to play safe: hit the high spots and leave out uncomfortable facts. Instead, he has an entire lyrical passage of her choreographed training schedule in picturesque surroundings set to a patriotic song in the background. There is no place for unsightly blood and sweat—except in the climactic bout in the ring when she finally knocks out her German opponent. This after a disastrous start; she is told one of the twins needs heart surgery and she becomes an easy punching bag for the rival bent on avenging an earlier loss. Mary Kom has gone on to even further wins and titles. The film ends with her title won in Ningbo in 2008.

Priyanka Chopra obviously trained hard to gain a muscular look—though she is much taller than the petite boxer—and this pays off for a film that follows the conventional route. It also veers between the pidgin Hindi Mary Kom speaks in real life and standard Hindi for wider acceptance by the audience. The local flavour of Manipur is superficial. There could have been more local music for creating ambient authenticity. Despite these shortcomings, *Mary Kom* tells us the inspiring story of how a feisty village girl was crowned Magnificent Mary.

If there is a text book on how to dramatize a real-life story, that film is *Dangal* (2016). The film's real hero is of course amateur wrestler Mahavir Singh Phogat (Aamir Khan) who finally realizes his dream of winning a gold medal for India through his daughter. Having to take up a regular job instead of wrestling—he does win state and national gold medals—he nurses the ambition that he can train his son to get an international gold. He is blessed with four daughters and is resigned to his fate … till one day, the two older preteeners, Geeta (Zaira Wasim) and Babita (Suhani Bhatnagar), come home dishevelled after beating up boys who made adverse comments. As the Hindi phrase says it so succinctly: *dimaag ki batti jal gayi.*[6] Mahavir sees the light: his daughters have potential. In the staunchly patriarchal Haryanvi society, he proudly declares: *meri choriyan choro se kum hai ke?* Are my daughters any less than boys? It became the famous tagline of a blockbuster and resonated beyond the film.

His methods of training them are harsh. Getting up at the crack of dawn to run, get muddy in the wrestling pit, be objects of shocked disapproval and ridicule ... life is indeed tough for the two preteens. Worse follows. When they complain of sand getting into their long hair, Mahavir has their locks chopped off and this adds to their dismay of wearing pants and shirts—their cousin's cropped off clothes. They silently curse their dictatorial, unnatural father for forbidding all feminine fripperies. He is a zealot, driving them hard to master the sport. They discover the tender father in him too: he oils and massages their blistered, aching feet as they sleep. And when Geeta wins her first prize money, beating boys in the arena, they know they have a future in wrestling. Elders of the community are aghast that he makes his daughters wrestle with boys but once Mahavir is set on something, nothing can swerve him from the chosen path.

Geeta (Fatima Sana Sheikh), now grown up, graduates to the National Sports Academy after she wins the national gold. But the newfangled, one size fits all methods of the official coach results in Geeta losing all her international bouts. She now doubts her father's coaching methods and gives in to her girly desires: nail polish, a stylish haircut and spends time watching TV. She is equally dismissive when she comes home to visit and beats her tired—also disheartened—father in a challenge bout. Her younger sister Babita (Sanya Malhotra) still adheres to her father's regimen and gently rebukes Geeta but to no avail. Repeated international losses make Geeta realize her folly and much drama ensues when Mahavir argues with the authorities for changing her weight category. He is banned from the institute but Mahavir is nothing if not ingenious. He watches Geeta's tapes and points her mistakes over the phone. The official coach is mean, petty, and jealous but Geeta triumphs over her old enemy—a big Irish girl—in the final, following her father's methods. Geeta is a flawed hero who comes through after egoistic bad choices. She finally realizes her true strength. She and her sisters are shaped into

---

[6] The brain lit up.

heroes by their mentor-father. Nitesh Tiwari knows the perfect graph of the sports film and imbibes the expertise—including sentimental manipulation and teary-eyed patriotism—to tell a finely crafted crowd pleaser with a message. Learning the lesson that ex-champ father knows best, both Geeta and Babita, who follows big sister's path of international success, finally have to rely on their own strength. As the adage goes, a coach can teach only that much. It is for the athlete to actually perform when it is crucial.

The real scene stealers are the two new actors who play young Geeta and Babita. Big cheers to Zaira Wasim (Geeta) and Suhani Bhatnagar (Babita) for bringing sinuous athleticism and tensile strength to their portrayal of reluctant wrestlers who go on to be champions. India needs such role models to tell girls that sports are an option worth pursuing. It is very ironic that in a state where Khap Panchayats form a parallel centre of authority, young girls are thronging local training facilities to learn boxing and wrestling: sports involving maximum physical contact.

The success of biopics created a buzz around reality-based stories than purely fictional films. If you look back and around you, there are brilliant untold stories of remarkable women. Two films share commonalities and yet are vastly different in the way they tell the stories of two intrepid young women from recent past within the memory of at least older generations.

Neerja (2016) recreates the drama of the Pan Am hijack in Karachi. It happened in 1986 and the number of that doomed flight was 73. The well-executed terrorist act was planned by the Libyan-backed Abu Nidal group. There were 379 passengers and crew on board and the eponymous heroine died saving 359 of them. Director Ram Madhvani's taut narrative (scripted by Saiwyn Quadras and Sanyukta Chawla Shaikh) gives the life and death situation on the plane a sort of paradoxical elasticity. There is immediacy of what will happen to them every minute at the hands of the terrorists and also a sense of time stretching with no end in sight. A sense of time suspended yet with minutes ticking loudly, threateningly. It is the kind of drama that Hindi cinema had not yet ventured to make. Encompassing it all is the public memory of mourning the death of the brave 22-year-old flight attendant Neerja Bhanot (Sonam Kapoor). Her journalist father Harish Bhanot and spirited mother Rama kept her memory alive by instituting the Neerja Bhanot Bravery Award, especially during the years immediately after her death.

The editing fluidly lets us into Neerja's troubled past, of an abusive husband during her brief marriage when she lived in Doha. These glimpses into her past are juxtaposed with the tense, suspenseful present at the right emotional moment. The shots from her marriage are just the right length, with telling close ups of a vulnerable young girl cut off from her family that dotes on her. Just as she had then found the resolve to get out of this abusive marriage, she now finds the ability to think on her feet, emerging from the plane's toilet after splashing water on her ravaged face. In a situation where there can't be conversations with her colleagues—the other flight attendants—gestures and body language have to be calibrated and eloquent. Neerja is able to do this most of the time, even when the maniacal terrorist Khalil (Jim Sarabh) singles her out as a special target, brandishing his Kalashnikov. He threatens to shoot at the slightest provocation. The group's plans of taking the plane to Libya are completely upended because Neerja manages to alert the cockpit crew to the situation. The American pilots escape from the overhead hatch, leaving the situation in Neerja's hands even though this is her first flight as chief purser. There are cutaways to the family in Bombay: her father reads the latest news on the teleprinter, stoic in his inarticulate forbearance. Shabana Azmi as her mother paces the compact apartment, telling herself that everything will be all right. She displays the Punjabi equivalent of the British stiff upper lip.

Back on the plane, the camera captures the varied reactions—selectively because there are over 350 people in there—and Neerja is trying to stay calm and normal, as she tends to two young children. When an Indian passenger is found to have an American passport, he is shot dead. Madhvani follows the advice of the master of suspense. Hitchcock had said: When the audience has more knowledge than the screen characters, they will be more engaged and emotionally invested. Neerja keeps us emotionally involved with her courage, compassion, and quick thinking. While the Pakistani authorities are trying to negotiate, Neerja quietly alerts her colleagues to hide or throw American passports in the chute. The hijackers want to see how many Americans are aboard. Time stretches to over sixteen hours, the auxiliary power shuts down. In the ensuing darkness, the terrorists think the Pakistani negotiators shut off power and start to shoot indiscriminately. Neerja risks her life to open the emergency exit, lets down the chute and guides the passengers to slide down to safety. She shields three children with her body to let them escape, is shot down and dies as she makes it to the chute. The postscript is a memorial meeting where the kid from the plane gives the grieving mother Neerja's last message: Pushpa, I hate tears. This connects to the film's opening scene, of a gathering of the housing society where the Bhanots live. The staid party is livened by Neerja's joie de vivre and the family's fan worship of Rajesh Khanna. The tagline of *Anand* in Rajesh Khanna's voice sums up Neerja's short but precious life: *Zindagi badi honi chahiye, lambi nahin.*[7] A sense of responsibility that went beyond duty to save so many lives made an ordinary young woman an extraordinary hero.

Another young woman exhibited tremendous courage and commitment to a cause at the behest of a dying father. *Raazi* (2018) is a spy thriller with a difference, based on Harindar Sikka's 2008 novel *Calling Sehmat*. The novel is an account of a young RAW (Research and Analysis Wing) Kashmiri agent who agrees to an arranged marriage to a Pakistani Brigadier's son. Sehmat (Alia Bhatt) is a 20-year-old studying in Delhi when her dying father Hidayat Khan (Rajit Kapur) summons her home. He is a spy, a double agent, trusted by Brigadier Syed (Shishir Sharma) for the useful information he passes on. Khan has come to know that Pakistan is planning something big—it is 1971, on the eve of the Indo-Pak war—but he has no time left to find out. He is terminally ill. He asks if Sehmat is willing to marry Iqbal (Vicky Kaushal), Brigadier Syed's younger son, also an army officer. Khalid Mir (Jaideep Ahlawat) is Khan's friend and handler. Mir is concerned if Sehmat is coerced emotionally but Sehmat is sure: the same patriotic blood of her freedom fighter grandfather flows in her veins.

Meghna Gulzar makes patriotism matter of fact, not succumbing to the chest thumping hyper-nationalism that has unfortunately become the norm for Indian films dealing with Pakistan and war. Gulzar's triumph lies in her restraint even as tension mounts. We are involved not only with what happens to Sehmat: the rookie spy sets up her Morse code equipment and gets to know members of the cell posted as anonymous people doing humdrum work. The Syed family is cultured and courteous. The

---

[7] Life must be lived large, not measured by how long. This expands the implied meaning of the succinct sentence.

father-in-law is affectionate, older sister-in-law is the one who shows her the household's ways, and her husband Iqbal is really sweet and caring. The sudden marriage is something both have to get used to. He gives her time to acclimatise to the new environment and she is to set the pace for the relationship to grow.

Alia Bhatt is a muted powerhouse here; you can't tell if her shy and decorous demeanour is an act to lull the in-laws and not evoke any suspicion. Or is she being herself? Sehmat's intense training under Mir lasts only a few weeks and she is left very much on her own to cope with the unexpected. The family servant who has been with them since pre-Partition days is the one who sniffs danger from the new docile daughter-in-law. And he is the first to be eliminated by Sehmat—a first kill to be followed by that of her brother-in-law who is investigating the faithful servant's 'accidental' death, run over by a jeep. Sehmat does find information about a submarine attack plan by Pakistan—the Brigadier is now a Major General and important papers are fortuitously sent to him. Mir passes on the information to the Indian army authorities but they are unwilling to act on a rookie agent's findings. Meanwhile Sehmat and Iqbal fall in love and the intimacy phase of the marriage begins. Bhatt's demeanour often hints of a gnawing conscience, because this family has given her nothing but trust and affection. Gulzar's strength as a storyteller is to make us aware of how like us the other side is. The Us versus Them rhetoric is so muted that it is inaudible. The suspense is not exactly nail biting but keeps us on the edge.

As the Pakistani authorities finally close in, our attention is divided: between Sehmat's safety and the poignancy of the painful scene between Iqbal and Sehmat when he questions if what was between them real at all? A grenade thrown by Mir leaves Iqbal's question unanswered. Perhaps he catches a glimpse of it in her eyes ... It is a question that will haunt Sehmat all her life, even after Mir manages to bring her safely back home. Sehmat discovers she is pregnant. She decides to keep the baby ... we last see her—not a close up—by the window of a lonely house. How did she spend the rest of her life? Was she given her due for alerting the army and navy about the nuclear submarine waiting to attack our aircraft carrier in the Bay of Bengal? The film's opening aboard the aircraft carrier speaks of the work done by an anonymous woman to safeguard the pride of our navy's fleet.

Raazi, which translates as *agreeing*, treats Sehmat's commitment to her country with restraint avoiding even a hint of hyperbolic exaggeration. She is a tragic hero who speaks beyond her particular time. Today, in the overheated, suspicion-laden, toxic triumphalism of the Right, Sehmat the woman is relevant. She reiterates that not all Kashmiris are militants/separatists, fanatic about their faith. They do not have to prove their nationalism when every little or big violent incident disturbs the uneasy calm—you can't call it peace—that is the new norm.

You can always trust Anurag Kashyap to be different. Kashyap reunites with Taapsee Pannu, his *Manmarziyaan* heroine to give us *Sand Ki Aankh* (2019). Bhumi Pednekar also co-stars in the project. The film, based on the exploits of India's oldest shooters, Chandro Tomar and her sister-in-law Prakashi Tomar, who started their careers when they were in their 50s, is authentic and inspirational beyond the confines of the particular story. They cunningly defy the patriarchal diktat of the feudal joint family to take part in competitions. The two no-nonsense, hardworking women finally shame the family patriarch into letting their granddaughters take up shooting. The girls are then set on the road to upward mobility, with opportunity to get government jobs set aside for women qualifying for the sports quota. Who says you have to be city bred to have millennial aspirations and a chance to achieve them?

Priyanka Chopra who has already produced a successful Marathi film made the heart-warming *The Sky Is Pink* (2019), directed by Shonali Bose (*Amu* and *Margarita with a Straw* are on her calling card). This film follows the classic tears-through-brave-smiles narrative arc, to describe the brief impactful life of motivational speaker Aisha Chowdhury (played by Zaira Wasim, in her last performance before she quit films) who died tragically young. Aisha, with her family's unstinting help, lives life fully to the extent possible without self-pity and infectious humour. Prinyaka Chopra, with not an iota of her glamour diminished, brings to life the tigress mother who gives her gifted daughter every chance possible to survive the compromised immunity she is born with.

The biopic *Gul Makai* (2020) on Malala Yusafzai, the youngest Nobel Peace Prize winner and advocate for girls' education was caught in controversy with objections raised by some people in Pakistan. It was woefully incompetent and did no justice to its famous protagonist. A slew of films are in varying stages of production about our women sports stars.

Saina Nehwal's biopic, with a change of lead actor, faithfully captured the graph of her career. Directed by Amole Gupte, the film stayed discreetly away from Saina's change of coaches. Sonu Sood is supposedly working on the life of P.V. Sindhu, the Olympics Silver medalist. He is keen on casting Deepika Padukone, who was a state level player and of course daughter of Prakash Padukone (he was the first Indian to win the All England Open Badminton Championship).

It seems to be the time to celebrate our sheroes in every sphere. The here and now has become exciting for filmmakers and actors, exploring every facet of woman the hero, to make the niche mainstream. In all this excitement, both film history and public memory seem to have forgotten the first true female action hero: Fearless Nadia who went on to be a legend in the decade she ruled the stunt genre in her trademark swashbuckling style, with poise and remarkable physical energy. A new name and career were destined for the Australian-born (1908) Mary Ann Evans in the land of Karma. Mary Ann came to India as a child with her Greek dancer mother and Scotsman father, a volunteer in the British Army. She learnt riding, hunting, and shooting in India's North West Frontier and later trained in ballet. Mary Ann Evans was a performer—in circus and on stage—discovered by her mentor J.B.H. Wadia, studio owner, producer and director, founder of Wadia Movietone. He was the Svengali to her blonde, blue-eyed, whip-wielding action star, the rage of moviegoers for a decade. He christened her Fearless Nadia and made 14 films well into the late 40s—the most important being *Hunterwali* (1935) and *Diamond Queen* (1940). Girish Karnad has described how he and his fellow schoolmates were agog with the thrill of anticipation when a new Nadia film was to be released in a lovely, nostalgic essay (*Cinema Vision*, a lively and informative quarterly published by Sidharth Kak that closed down to the lasting regret of cineastes). Nadia jumped off running trains with aplomb, evoked awe as a masked and cloaked avenger and rode like a champion. She was the redresser of injustice and helped the poor.

All this ought to have made Fearless Nadia a feminist icon. It is a curious and rather tragic paradox that a star of this magnitude with such a fan following, who lived on till 1996, went largely unrecognized by later generations. Her great-grandnephew Riyad Vincy Wadia made a much admired and well-travelled documentary: *Fearless: The Hunterwali Story*. After watching the documentary at the 1993 Berlin International Film

Festival, Dorothee Wenner, a German freelance writer, and film curator, wrote *Fearless Nadia–The True Story of Bollywood's Original Stunt Queen*, which was translated into English in 2005. The film was screened to admiring audiences, largely limited to film history mavens. Why has Fearless Nadia remained outside the pantheon of icons? Was it because in the pre-Independent days, though this Anglo-Saxon beauty ruled the box-office, free India subconsciously associated her with our erstwhile White rulers? Her accented Hindi did not come in the way of public adulation, which was anyway more enthralled by her unbelievable stunts that she performed herself. Perhaps it was the latent bias against her White origin—though she was married to Homi Wadia, brother of J.B.H. Wadia—and the stunt film was déclassé compared to the socials, mythological and historical spectacles that found favour.

Vishal Bharadwaj's ambitious epic *Rangoon* (2017) cast Kangana Ranaut as an action star of the 40s, as homage to Fearless Nadia. She is caught in a triangular relationship with her Parsi mentor (Saif Ali Khan) and a mysterious soldier (Shahid Kapoor)—ostensibly serving the British Army but secretly an agent of Subhash Chandra Bose's Indian National Army. The flawed film—brilliant in parts but not cohesive as a whole—failed and so did the resurrection of Fearless Nadia's new avatar.

5
Woman at Work

Vintage Bollywood had really no place for the working woman in its narrative, except a token mention that she works. The exceptions are few. Radha of *Mother India* was rooted in the soil, tilling the fields and making her shoulder the yoke for the plough. It minted an iconic image for all time. A desultory teacher here and district collector there no less, to fulfil middle-class India's ultimate aspiration in the melodrama-addicted 60s are noteworthy. The norm was to raise domestic drudgery to be the ordained duty of the sainted *grihalakshmi*. To be the domestic goddess was the ultimate dream.

It was easy to banish the working woman to penumbral shadows earlier but her presence is widely acknowledged and given space now. That is because the millennial woman is working in many fields and her presence is unmissable. You see the local trains in Bombay, Chennai; or metros in Delhi, Kolkata, Bengaluru; and those who want their own mobility, on two wheelers in Pune, Mysore, Bengaluru; and smaller cities that are deemed safer. You see her behind the counters in shopping malls, front desks at many offices, teachers in schools and colleges, cashiers and clerks in banks and the media in its many avatars. Amitabh Bachchan in promotional interviews for the thriller *Badla* (2019) talked admiringly of the young women he is surrounded by on the sets—as production and costume designers, make-up specialists, assistant directors, cinematographers—all working hard and efficiently (NDTV, 17 March 2019). They are fifty percent of the crew, he said. There are of course behind the sets professionals: writers, editors and marketing mavens that he did not mention. Bachchan recalled that in his heyday, there were just two women on the sets: the heroine and her mother.

The numbers of women in the workforce are cold statistics. It is easy to see for oneself the empirical evidence all around. There are trustworthy professionals speaking from personal experience of qualitative field research. Meet Preethi Maroli, Ex-global business director at J. Walter Thompson, London. She used to head the global communication business on Sunsilk. This brand of shampoo was targeted at the lower middle-class women, the B and C category. As part of the research methodology, Maroli spent two to three hours with young women in their homes, talking to them about their aspirations, fears, career aims, and general expectations from life, safety while commuting specially in a city like Delhi. These interviews were conducted during 2016–2017 across India. Most revealing is Maroli's interaction with a 22-year-old who got her first job in the Accounts Department of a small firm. When asked if she shared any untoward experience of travelling by Delhi's notorious public transport with her parents, her answer was an emphatic no. Her can-do attitude was: I will deal with it myself. I don't want to be stopped from working. Her plans were well set. Saving money to buy an air-conditioner for the parents; then save over three years to start a business of her own. This girl was thinking like a boy with long-term goals, muses Maroli. For so many young women she met, the present circumstances were 'just current' and they were sure their ambition and hardwork will take them to a better future. Ambition was the key word, Maroli noted. This was across developing countries and over continents, be it India, Thailand, or Brazil. Maroli sets the India story in the context of the wider research she headed. She confesses: 'I found these women truly inspiring and the only word for me to describe them is awesome. No matter which country, these women were consistently awesome in each of them. It was fascinating to discover a silent but sure movement happening amongst young women across the globe, a movement to assert themselves and make their place in the world. Most of them were first jobbers and one of the first women in their family to be working. Marriage was very low on their priority list. They wanted financial independence, a chance to live life before they were tied down with responsibility of a family.' Similar were the findings of Thomas L. Friedman, three times Pulitzer winner. His bestseller *The Earth is Flat* describes encounters with young women (many from outlying small towns) working in Bengaluru's thriving IT industry with big dreams for the future.

Bollywood is alive to this reality but the career it chooses for its heroines is more glamorous—not the routine office job in small and big firms. The ordinary job is more the exception to Bollywood's requirement of the glamour quotient. Kriti Sanon works in the electricity board in *Bareilly Ki Barfi* (2017)—a typical rundown municipal office, none of the gleaming glass and chrome offices films bedazzle us with. Usually, heroines in staple rom coms are working women who treat it as a career, not just a job, as described in Chapter 1. Deepika Padukone is a serious doctor who prefers not to express her feelings for the wanderlust-bitten hero Ranbir Kapoor in *Yeh Jawaani Hai Deewani* (2013) when they first meet on a trek. They meet years later, and romance is rekindled but she is also committed to her vocation. Kareena Kapoor is a doctor in *3 Idiots* (2009). In the bromance *Zindagi Na Milegi Dobara* (2011), Katrina Kaif has an unusual profession: deep sea diving instructor, an interesting departure from the regular teacher, lawyer or doctor—professions deemed suitable for women. Look more searchingly, and we find that Bollywood has a strong penchant for media professionals for the female lead. Symbiosis at work, apparently. This is part acknowledgment of Bollywood's sometimes patronizing, sometimes admiring relationship with television. The sibling rivalry was always weighted in favour of cinema (all over the world) while upstart TV was relegated to a poor, imitative relation. Not anymore. Films need TV for promotions on its most popular programmes and the trailer blitz starts months before a film's release. TV has not gotten over its awe of big glamorous cinema but soaps with the highest TRPs know that they have a long lease to get viewers addicted, even across those mandatory generation leaps. Familiarity breeds a strange kind of affection for characters you meet on a daily basis. Films face the dreaded Friday verdict followed by the tension of weekend collections. TV actors still aspire for the Bollywood break but not all can be Shah Rukh Khan. A few actors, who have a big fan following, if we go by internet forums dedicated to soaps and proliferation of fan fiction based on these serials, have transited to films with minor to middling success.

But the biggest impact TV has had on Bollywood is how the well-known anchor Barkha Dutt shaped some memorable characters in films. It all started with *Lakshya* (2004), Farhan Akhtar's second film. A difficult task to match *Dil Chahta Hai*'s (2001) fresh energy, which epitomized male bonding that survives mistakes and wilful misunderstandings. *Lakshya* is the coming of age of a confused young man, a drifter through life, inured to his father's disappointment and steady girlfriend's exasperation with his aimless attitude. *Lakshya* has also been called a poster film for the Indian army. Kargil War was a recent event and that no doubt shaped the script. Hrithik Roshan played the non-hero Karan Shergill who finally finds his vocation in the army after initially rebelling against its strict regimen during training. Romila Dutt (Preity Zinta), Romi for short, is Karan's college friend who has sort of graduated into girlfriend. She is the total antithesis to Karan who looks for an excuse to goof off. Romi is the daughter of an academic; the atmosphere at home is intellectual and politically aware. Romi is an activist for women's causes and a budding journalist. It is Romi's final rejection when he runs off from NDA (National Defence Academy) that chastens and shapes up Karan. He needed the rejection to kick start his motivation. He is inducted into the army and posted to Kargil when the war with Pakistan has started.

Kargil was the first war that was brought home to viewers on TV. Cynics called it made for TV war. That is unjustified but the excitement—thrill of a minor victory in an arduous war in difficult terrain, fear for our soldiers on the front, the tragedy of lives lost—was something new for India. NDTV's Barkha Dutt was the most famous face reporting on the war, its human stories and its fall out. Romi is obviously modelled on Dutt—professionalism coming into its own when guns are booming across the mountains, searching for the smaller stories embedded in the larger narrative. Romi's fiancé doesn't want her to go to the front as a reporter and she breaks off the engagement. She sees a new Karan, dedicated to his mission when she starts her reporting stint. Karan emerges a hero from performing an extremely challenging mission of capturing the peak in a specified time, within shooting range of Pakistan's bunkers on higher ground. He is exhausted and deeply sad at losing half the men that set out. Romi is truly impressed, not only with what his unit achieved but the whole change in his attitude. Karan has found his vocation. Next mission for Karan: get Romi back. Reportage under fire became glamorous in Bollywood, reel taking a cue from real.

TV newsrooms continued to fascinate filmmakers. Next was *No One Killed Jessica* (2011), a docu-fiction based on the shooting of Jessica Lall, Delhi's popular model, working at a hotspot restaurant frequented by Delhi's happening crowd. The man who shot her—the son of a Haryana politician boasting powerful connections—was acquitted for lack of evidence. This was the first time that ordinary citizens were outraged by this gross miscarriage of justice and blatant manipulation of evidence. Their protests were highlighted by the media, more so by TV channels that were competing for eyeballs in the breaking news race.

What is the most engaging way to tell a story based on real events? Documentary? Mockumentary? Or a 'hybrid of fact and fiction' as director Rajkumar Gupta announces with commendable rare honesty in the pre-credit titles of *No One Killed Jessica*. That too raises a question: is it to pre-empt the inconvenient fiction that he gives NDTV all the credit for a messianic campaign to right the grievous miscarriage of justice when it was *Tehelka* that staged the sting operation? *Tehelka* got the crucial evidence to nail the trigger-happy brattish son of a politician. When Gupta had the courage to take up a high-profile case and set it in the context of Delhi's naked power play, was it so difficult to give credit where it is due? He does insert a couple of lines as the end credits roll that *Tehelka* was one of the news organizations that contributed to media activism. The fact is, *Tehelka* (the leader of sting operations before sting became synonymous with sleaze) exposed how the aspiring actor Shayan Munshi was bought off by Manu Sharma's (the murderer) father, a minister in the Haryana cabinet. Well, it's a truth universally acknowledged that TV is much sexier than print, and easier for the audience to get co-opted into a story. It is story that has no romantic angle, no conventional hero, no gratuitous item number, and goes on to test our recall capacity of the case that stopped making headlines when it was dragged through the court for six long years.

Moreover, Gupta casts two fine actors against the grain and doesn't give them too many scenes together either. That is either chutzpah of the most daring kind or trusting his dramatic instincts and faith in the story to keep us riveted through a fast-paced narrative. Another fact-fiction conundrum. Except for Sabrina and Jessica Lall, all other names are changed. Once past these sticking points, *No One Killed Jessica* is a good film that works as a thriller and conscience-rouser. What he achieved is rekindle hope that justice can be obtained through collective action and dogged commitment, that the media (especially in the post Radia-gate age)[1] can play the activist for a good cause. Gupta is able to create the

---

[1] A scam cum scandal that embarrassed ministers and business houses in 2008–2009. It was centered round the tapes of Nira Radia, a well-connected lobbyist and her conversations with power wielders including TV journalists.

feel-good factor that is intelligent and emotional—not manipulative and sentimental.

The lapidary barrage of headlines is followed by Rani Mukherjee's husky voice over, giving quotable sound bites of what Delhi is all about, the city where who you know matters more than what you are. We go along with Meera Gaity (a feisty, foul-mouthed, no nonsense star anchor of NDTV) on her star-making Kargil assignment, followed by the Kandahar highjack. You can see the sexy strut of power and self-confidence oozing out of the diminutive dynamo. Barkha Dutt must have felt gratified after *Peepli Live's* (2010) smart take down and red-faced embarrassment following Radia gate. You wonder if she is flattered or discomfited by Rani Mukherjee's self-conscious use of the F word and the untranslatable Hindi abuse she hurls—and repeats for his shocked disbelief—at a silly sycophantic man on the plane. Rani as Meera revels in shocking everyone around and wears the title bitch as a compliment. Are we creating a new stereotype of the media star as a brash, abrasive bitch? Meera passes up the Jessica Lall shooting as an open and shut case where there were 300 witnesses at Beena Ramani's exclusive club.

Not so exclusive after all, where Manish Bharadwaj and his loutish companions brandish 1000 rupee notes and a pistol at Jessica (Myra, a fetching new face) and demand a drink when the bar has closed. Half the public interest in the Jessica case was because it featured cowardly socialite-designers, equally cowardly well-heeled society types and wannabe actors. The cop on duty (a brilliant Rajesh Sharma) expresses his disgust at these spineless socialites. He is a most intriguing character, looks thuggish but looks can be deceptive. He has to struggle to keep his hands to himself while he questions Maneesh at the police station, because he has taken 70 lakhs not to hit the tender flesh of the politician's son. He also has the foresight to record the suspect's confession and keep it for later use, because he knows how corruptible the police force is when a politician in power can tamper with evidence and coerce/bribe/threaten witnesses. Everyone takes bribes, but the difference is for what, he rationalizes.

He keeps Sabrina's (an expressively subdued Vidya Balan) faith going as she wearily makes the rounds of the police station, courts, and evasive witnesses who promise to speak the truth. The first half of the film, though it starts with show—casing Meera's professional success is centred around Sabrina—despairing yet determined, propping up her grieving parents, trudging along narrow lanes and braving Delhi's buses with quiet fortitude and sinking hope. She wants justice for her chirpy younger sister, killed so senselessly. It is easy for an actor to invite us to share the highs and lows of emotion. But to create empathy for the slow poison of helpless despair, the descent into apathy, and non-caustic cynicism calls for understated skill. And shedding of star ego when there are other characters that are perky (Myra) or flamboyant (Meera). The film offers contrasting working women: Sabrina's is a routine job at a travel agency, bright touristy posters contrasting with her dull despair; Meera is a flashy media star, taking her celebrity status for granted. Her setting is jazzy with bright studio lights.

Gupta limns the screen with flashbacks, of a chirpy, ambitious Jessica who cajoles and bullies her indulgent older sister with gamin charm. This establishes the bond between sisters and makes us understand Sabrina's bitterness when witnesses—one of whom she has paid when she could ill-afford it so that he will not be bought over by the minister—lie through their teeth. Rage spent, cynicism sets in, and her shoulders droop in defeat. A deglamorized Vidya Balan reins in her lovely warm smile and defines body language as an underused tool in the actor's armoury.

Her quiet despair and mutinous apathy throw Meera's energy and efficiency into high relief. This is the subtle dramatic dynamics that Gupta brings in so effectively to propel the taut story forward. It makes us finally overlook the fiction part of the film, of making NDTV the prime mover of events, galvanizing the country into sending SMSes by the thousands. To be fair, NDTV was the premier news channel in 2006. And more importantly, we were not so cynical about the media and its hidden agenda.

Anushka Sharma played a spunky TV reporter in Raju Hirani's satirical exposé of our dependence on godmen and charlatans of all hues through the eyes of a stranded naked alien, a humanoid of exceptional intelligence as befits a specimen from a far advanced civilization. *PK* (2016) is the eponymous hero who gets this sobriquet because his erratic (by our human standards) behaviour makes people assume he is drunk. Hence the question: *Peekay ho*? Chaplinesque sight gags careen into screwball comic frenzy in the riveting first half. His remote has been stolen and without it, he can't connect to his spaceship. He is sent to research our species and comes with the telepathic gift of transferring all the memories of a person whose hand he holds for a given length of time. This of course leads to hilarity of various hues.

PK discovers clothes in dancing cars—as couples make out—and this becomes a recurring gag. His attempts to find his remote lead him to shrines of all religions and the ensuing satiric outcome spares no faith. Soon, he discards all the idols, holy beads, and threads as fraudulent devices to exploit the gullible, looking for easy fixes for life's problems. PK's escapades cause a stir and he becomes an object of general curiosity. Jaggu's reporter's nose is now twitching at the scoop that can lead to a major exposé, fed up as she is with inane stories of suicidal pets.

Jaggu (Anushka Sharma) is the rebellious daughter of a rich father, a devout disciple of Tapasvi Maharaj (Saurabh Shukla), a fraudulent god man with a huge following. Jaggu (who has truncated the unwieldy Jagadambika she was saddled with) nurses a particular grouse against this guru. It was at his bidding that her father had refused to let her marry Sarfaraz (Sushant Singh Rajput) a Pakistani she had met in Bruges as a student. The intolerant god man brainwashes her father that all Muslims are not to be trusted. She still goes ahead with her plans of marriage, except that Sarfaraz fails to turn at the venue. There is only a letter for her. For a climax, their teary reunion in a studio with live audience is taken care of by PK's omniscience and faultless logic. So we have a happy end to a cross border love story even though PK has by now fallen in love with the girl who not only believes him but is bent on getting back the remote that will take him home. Inter-galactic love stretches believability and it is politically suave to unite Indo-Pak lovers. This balances the earlier scene where Hirani shows a Jihadi bombing of a train that leaves PK in despair, losing the first human who befriended him—the Rajasthani band leader played with gusto by Sanjay Dutt, the filmmaker's talisman.

The second half is full of too many threads that need all of Hirani's editorial expertise to weave into a smooth narrative. It is still engaging, and takes us on a rollercoaster of emotions, though the pace feels flaccid. The arguments of religious 'managers' using the human need for hope get repetitive even though the points made are both familiar and relevant. Tapasvi displays PK's bright blue pendant as a piece of Shiva's damaru fallen in the Himalayas and wants funds to build a glorious temple. A sly reference to Ayodhya and Ram Janmabhoomi temple? The allusion is unmistakable and brave in the climate of triumphalist Hindu majoritarianism.

So far so acceptable, even if the simplistic arguments are set in a rationalist's echo chamber. PK's arguments are on the wellworn lines of *O My God* (the play was far superior to the film). You could say they need repetition in a country where *swayambhu* idols—daub with vermillion and presto, a new temple is born!—sprout like umbrellas in the monsoon and god men take new avatars every other day. Hirani understands and condones our need for hope and how we find it in faith. But he is no latter-day Charvaka or a follower of Richard Dawkins and Christopher Hitchens school. He does not ask why we need religion at all. Even his protagonist, the holy innocent from an advanced civilization that does not need religion, in a way validates human need for faith instead of posing logically irrefutable questions based on material reality. But then, that would make the whole clever premise too discomfiting—cerebrally, philosophically, and commercially.

It would be interesting to know what the late Father Gaston Roberge, the distinguished Kolkata-based film academic and researcher, would have made of Hirani's use of the holy innocent as the vehicle of enlightenment (in a limited sense). At a paper presented in Bombay a few years ago, he posited that Rancho of *3 Idiots* had Christ-like qualities and his ongoing research was to survey how students responded to the film. Is religion to be debated in metaphysical terms or at the level of simplistic exposés of god men materializing gold chains from thin air and Jihadists carrying out killings in the name of Islam? The choice settles for simple answers that make us feel good about ourselves. It is content to skim the surface and not subvert deeply held beliefs. We cannot ask for profundity when the director's intention is to tell an agreeable, entertaining, and safely provocative story with grace, wit, and superior sentimentality. The operative word is superior.

Hirani's impeccable casting—from the superstar Aamir Khan who blazes curiosity and intelligence in place of his usual square-jawed earnestness, a poised yet vulnerable Anushka Sharma, the underestimated brilliance of Saurabh Shukla, a restrained and thus far more effective Boman Irani and the reliable supporting actors—delivers a winner. Sharp dialogue (part of the credit must go to regular collaborator Abhijat Joshi) and first-rate cinematography all contribute to make *PK* an important film but not path-breaking. Jaggu's journalistic instincts are satisfied with the headline making exposé; the script does not allow her to take the argument further, nor does it hint at her intellectual capacity to do it.

A final thought that leaves me intrigued. *PK* is not a sci-fi film in the true sense of the term nor is it set in some distant future. Indian cinema in general and Bollywood in particular does not make futuristic films and if they do venture into alien territory, the future for humankind is generally optimistic, if not Utopian. Unlike films from the West, where the future is always dystopian—be it *Interstellar* (2014) or *Hunger Games* series (2012, 2013, 2014, and 2015) and even garden variety Sci-fi films—our imagination distances itself from a bleak future in store for humanity. There is sanguine hope that the world will be a better place despite all the ills that bedevil us. What makes us so optimistic? Perhaps it is because the creation and destruction myths are cyclic in nature in all Indic faiths.

From sanguine futurism to the rough and tumble of politics at its worst: Prakash Jha's political dramas usually centre on the conflict between idealism and the pragmatic amorality of politicians and their crony capitalists. *Satyagraha*'s (2013) protagonist is Dwarkanath (Amitabh Bachchan) a retired principal who lives in a small town with his upright engineer son Abhishek and daughter-in-law. Manav (Ajay Devgn) though diametrically the opposite of Abhishek—he wants to be an entrepreneur and will make the compromises it requires—remains good friends with him. Abhishek's death in a staged accident—actually a commissioned murder by a contractor who is also the brother of a minister—triggers protest. The compensation announced is also not paid. Dwarkanath mobilizes a mass protest and goes on a fast—no doubt inspired by Anna Hazare whose movement was in a way one of the causes for the UPA government's defeat in 2014. Yasmin Ahmed (Kareena Kapoor) is a TV journalist who believes in ground reporting than be a glamorous talking head in the studio. She chronicles the events as they happen and meets her estranged boyfriend Manav. They had parted because she does not approve of his capitalistic views, for she believes in an egalitarian society. Unfortunately, the conflict is mere verbalization and we don't really get into their minds. It is still an attempt to show the non-glamorous side of television journalism.

From reportage to filmmaking is logical progression. Akira (Anushka Sharma) is a documentary filmmaker for Discovery channel no less in *Jab*

Tak Hai Jaan (2012), Yash Chopra's swan song about the need for trust in love, whatever impediments come in the way—like accidents causing and restoring short time amnesia. Akira comes across Samar Anand (Shah Rukh Khan) a taciturn bomb-defusion expert in Ladakh when he saves her from drowning in the lake. She develops an almost immediate crush on him but accidentally finding his diary makes her more of a determined cupid trying to unite Samar and Meera (Katrina Kaif), the love of his life and a London businessman's adored daughter. Meera has issues of trust because her mother had left her when she was twelve for another man. The diary introduces Akira to Samar as a young, hopeful immigrant in London, a struggling street musician when he is not waiting tables. Meera's prayers and obsessive faith in God is an irrational impediment to being together even though she does love him.

Akira—inevitably hailed with the Hey Kurosawa greeting—makes a documentary on Samar's bomb disposing expertise and invites him for the London premier. Akira, playing fate's agent, brings Samar and Meera together after a few hiccups and some well-meaning pretence. Akira is one of those young women who are happy for others when she knows she has absolutely no chance with a one-woman man. We first meet her in shorts and Tee in freezing Ladakh, while soldiers around her are warmly dressed. She is so happy singing *jiya re jiya* where one of the lines goes:

> *pinjre se uda, dil ka shikra,*
> *khudi se maine ishq kiya re*[2]

Even the eminently forgettable *Tees Maar Khan* (2010) is only remembered for Katrina Kaif's sizzling dance to *My name is Sheila, Sheila ki jawani*. After announcing she will not belong to anyone though the whole world wants her, the song confesses:

> *Ab Dil Karta Hai Haule Haule Se, Main Toh Khud Ko Gale Lagaun*
> *Kisi Aur Ki Mujhko Zaroorat Kya, Main Toh Khud Se Pyaar Jataun*[3]

---

[2] My heart flew out from the cage, I have fallen in love with myself.
[3] Slowly, my heart wants to embrace me, why do I need anybody else, I can express love for myself.

Is this arrogant self-love healthy confidence or narcissism? Given Akira's cheerful insouciance, it speaks of self-confidence that her clothes attest to. She ignores the first rule of a documentary filmmaking. The filmmaker ought to blend with the milieu and not draw attention to herself. She seems not to be even aware of inappropriately prancing in her shorts for a whole troop of men. Well, if the intention is to display Anushka Sharma's long toned legs can commonsense quarrel with the king of romance's sartorial choice?

With so many women wielding the camera so efficiently—Anjuli Shukla won a National Award for Best Cinematography in 2010—it was time for a cinematographer as the lead. In Gauri Shinde's *Dear Zindagi* (2016), Kiara (Alia Bhatt) is a budding cinematographer who dreams of making her own film. She has just come back home—a colourfully untidy flat in Bombay screaming 'personality'—after packing up a shoot in London. The handsome producer with whom she is romantically involved vaguely promises to produce her film but he gets engaged to another woman. Kiara is venting with her three best buddies, the only people to whom she opens up—but again, she holds back. A layer underneath is out of bounds for everyone. Even she is unwilling to look within.

Kiara has one more trouble staring her in the face. The landlord wants her to vacate; he will let it to only a married couple. So many women not in a regular 10 to 5 job face this problem even in cosmopolitan Bombay. She goes home to her parents in Goa, not with the joy of homecoming but wary and defensive. Her behaviour with the equally wary parents, cheery extended family, and old friends borders on uncalled for rudeness.

Shinde has made sure that the coming-of-age theme is not an exclusive male domain. Even young women who apparently have everything find it difficult to focus. So is the case with Kiara. Instead of Goa's famous laidback lifestyle relaxing her, Kiara is so restless and angry that insomnia is a constant companion. It is fortuitous that she chances upon Dr (Jahangir) Jug Khan's (Shah Rukh Khan) unconventional talk at a psychiatrists' conference, totally free of seminarese jargon. She decides to consult this nonconformist therapist and it is this interaction—sometimes cerebral, often seemingly desultory and inconsequential—that is the strength of the film.

Intelligent conversation is a rare delight in our films. Slowly, Dr Khan gets to the core of her problem: Kiara's fear of abandonment that has haunted her since childhood when her parents left her in her grandmother's care for years. That is why she leaves a relationship before the other could leave her. She meets a singer and is attracted to him but leaves before it could lead to something more. Finally, knowing the root of her problem allows Kiara to make peace—tentative but it is a beginning—with her parents. What works for *Dear Zindagi* is the chemistry between Bhatt and Shah Rukh Khan. Chemistry doesn't always have to be sexual. They share an intelligent and encouragingly receptive relationship though Kiara does admit to her romantic feelings for the good doctor. It is perfectly normal to fall in love with your therapist, part of the healing process, reassures Dr Khan. There is a hint of attraction on his part too; he retreats, with the memory of a broken marriage behind him. We last see Kiara interacting animatedly with a furniture designer and her first film is screened to high praise. Rather neatly tied up, because deep-seated anxieties are not so easily resolved. The infectious vibes between the unlikely pair who are not romantically involved charm us into believing that all's well. It is not often that a millennial woman's anxieties are addressed with honesty.

Call it tokenism but unusual professions for women are not only recognized but lauded too in the alpha male world of the army. *Uri: The Surgical Strike* (2019) is a well-made action film high on nationalism that thirsts for revenge for the loss of our soldiers' lives. 'How's the *josh*' is the famous tagline appropriated by the BJP for electoral gain. Amidst this high-octane action riding on high levels of fiery enthusiasm, we come across two women professionals, dedicated to their high-risk jobs. Yami Gautam is actually an Intelligence Agent Pallavi Sharma disguised as nurse Jasmine Almeida sent to care for Major Vihan Singh Shergill's (Vicky Kaushal) Alzheimer-stricken mother. The major, who leads handpicked commandos to go across the border and eliminate terrorist cells, is impressed by Pallavi's quick thinking. He is also furious when his mother goes missing. The major selects Seerat Kaur (Kirti Kulhari), a pilot grounded for saving a family stranded in Kashmir's floods against orders to return to base: her highly risky job is to paradrop his unit in enemy territory. The drop is cancelled. Seerat Kaur is the widow of an officer who died on duty and she brings them all back to safety, dodging enemy fire. There is no combat role for women in the army but highlighting the professional commitment of these two women might help them breach a male bastion inch by inch.

There is something about the uniform. If it gives men authority and makes them sexy (if the men don't have a paunch that is), on women it often looks as if they are trying hard to assume authority and mimic men. But when it comes off, women in the full accoutrements of a police officer give femininity a new definition. The gung ho woman cop who can fight as well as any male colleague is very rare in mainstream Hindi films. Vijayanirmala of South Indian cinema, and especially Telugu films, was hailed as 'Lady Superstar' and 'Lady Amitabh' for her many roles as the super-efficient, super-brave police officer who excelled at action without sacrificing her femininity. She won a National Award for Best Actress for the Telugu film *Kartavyam* in 1990. There has been no equivalent of Vijayanirmala in Hindi films. The South superstar was a producer and went on to become a politician too. Is it an idle speculation to hazard that the North Indian audience—the primary viewers—feel threatened when they see a rampaging female cop? *Mardaani* (2014) a specially crafted vehicle for Rani Mukherjee in a new avatar was successful at the box-office to prove this speculation wrong.

Rani Mukherjee inhabits the uniform of a senior inspector with Bombay police, physically and mentally. Shivani Shivaji Roy has strong views on not letting the system deter her from single-minded pursuit of Karan Rastogi (Tahir Raj Bhasin), the Delhi-based elusive kingpin of a drug cartel involved in trafficking young girls. Shivani takes no prisoners and devises punishment that may not comply with rules. A bit of vigilantism is always attractive to storytellers who play on society's perception of the judicial system hampered by shoddy prosecution. For Shivani, trafficking in young girls becomes a personal emotive issue. One of the girls kidnapped is teenager Pyaari, very dear to Shivani. She had rescued the girl from an uncle who was about to sell her and since then, Shivani has regarded Pyaari as her own daughter.

Pradeep Sarkar is known more for romantic dramas than thrillers. *Mardaani* is paced and narrated with all the twists and turns, dangers and deceits, rousing action and cunning ambushes the genre thrives on. Rani Mukherjee is taut as a drawn arrow poised to pierce the target and fleet footed as she chases down a man through crowded streets. The upward tilt of chin spells challenge, blood trickling down her mouth subtly invokes Kali, and her steely glare promises retribution. Mukherjee masters body language and uses her husky voice to send a chill down the spine of even a hardened criminal. When she utters her full name as if it is a royal proclamation, it reverberates with self-confidence: she can nail her target, however clever he might be, and whatever powerful connections he may have.

Shivani goes to Delhi to hunt her prey by luring him into a trap with Nigerians posing as dealers of rare and very expensive cocaine. She is as good a strategist as she is courageous. Rastogi's right hand man is caught but he erases all information and leads from his phone before shooting himself. Shivani is kidnapped by Rastogi and brought to a party he is hosting. She finds Pyaari and other missing girls there. They are forced to work as prostitutes. When Shivani finally corners Rastogi, she takes the law into her hands. No, she doesn't shoot him but hands him over to the girls who beat him to death. She is a true *mardaani*, a word used to describe the legendary Laxmibai of Jhansi and her skills as a warrior who fought like a man. Here *mardaani* connotes celebration of bravery on par with a heroic man, not the literal mannish woman. There is a subtext: what motivates Shivani is not just her resolve to root out a heinous crime like trafficking in young girls. It is her personal emotional involvement with Pyaari, her maternal attachment that gives the extra edge of focused rage. Even for a committed professional, the personal does become political.

Drishyam (2015) is a thriller that plays out like a cat and mouse game, between no less than the top cop of Goa, a hard-nosed woman is the IG, and a common man who is an elementary school dropout. At stake are her missing son and his victimized daughter—both teenagers—that makes it a knife-edge conflict. Vijay Salgaonkar (Ajay Devgn) is a law-abiding cable TV operator, well-liked by the people of a sleepy small town as a devoted family man. He is a fiercely protective father of two daughters—the older Anju is adopted and a much younger Anu is his biological child. He will do anything to keep them out of harm's way. There are no 'actual surprises' about the crime and its punishment. The suspense is how Vijay creates the perfect alibi for the entire family when Sam Deshmukh, the IG's son, uses a video of Anju bathing to blackmail her for sexual favours.

They were both participants at an interschool nature camp and a lawyer's daughter calls out Sam for taking photographs of the girls at the camp. He comes to Anju's house, and threatens to make the video public if she doesn't agree to his demand later that night. Ajay usually stays late at his office, watching films: the class 4 drop out as he repeatedly calls himself as do others, owes his practical knowledge and linguistic skills to his film addiction. He comes home to discover his wife Nandini and the two girls cowering in fear. Anju had hit Sam on the head with a rod when he tried to misbehave with the mother, as a diversion from threatening the daughter. Sam is dead. They are petrified. Nandini and Anju bury the body in the pit Vijay had dug in the back garden for composting.

Reassuring his wife and kids that nothing will ever harm them, he spins the elaborate story of them attending a Pravachan in Panjim over the holiday weekend—complete with bus tickets, hotel bills, chatting up conductors—to account for their absence. Sam's bright yellow car is parked nearby. Vijay drives it away and a particularly inimical, bribe-taking sub-inspector Gaitonde who dislikes Vijay's honesty sees him get into the car. He is the prime witness and accuser when Meera Deshmukh (Tabu) mounts a discreet investigation into her son's disappearance for over two weeks.

Meera Deshmukh's entry is dramatic and creates the mise en scène normally reserved for a male action star. We hear her threatening, ruthless voice emerging from the dark while two men are being mercilessly beaten up in a cell. As she rises and walks into the frame, her cold composure is as striking as the uniform. The cap casts a shadow on her forehead. Her chiselled cheekbones and mouth set in implacable straight line are highlighted. You know that here is a woman you can't mess with. Every word she speaks is calculated to strike fear.

Sam's phone is traced up to Coimbatore and then it goes into permanent silence. The car that Vijay had pushed into the pond of a disused stone quarry is fished out but there are no clues. Gaitonde's report of having seen Vijay driving it incriminates the entire family. Anticipating the contingency, Vijay has tutored Nandini and the girls to stick to their story, with minor variations from the girls to make it more natural. Meera Deshmukh is a relentless avenging angel now, her intelligence picking holes in Vijay's cast iron alibi. She orders and presides over the concerted effort to break Vijay, and has him beaten up before his family.

Nandini is the next target of violence. But no one, not even the little girl, breaks. Mahesh (Rajat Kapoor), Meera's businessman husband, repeatedly asks her to stop it. But Meera is now both the wounded tigress mother and implacable cop rolled into one. She mocks herself for being bested by a fourth class fail. The contempt of her class for an uneducated man is implicit in her hauteur, her upright bearing even when she is not in uniform. All the interrogations and thrashing are done in her home, away from the public eye since Meera doesn't want news of her missing son to come out.

When kicking and thrashing do not yield information, Meera decides to question the little girl Anu alone. Gaitonde, unleashing the brute in him, is ready to bring down his boot on the sobbing child on the floor. Mahesh can't take this anymore. Meera cries stop but the frightened little girl is ready to tell them what she saw that night from the window: something was buried in the backyard late at night.

Now the matter is out in public. The pit when dug up reveals the stinking, skeletal remains of a dog. The media is now involved and the court intervenes: Vijay can be interrogated only under its orders. A friend of Sam surfaces and at last, Meera finds out the despicable thing her son did. Gaitonde is suspended for excessive violence and there is a new inspector who has come to take charge in the newly built police station.

Meera resigns. The Deshmukhs want to apologize to Vijay and he meets them by the seaside. It is Mahesh who apologises and explains that they indulged their only child born late in their marriage. They just want to know if Sam is alive before they leave for London to settle down there. Meera is silent, and stony faced throughout. Vijay's cryptic answer implies that the intruder into their family will not return from where he has been sent. Meera finally breaks down sobbing. Is she crying for her son or is there some remorse for the brutality unleashed on Vijay at her orders? Director Nishikant Kamat leaves it ambiguous.

Meera's dark side could also be read as subterranean reference to Tabu's character in *Maqbool* (2003), the first of Vishal Bharadwaj's brilliantly creative adaptations of Shakespeare. Tabu is a Lady Macbeth-like woman with great ambition. Filmmakers who want a star actor to play characters with negative shades seem to prefer Tabu and her subliminal association with amorality. One should not underestimate the connections audience make—if an actor has made a memorable character her own, echoes from that performance sometimes colour our reading of her in a different context.

Drishyam is a remake of a Malayalam hit of the same name. The implied ambiguity that questions the ethicality of actions by both families is only superficial. The answers are implicit in the narrative, in how it valourizes the common man's love for his family through every means available to storytelling. It is interesting that both *Mardaani* and *Drishyam* recognize and to some extent validate (in different degrees) the maternal instinct under the starched uniform. But does it condone Meera's cold-blooded violence, coming from mixed motives? Meera is a warning couched in dramatically engaging narrative. The streak of ruthlessness, lack of any compassion, is portrayed as doubly reprehensible in a woman. It is par for the course in a male protagonist as we have seen in countless films.

Another top actor dons an IPS officer's uniform in *Jai Gangajal* (2016), Prakash Jha's sequel to his 2003 blockbuster starring Ajay Devgn as the dedicated cop who is set to clean up Bihar's lawless hinterland. This is a recurring theme running through Jha's oeuvre, concerned as he is with his home state's legacy of feudalism, corrupt police doing the bidding of criminals, and manipulative politicians poking their dirty fingers into a messy pie. *Jai Gangajal* brings Abha Mathur (Priyanka Chopra) to yet another benighted district where land grabbing is the norm and farmers unwilling to sell their meagre holdings are killed, and their strung-up bodies passed off as suicides. Abha Mathur's efforts to bring the criminals—who run riot in the district with the connivance of a corrupt higher up police officer played by the director himself—are doomed. Such narratives littered with corpses and driven by a righteous mob finally wreaking its own version of justice are yawningly predictable. There is nothing much that Priyanka Chopra brings to the film except the novelty of her unmadeup face. Just changing the gender of the crusader doesn't change anything, except the innovation that wears off soon enough. The film raises a troubling question. How different is a mob of oppressed people killing class enemies en masse different from lynchings of Muslims by cow vigilantes or Dalits by upper-caste armies? Doesn't this endorse people taking the law into their hands?

Do these three films augur change in how Hindi cinema portrays women police officers? Three films don't really set a trend but they are indicators of change. *Mardaani*'s sequel, with its predictable narrative, did fairly well. Rani Mukherjee as wife of Yash Raj films' head honcho can commission scripts that can create a new image and boost her career in an industry crowded with young actors doing commendable work. Comparing these three films with an obnoxious obscenity perpetrated in the name of woman empowerment thirty years ago tells us that the industry has moved forward. The said obscenity is *Zakhmee Aurat* (1988) starring Dimple Kapadia and directed by Avtar Bhogal.

Feminism needs saving from so-called filmmakers like Avtar Bhogal. This was how women felt—not all of them card-carrying feminists—when this travesty of women empowerment was paraded as a victim of censorship. The producer had screenings especially for groups of women to sell his idea of what rapists deserve. *Zakhmee Aurat* took off from the success of a few female avenger films made in the 80s and sought to capitalize on a raped police officer's revenge, as she leads a group of other victims on a castrating spree. The film is crude and reworks the Hebraic law of an eye for an eye. To drive home this idea, Bhogal lets loose an army of rapists and an assorted band of rape victims to package this atrocity. He needed a leader and a catalyst and who better than the gorgeous Dimple Kapadia (who had made a comeback) as Kiran Dutt the police inspector? Notice the first name Kiran—Kiran Bedi was very much in the news then. Kiran Dutt likes to jog on Juhu beach in the morning, letting the breeze play with her magnificent mane for our visual pleasure. She rescues a rape victim after the fell deed has been committed in a red Maruti van. Her karate chops are enough to subdue the culprit and handcuff him. He has a wily lawyer who specializes in defending rapists. This man can prove that the accused was in Pune that day and the man walks free.

Next, you have four creeps invade Kiran's spacious bungalow where she lives alone. The director takes sadistic pleasure in showing Kiran's prolonged struggle, positioning the camera to frame the gang rape for cheap voyeuristic thrills. Worse follows: Kiran internalizes the violence to succumb to self-hatred. The men are acquitted because the same clever lawyer argues that it is Kiran who raped the men to satisfy her lust. He produces a newspaper cutting that says women can commit rape as evidence. It convinces the credulous judge who lets the four goons off.

Kiran meets a doctor whose young daughter was raped and soon finds other victims. Now the project is on: each of the women will find her rapist, almost seduce him to come to a particular place. The doctor is ready with her implements to castrate each of them. Many of the rape stories are shot in a manner to titillate the audience. Luring rapists to come to designated spot is done through even more titillating songs and gyrations. The subliminal message, of Kiran Dutt inviting rape as punishment a professional deserves, is the worst offence a film can commit. A beautiful woman wearing the police uniform riding a powerful bike—the most obvious phallic symbol—invites reprisal for daring to encroach on male territory. The gangrape is a statement of power by men to subjugate this pretender who claims the authority of an office that is an exclusive male privilege. When the subtext is so blatantly sexist, how does the filmmaker have the temerity to pose as a champion of women? *Zakhmee Aurat* caused outrage because it showed how easily a film with known names can pass off crude sexism as a fight against rape culture.

For all the adrenalin rush of live television reporting, there is more permanency in the written word—even if it gets outdated. Mehul Kumar's high decibel vigilante drama *Krantiveer* (1994), dependent on Nana Patekar's histrionics, created an inspirational journalist who aids the angry hero. The angry hero calls Dimple Kapadia, who plays an unlikely journalist who chooses to live in a slum, *Kalamwali Bai*.[4] We never actually see her in a newspaper office or doing legwork researching for her angry polemics. She is hunched up on a bed, furiously filling up reams of paper resting against her knees: an image that stays in the mind minus the echo of written words. It is very different in Madhur Bhandarkar's best film, *Page 3* (2005) where we see the habitués of this exclusive world through the eyes of Madhavi Sharma (Konkona Sen Sharma). She is a rookie journalist, newcomer to Bombay's glitz, glamour, and the grime she discovers late. When Bhandarkar set his film in this rarefied section that features the who's who of society, the whole phenomenon was still relatively new and at the peak of popularity.

Pradeep Guha, president of the *Times* group, is the pioneer of celebrity journalism on a daily basis in India. It was dedicated to celebrating celebrityhood without the catty commentary and assumed dismissive tone of say *Stardust* or *Savvy* to a lesser extent. He rationalized that unlike papers in New York, the main sections of our papers did not give space to the doings of the rich and famous and their party circuit. Guha

---

[4] Lady with the pen.

was visiting the *New York Times* offices 'where he caught a glimpse of a new genre of news—celebrity reportage—and how popular it was becoming. That was the beginning of the idea for *Bombay Times*.'[5] He cited particular examples of Aishwarya Rai and Sushmita Sen's wins not getting the column space they deserved. Thus was born *Bombay Times* and its famous page 3 in 1994. So successful was this supplement that soon, *Times of India* started local versions to cater to local celebrities with their other city editions. Rival publications were forced to follow suit with their own versions but the *Times* has enjoyed the advantage of being first in the field.

Page 3 was the space where photographs of parties and important guests were splashed. It was assumed that if you did not make it to page 3, you had not arrived. The beautiful people featured were businessmen, socialites, models, designers, VIPs (self-proclaimed or the genuine article), and wannabes gate-crashing their way. Bombay had the additional cachet: it could exclusively flaunt Brand Bollywood.

Bhandarkar is nothing if not market savvy, of catching a trend and cashing on it. *Page 3* makes its protagonist Madhavi the observer and observed as she moves through the party scene, night after night, with practiced ease. There is the delicious irony that the air-kissing socialites busy with their bitchy backbiting are so friendly with a young woman who is not their equal in terms of money, status, and background. But the journalist needs to be cultivated because she is the one who will decide who will feature in her column. Madhavi is a mass communications topper and an ex-army officer's daughter from Bangalore. She has established her footing in the party scene, and at work, not afraid to argue with the Editor Deepak Suri (Boman Irani) for what she wants and gets it—to the chagrin of colleagues. However, when she wants him to carry a 500 word piece on a new obscure painter, the pragmatic Suri metaphorically runs a blue pencil across it.

The film introduces us to the other feature of a working girl's life in Bombay. Madhavi shares her apartment with the motormouth without brakes, the airhostess Pearl Sequeira (Sandhya Mridul typecast as the 'yes man' spouting Goan) in search of a rich man to give her the life of luxury she wants. Soon, another flatmate is added by the ever-friendly Madhavi.

---

[5] (*Nisha Menon, afaqs!, Mumbai | In Media Publishing*).

She meets Gayatri, an aspiring actress from Delhi looking for more congenial accommodation than her PG digs. To make for tighter storytelling, both the girls meet the men who can help them through Madhavi. Pearl starts dating a very much older hotelier based in the US while Gayatri is introduced to a leading star Rohit Kumar who readily gives an interview to Madhavi—much to the resentment of vernacular journalists who don't get the time of day from the star while they hang around his vanity van for hours. Privileges the English press enjoys over a Hindi paper that might have a much larger circulation, moans the disappointed journalist.

Madhavi's friend, the rising model Tarun, soon becomes her boyfriend. Everything is going swimmingly well until Madhavi discovers him in bed with her gay best friend, the makeup artist Abhishek. Madhavi gradually turns blasé when it comes to relationships—gay and heterosexual—because she has become cynical as a society columnist, where she sees lovers used and discarded like last season's fashion.

The next shock is Gayatri's attempted suicide. Madhavi and Pearl rush her to a hospital but face the hurdle of a needing police clearance. Vinayak Mane (Atul Kulkarni, effective as ever even in a brief role) is a colleague who works on the crime beat is at the hospital and helps with the admission. He is rather scornful of Madhavi's brand of writing: it is entertainment, not journalism, he pronounces rather judgementally. Madhavi ignores him, but it rankles... it is the beginning of questioning the worth of what she is doing. Far more urgent matters are at hand. Gayatri is safe but has lost the baby. The others don't know of her affair with Rohit and his curt order to get an abortion. Cut to an earlier scene: Rohit at a public appearance talks of the need for safe sex and Gayatri lands up there to tell him she is pregnant. Trust Bhandarkar's shoot and scoot style for this heavy-handed irony.

The one person Madhavi respects in the snobbish socialite set is Anjali Thapar (Soni Razdan) who runs a home for abandoned children. Madhavi's article on her laudable work gets cut because of a last-minute ad. She apologies to Anjali but the amiable lady laughs it off. She is more concerned with the excessive partying of her daughter who ignores her. Her husband, the head of the Thapar group has no time for her either. To the shock of everybody, Anjali Thapar commits suicide. Madhavi really grieves for her but is disgusted by the page 3 crowd's behaviour: they are all tears with heartbroken words for the microphones and busy planning the next party or what jewellery goes with the mandatory white for the funeral. They always wear their public face for the camera. With tears streaming down her face, Madhavi refuses to write the expected mushy article on Anjali's death but the editor will have none of it. She quits page 3 to accompany Vinayak Mane on his crime beat.

This is her brush with the tragic truth of Bombay's other side: bomb blasts, Muslim young men whisked away as terror suspects and finally, the racket of child trafficking that leads directly to Thapar where some of the children end up for the pleasure of paedophiles. Anjali had discovered the truth of how children of her home have been his victims and that is why she committed suicide. Madhavi writes a lead article with damning photographs as evidence late at night to make the front page the next day. But the final nail is driven home by the editor forced to kill the story by the proprietor who doesn't want to lose Thapar group's ads. It is the basic truth of publishing. Madhavi gets her termination notice the next morning, even though Deepak Suri admits it was a good story. She looks for work but finally finds a page 3 reporter job in another paper. Madhavi learns some basic lessons of journalism from Vinayak who was away on an assignment when all this happens. He upbraids Madhavi for parting with all the evidence and tells her, you must be in the system to fight the system.

The last shot of the film is close up of Madhavi as she moves through the swirling party scene merging in the background. Her wry cynical smile is the comment on her education in the ways of the media. Konkona Sen Sharma is the spine of the episodic narrative that aims to hit too many targets with a magic bullet. Bhandarkar opts for shallow breadth over depth. That has always been his choice, of tabloid style filmmaking with high-sounding rhetoric. Even within these constraints, Sen Sharma gives a sterling performance that is pitch perfect. It is a 22-year-old's journey from enamoured innocence to cynical maturity all within a year.

An evitable postscript is mandatory to the Page 3 world described, derided and yet celebrated by Bhandarkar. Today the Crème de la crème will not be caught dead on page 3 that has become tacky. Its claim to exclusivity has long been gone. Lifestyle magazines and TV shows give both the featured celebrities and curious viewers instant gratification with far better visual content. That said, the cult of celebrity will never die out. The dilemma for journalism and individual journalists remains: how much can they compromise their integrity to cater to this rather trivial pursuit?

It seems an unwritten rule that when you need a young woman who wants to be a writer, you pick Konkona Sen Sharma. Not at all surprising given her credentials: daughter of eminent filmmaker Aparna Sen and respected writer-journalist Mukul Sharma, granddaughter of late Chidananda Dasgupta, the doyen of film critics. Ayan Mukherji's first film *Wake up, Sid* (2009) is an understated ode to Bombay in all its moods and the chances it gives those who will seize it. It is also a coming-of-age film, of a spoilt rich brat Sidharth 'Sid' Mehra (Ranbir Kapoor) going through life as if it is an unending party for carefree collegians. We meet him and he meets Aisha (Konkona Sen Sharma) on the last day of his exams. After an initial minor fracas, Sid and newcomer to the city Aisha take a walk by the sea and connect. She is a roommate of Sid's friend and Sid, along with the rest of the gang, help Aisha to get a cosy apartment to rent. If you crane your neck on the terrace, you might even be rewarded with a view.

The gang unravels. Sid is the only one who has failed and he can't take the humiliation. He vents on his best buddy and is in a perpetual sulk. Fights with his doting mother and refuses to work in his businessman father's office. He impulsively walks out of his home, with his camera and finally ends up at Aisha's flat. Aisha Banerjee has come from Kolkata to be a writer but is willing to wait while doing clerical work at *Bombay Beat*, a hip magazine on the lines of *Time Out*. She lets Sid stay with her (temporarily) and it is a purely platonic relationship—a relationship severely tested by Sid's habitual untidiness, expecting others to pick up after him, and useless when it comes to chores. One day when an exasperated Aisha yells at him, Sid is willing to admit he must improve. A while later, he surprises Aisha with his newly acquired neatness and ability to rustle up a simple meal. Sid has been roaming aimlessly with his camera, taking photographs at random. Some of the photos interest Aisha enough to get him an internship with the photography section. It is as if a light is switched on. Sid finds his vocation and the picture editor is so impressed that he chooses one of his photographs for the magazine. Euphoric at getting his first cheque, Sid goes to his father's office to show it to him. Earlier, the father had blocked Sid's credit card. He enjoys his I-will-show-you moment, not realizing how pleased his father is.

Aisha is attracted to the editor Kabir (Rahul Khanna) and he too is interested in her. He is an intellectual and spells coolth. When they start dating, Aisha finds that they are incompatible: he likes jazz and she is die-hard Bollywood fan. Unconsciously, she is comparing him to Sid and the comfort level they enjoy. Aisha's inability to introspect why she resents Sid's closeness to the design intern Tanya adds to the emotional fog enveloping her. Aisha is older to Sid perhaps by a couple of years but now, she sees him in a new light. When Sid packs up to go home, she is angry and fights with him—both not recognizing their feelings for each other. It is when Sid reads Aisha's first column about her impressions of Bombay and feelings for an unnamed person, that he realizes he loves her. Charging out in the pouring rain, he meets Aisha for their rendezvous by the sea—where they first walked together—for the magic of monsoon to weave its spell.

Wake up, Sid avoids sentimentality to create casual warmth, of letting a relationship grow over time. The fact that Aisha is older doesn't matter. This goes against the convention of a girl always looking for an older man and the unwritten rule that the woman must be younger in a relationship. Like Rumi in *Lakshya*, Aisha plays the catalyst to Sid's maturity. He realizes he must not fritter away his life aimlessly. She is the anchor. We are certain that Aisha will one day be a writer of substance.

If this seems like a Sen Sharma trilogy, so be it. She is the foil to Farhan Akhtar in *Luck by Chance* (2009), Zoya Akhtar's unflattering exploration of Bollywood with an insider's knowledge and the affection of its child. An already over-the-top Bollywood is not easy material to satirize but Akhtar does it deftly. It is sharp but without malice. The film follows two parallel careers ending differently. Vikram Jaisingh (Farhan Akhtar) comes to Bombay with the dream of an acting career. He has two hometown contacts: One, an actor doing small roles and the other, working with studio props. The round of auditions and the endless waiting come across with the feel of real time, dramatically compressed. Vikram meets his friend's neighbour Sona Mishra (Konkona Sen Sharma) an actress waiting for the big break and sustaining herself by acting in regional films and bit roles in Bollywood. Initially, she seems to have her foot in the door, just waiting for it to open to let her in. When she meets Vikram in the waiting room of a producer's office, she oozes confidence of getting a parallel lead. And she infuses confidence in the new friend: she reassures him, for he has that 'something'. After a time, the two get romantically involved.

Sona has been the mistress of a small-time producer Satish Chowdhury (Alyy Khan) who has been promising for three years that he will cast her when he finds funding for a dream project. But when he does, Chowdhury evades the commitment trotting out the excuse that he needs a fresh face and Sona is no longer one. In tears at the heartless betrayal, Sona runs into Chowdhury's wife and hastily makes up a story of trouble back home. She leaves behind Vikram's photograph and this leads to Romy Rolly (Rishi Kapoor) a big producer to short list him for his upcoming film with a new heroine. Rolly does it at the urging of his insistent wife (Juhi Chawla)—part of the Bollywood wives' kitty party circle. Zoya Akhtar has fun at the wheels within wheels grinding to keep the Bollywood machine running. Vikram encourages another actor auditioning for the role to overact—says that's the director's preference according to the grapevine—making sure he is rejected. Vikram makes the short list and is chosen by Neena (ex-star), Rolly's wife and the director.

The hitherto straightforward Vikram learns to be devious and manipulate people to get ahead. The ingénue Nikki (Isha Sharvani) he is paired with has been groomed by the dragon mother Neena who was a top star in her day. Dimple Kapadia plays this prima donna (even when she is past her prime) sportingly, veering between warmth when she is flattered by Vikram's adulatory fan act and a hysterical virago when things don't go her way. Rolly mollifies her, assuring her that Nikki is the important star, the hero is secondary.

While Vikram succumbs to Nikki's overt seduction, Sona has been waiting patiently. She comes to know of the affair and a journalist friend working with a tabloid is also in the know. He in turn writes a stinging piece on Vikram's manipulation of Neena and her debutante daughter. The damning article goes into his struggling days and his discarded girlfriend who had helped him. Sona is not really responsible for the leak but Vikram blames her and the estrangement is permanent. Vikram's first film is a hit. A talk with none other than Shah Rukh Khan post the success infuses a small dose of introspection. Vikram wants to mend fences with Sona who had been such a pillar of support all through. Meanwhile, Sona has learnt her lesson. She knows time for the big break has gone. Instead, she is more secure with her TV career that offers her good roles and a growing fan following. Sona is being interviewed by a fawning journalist who tells her she is very popular with viewers. It is true women who make the biggest audience of soaps prefer women-centric stories and this offers actresses better roles.

A bittersweet ending with two career paths leading to different conclusions is the only one possible. A contrite Vikram comes to Sona's set while she is shooting a typical soap in a decked-up mansion. Sona emerges stronger, clearly able to see through Vikram's apology, of missing her constant support, of her belief in him. As she finally says without accusing him: it is all about you, how you felt but there is nothing really about me. Renewal of a relationship gone cold is not worth the emotional cost it may extract in the future with one more betrayal. It is an ending without loud recriminations but Sona's quiet statement of truth says it all.

Neither Vikram nor Sona is perfect. Both make compromises the industry demands. But on the moral scale, there is no equivalence. Sona's affair with a married man hurts only one person, his wife. Vikram has lost his moral centre while he plots his way, to get past rivals and climbs on the shoulders of others. Zoya Akhtar writes characters with grey shades without being judgemental, yet shows the difference between the two, Sona coming out the better person.

The film ends with Sona in a taxi on the way to Film City. Her voice over monologue remembers her past in Kanpur and wonders if her conservative parents will ever reconcile to her leaving home. She occasionally talks to a sister and knows her parents see her on TV. Sona takes justifiable pride that she is the first in her family to stand on her own feet. That is an achievement for a girl alone in a city without family support. The best part is, Sona doesn't repine or dwell on what might have been. She is content to work, earn her living—the only one among three sisters—and quietly self-assertive. She emerges a strong, grounded young woman making her mark in the daunting metropolis. She is not to be swallowed up in anonymity.

A postscript is in order for fandom. *Luck by Chance* is a Bollywood fan's dream of heaven. So many big stars from Hrithik Roshan to Aamir Khan and finally Shah Rukh Khan play brilliantly written cameos to justify their presence. This is the reward for being an industry child making her debut.

All the films discussed have women working in various media. The reality is, there are more women working in corporate offices. Trust Madhur Bhandarkar to hit on this virgin territory with *Corporate* (2006). It is a convoluted plot centred on the bitter rivalry between two groups, both in the Food and Beverages industry vying to launch a new minty drink, all kept under wraps. Corporate espionage is part of a vice president's job description according to the plot torn from a pulp novel's page. Spying is made the woman VP's responsibility and we can see miles ahead that Nishi Dasgupta (Bipasha Basu) will be the pawn sacrificed in the corporate war. This is the time before rules prohibiting relationships between staff members came into existence. Nishi is involved with Ritesh, the CEO and brother-in-law of the company's owner. So many factors are in play—FDA, environmental protection agency, foreign investors, central and state ministers, enquiry commission into contaminated soft drink—and before our spinning heads go faster and out of control, a murder made to look like an accident takes place. Things get worse for Nishi, pregnant with the dead man's baby. She is talked into being the sacrificial lamb and assured she will be released very soon. But the politician finds it inconvenient and so she is not released from custody by the enquiry committee as agreed. Rival groups are doing business as usual, while Nishi continues to fight even after two years. She has her child with her now. What the film tries to show is how implacably hostile the corporate world is to women and even senior executives are expendable. Bipasha Basu looks professional in power suits but that's all. The double and triple crosses are beyond credibility, because Bhandarkar's weakness for the topical quickie takes toll on the script and characterization.

Sudhir Misra, notable for some very fine political films, plunged into corporate affairs—this time literally—leading to sexual harassment charges by a female executive against the Ad Agency CEO. *Inkaar* (2013) pits the deadly charms of Maya Luthra (Chitrangada Singh) against the cool handsome hunk Rahul Verma (Arjun Rampal). Spanning seven years, a love-hate relationship spirals into Maya's charge of sexual harassment against the man who was once her mentor.

Sudhir Mishra's film does not do for sexual harassment what the Hollywood classic *The Accused* did for rape. As if he is conscious of the difficulty of what he has undertaken, the director has Mahabanoo Mody-Kotwal (the theatre personality playing a lawyer) tell Maya that it is easier to prove rape than sexual harassment. She advises her client to make an out of court settlement, and not pursue the matter in court. Right now, Maya doesn't seem to have much faith in an ongoing internal investigation at the ad agency. It is good that Mishra knows the complexity of what he has set out to do, because of the structure he has chosen. The events of *Inkaar* unfold over two days and the investigation is intercut with flashbacks of what happened seven years ago. This going back and forth over a tight time-frame in an enclosed space is a challenging device and Mishra has done similar films before—*Is Raat Ki Subah Nahin* (1996) and *Chameli* (2003). Incidentally, you can't miss the self-referential bit in *Inkaar* when the punch line of a condom ad is: *Is Raat Ki Subah Nahin*! Mishra is entitled to self-congratulation given the range and depth of his work.

The theme is ambitiously layered in *Inkaar*. Maya has now outgrown her mentor Rahul with whom she had an affair—an affair with no commitment on either side. From a raw smalltown girl whose idea of sophistication is a pierced chin, to an alpha female (to survive among the alpha males as she tells us), Maya had moved to New York and come back as the national creative director of the ad agency where Rahul is the CEO. Social worker Mrs. Kamdar (Dipti Naval) presides over the internal investigation where colleagues expectedly take sides. Maya and Rahul both put forth their versions that sound credible and a key incident is told *Rashomon* style from two different points of view. The key question that Mishra poses—and evades—is when does flirtation that was once mutually welcome become harassment? More so in the glamorous world of advertising where the sexual content of what they are packaging to sell is so palpable. When do competing ambitions come into play given the emotional baggage of an affair gone sour?

Mishra succeeds in posing these questions convincingly. He also takes you to Rahul's childhood in a small town and his father's work ethic that has embedded itself into the successful, sexy CEO who now seems to feel threatened by his own protégée. The glamour comes with the stress of deadlines, of fierce competition and appropriation of ideas, the partying and bitching ... it is all captured in essence if not detail. Visually, the film has interesting grey tones, like a black and white film whose contrasts have been bleached out. With so much going for it, it is the last fifteen minutes that are a letdown. *Inkaar*'s foggy ambivalence—some of it intended to not oversimplify a complex, explosive issue—is bogged down in a swamp of moral equivalence. *Inkaar* finally is a cop out—not because both Maya and Rahul have valid reasons for what they do and say—but because the blame shifts finally to the big bosses who want to create different power centres. A pity really—though Chitrangda Singh looks the part even if she can't act all that well, Arjun Rampal gives the best performance of his career after *Rock On* (2008). It seems the dice are loaded after all when it comes to proving sexual harassment.

If the corporate world is not conducive to women breaking the glass ceiling, science and technology recognize and reward merit. In a quiet, unobtrusive way. Departing from the norm, 2019 turned the spotlight on our unknown women scientists and engineers, working in the beehive that is Indian Space Research Organisation (ISRO). *Mission Mangal*, directed by Jagan Shakti, who collaborated with the writing team, celebrated Indian women power for their work behind the successful launch of our Mar's orbiter on the very first attempt. Shakti's sister is a scientist and that may have germinated the story in his mind. ISRO highlights male rocket and space scientists whenever there is a successful mission. Like all bureaucracy, even the scientific one, it is male dominated in public perception.

Mission Mangal is fuelled by committed women scientists and engineers. A woman makes rocket science as easy as frying puris when the gas is getting over in the cylinder. Start and stop the flame is Tara Shinde's (Vidya Balan) answer to making use of an available PSLV rocket that can't carry enough fuel to reach Mars orbit. Her solution is the puri-making analogy. You don't need the flame to be burning once the oil reaches a certain temperature. You can start and stop the precious fuel consumption in the absence of the more advanced GSLV rocket ISRO can't spare for a failed team. A minor error by Tara is responsible for a failed GSLV launch. Her boss Rakesh Dhawan (Akhsay Kumar) takes the blame and the project is taken over by the condescending Rupert Desai (Dilip Tahil), an import from NASA. Rakesh and Tara are relegated to a back room and entrusted with the Mangalyaan project with a negligible budget and a team of junior scientists. They are expected to fail.

Tara comes up with the puri-frying analogy to get this mission impossible going. You question if it is necessary to dumb down rocket science not only for a largely ignorant *aam janta* but also to demonstrate it to the sneering NASA expert. Though Akshay Kumar plays the titular hero, the whimsical Rakesh Dhawan who hums old Bollywood favourites, it is Tara Shinde who takes control with her enthusiasm, never say die optimism and nurturing qualities when it comes to building a dedicated team that can think on its feet. India's Mars mission did have a strong contingent of women engineers and space scientists, a fact acknowledged in the end credits with their photographs, titles, and names.

Like the Hollywood Oscar nominated *Hidden Figures* (2016) that also took dramatic license to underline the racism and sexism gifted Black women mathematicians faced in the days of segregation while they did significant work for NASA, *Mission Mangal* also highlights the personal problems of these anonymous women. It builds engaging backstories for Tara and her team, dominated by young women.

The film lapses into cheesiness at times but the overall impact is the dedication and problem-solving abilities of the derided team. Vidya Balan's Tara Shinde is the best thing in *Mission Mangal*. She is much more than the project manager with a can-do attitude. She tries to convince the sceptical inexperienced team that they can pull it off even with a curtailed budget and impossible deadline. The women are as different as can be. The propulsion control expert Eka Gandhi (Sonakshi Sinha) is sophisticated and modern in her attitude to relationships, aiming to join NASA. Neha Siddiqui (Kirti Kulhari) is the spacecraft autonomy designer, facing the problem of finding living space because of her Muslim background. Ironically, the staunchly religious Brahmin older colleague, the structural engineer Anath Iyengar, offers a home with his wife and him. Kruttika Aggarwal (Taapsee Pannu), the navigation expert keeps away from work to care for her husband, an army man severely wounded in action. He motivates her to go back, equating her work with his on the border. Varsha Pillai (Nithya Menen) is the satellite designer who has a running battle with her carping mother-in-law who wants a grandchild as soon as possible. Parmeshwar Naidu (Sharman Joshi) is the payload expert but he haunts priests and astrologers since he is unable to get married.

Tara is the central character. She exudes warm wholesomeness along with dedicated professionalism, a cool mom to her teenaged kids unlike her uptight husband who gets hassled when the daughter comes home late and loses his temper when the son reads the Koran and offers *namaaz*. Guitar-strumming teenaged Dilip's idol is A.R. Rahman. The necessary dose of secularism is dispensed casually without laying it on by Tara who will perform arti to Ganesh but encourages her son to delve into other religions. Worship the power, not the face is her statement. She is both a domestic goddess and a calm scientist who tries to whip up sagging spirits by hosting a birthday party: to celebrate the day when they all decided to be scientists. Balan also makes a quiet statement that a highly qualified professional woman need not wear business suits but be in the comfort zone of saris and gajras in her hair. Her attitude is modern and accepting: be it her son's insolence or the daughter's partying. Tara's openness to ideas, at home or at work, makes her a leader—inspiring, yet approachable.

Now to the other extreme end of the working woman spectrum.

The dance bar and its dancers have had a contentious existence. Dance bars are not unique to Bombay, their clones or variations do exist in Delhi and other cities. Yet the moral brigade has made Bombay dance bars their particular target at regular intervals, when they have run out of other causes. The crusading zealots see the bar dancer as the active agent of original sin, destroyer of families, and equate her gyrations to Hindi hits with prostitution. They are blind to their own hypocrisy. These same dances can be seen—by children too—on cinema screens and television. They don't corrupt public morality then. Governments and municipalities routinely try to close the bars or lay down such stringent rules in the name of regulation that they find it difficult to survive. Dance bars have been shut down, briefly revived with ridiculous restrictions and again closed indefinitely till the Supreme Court ordered them to be open in January 2019, laying down a few reasonable conditions. The basic right of women to earn their living has been restored.

Chandni Bar (2001) is Madhur Bhandarkar's first foray into his brand of realism. He has made a rather questionable reputation (stringent critical standards don't buy into his claims of being an 'experimental filmmaker') for hard-hitting realistic films. *Chandni Bar* is reasonably accomplished, marrying the bar dancer phenomenon that was very much in the news, to the cinematic legacy of the *tawaif*, by implication. While Bhandarkar piles misery upon misery on his protagonist Najma (Tabu at her brilliant best), he upturns Bombay's sleazy underbelly to our judgemental gaze. It is fascinating in a horrifying way. Najma is a victim twice over: a teenager, she is a survivor of communal riots that burnt down her village in

UP, leaving an uncle as her sole support who brings her to Bombay; the uncle turns rapist who also lives off her earnings as a bar dancer. Chandni Bar where she works is not all roses and moonlight. Initially, Najma is uncomfortable in this unfamiliar setting, waving her arms stiffly while the other women sinuously sway their hips. Over time, she finds that hers is not the sole story of pain and exploitation. Others have gone through wrenching experiences.

In a reprise of the classic whore and criminal/cop trope, Najma is the object of a petty criminal Potya Sawant's attentions. Atul Kulkarni brings to life the epitome of the tough male with a vulnerable side. He pays her to sleep with him since she is not amenable to his rough wooing. Najma is unable to go through with it and confesses how she has been raped. Potya is nothing if not volatile. In an explosion of rage, he kills the rapist uncle and marries Najma. Then ensues a brief idyll away from the world of dance bars. She does choose the small-time gangster, with full knowledge and acceptance of her own emotional and sexual needs. Najma has two kids, a boy and girl. She is determined to educate them so that they are insulated from the world of dance bars and crime. But fate decrees otherwise. Potya has now climbed up the gang hierarchy. His old failing resurfaces and he kills a rival gangster. In turn, the cops shoot him down in an 'encounter' and pass it off as part of gang wars so endemic to Bombay's underworld.

Najma returns to Chandni Bar to raise her small children… years roll by and her children are teenagers and she is now a waitress. Her studious son Abhay gets into bad company and cops place him in juvenile custody, not heeding his protestations of innocence. Older inmates rape him. He comes out of detention, hardened and cold, and becomes a criminal. History repeats itself. He too shoots a rival and this time, Najma tries to reach those proverbial men with influence to save her son. To meet their demand of money, she prostitutes herself and yet, falls short. Her 15-year-old daughter Payal becomes a dancer at the same bar. Lives caught in a vicious circle from which there is no escape. This relentless tragedy is not destined to scale the heights of Greek tragedy. It is a recurring tragedy in the bowels of the city's seamy underworld. Life is a sentence to be eked out. Bleakness is all.

Tabu won a National Award for Best Actress along with many popular awards; Atul Kulkarni for Best supporting actor and Ananya Khare who plays Deepa Pandey, another bar dancer, for best supporting actress. *Chandni Bar* becomes a case study—unwittingly perhaps—for tracing the decline of the *tawaif* displaced from the courtly *nawabi* culture of its heyday—*Pakeeza (1972), Umrao Jaan (1981), Mere Mehboob (1963),* etc.—to the dingy grime of a Bombay slum. The *tawaif* is in a way descended from the cultivated courtesan of Hindu classical culture, celebrated in drama and discourse for her mastery of the arts, literature and cultivated ways of pleasing men of discriminating taste. She is then blended with Mughal India's courtly *nawabi* culture—she embodies *tehzeeb*,[6] is adept at dance and music, poetry and conversational skills. The late Iqbal Masud, writer of distinction and film critic who insisted on connecting cinema with its historical, cultural and social roots, held that the *tawaif* is unique to India. She has no counterpart in classical Islamic culture, be it in Persia, Arabia, and Turkey. This is one of the reasons why the *tawaif* is the apotheosis of the desired but unattainable Other in her pure essence. Films that celebrate and commiserate with the *tawaif*'s pitiable plight are an apostrophe to her Otherness and the beauty of melancholy. That was the romance. We now come to the reality of the *tawaif*'s descendants.

Sameena Dalwai, professor at Jindal School of Law, has based her doctorate on bar girls. She points out to the clear class and caste line that divide the patron and the bar dancer. Dalwai writes in the *Indian Express*. 'The demand for the ban came disguised as discourses of gender rooted in nationalism, culture and the dignity of women. The state was called upon to protect the family and the good wives, the helpless youth and the Maharashtrian/Indian culture from the dangerous lure of bargirls. In the Maharashtra legislature, the need for a new law was justified as a need to discourage men from going to the bars and throwing money at "bad women". In this scheme, the upper caste/class men seemed to need the protection of the state from the lower caste/class women. The bargirls became the 'bad women' who danced before men and seduced them with obscene attire and gestures. They were accused of avoiding honest labour and earning "easy money", unlike the toiling, good poor women.'[7]

'Caste and gender hold the key to understand the politics that unites parties on the dance bars issue. The emergence as well as the ban of

---

[6] Cultured manners.
[7] 24 January 2019, *Indian Express*.

dance bars in Mumbai can be seen as symptoms of globalisation in India. Dance bars emerged as a site of opportunity for customers to flaunt the wealth they had accumulated through their association with a globalised India. For the bar dancers, a majority of who came from the traditional dancing communities of North India, it offered a new employment opportunity. The demand and supply sides of dance bars comprised two distinct classes, which fit uncomfortably into the narrative on globalisation in India. The first class is the vernacular "new rich", linked to the black economy, government contracts, political connections and religious consumerism. This class constitutes the bulk of customers of the dance bars.'[8] Shyam Benegal's rambunctious brothel comedy *Mandi* (1983) is a biting satire that exposes the political and religious underpinning of sex trade set in pre-globalized economy.

To continue with Dalwai's exposition, she describes the second class of clientele: 'The second class comprises the lowly-paid irregular workers; a class of people who are not just poor but are surviving with limited means. Bargirls hail from this class. Since the 1980s, these two classes have come together to create the dance bar market, which has upset and irritated both the ruling ideology as well as the popular script of globalisation.'

Dalwai then describes what the clients get from their patronage. 'The dance bar market offered its customers song, dance, Bollywood imagery and a pretence of royal mannerisms in the tawaif culture. It enabled customers to escape reality, feel like royalty, and fulfil the need for affirmation of their new status that the seemingly charmless capitalist economy—while providing unprecedented cash—fails to provide.'

'The dance bars used the power of musical performance in arousing feelings and deployed the established idiom of the Hindi film songs to attract customers to the bar and the bargirls. For customers, the dance bars offered a sense of fantasy, drama, adventure, addiction and competition. Though the dance bars were lucrative, they had remained almost hidden from the mainstream public for nearly two decades.

'The bar dancers from traditional dancing communities can be seen as "performing their castes": They were redeploying their caste capital—skills of dancing, entertainment, care, hospitality and the use of sexuality—to occupy the new space created by the globalising dance

---

[8] 24 January 2019, *Indian Express*.

bar market. However, as their traditional skills gained unprecedented demand and monetary value in the globalising market, the bar girls seemed to occupy a space of high economic gain and challenge the gender, caste, class borders by performing their caste occupation in the global market.[9]

If the bar girl is the current, down-market avatar of the *tawaif*, there is a counterpoint in the women who perform in cabaret clubs. The cabaret has a more upmarket, Western association even though the lives of the dancers are basically similar. Meera Nair's documentary *India Cabaret* (1985) explored the attitudes of the 'respectable' men who patronized the cabaret clubs and the pragmatic lives of the dancers. The hypocrisy of patriarchy is self-evident in the way the men speak in derogatory terms of these 'loose women' whose performance they enjoy. Nair's film interviewed at length the outspoken Rekha, a star and camera natural. Vivacious and forthright in speech, she talks of her village in Andhra Pradesh and the family she supports without a trace of self-pity. Many feminists faulted the film as being voyeuristic, using the camera to film the women's bodies in a fashion similar to the way men use to objectify women. *India Cabaret* is notable for drawing out the life stories of these women with honesty. The unexpected, earthy humour is a bonus.

---

[9] 24 January 2019, *Indian Express*.

6
Sisters under the Hood

Sisterhood is a concept taken for granted in a subliminal fashion in both life and films. Pop psychology and professional therapists emphasize how important it is for women to have close friends of their own gender for emotional health. It is almost like spouting another cliché: women are naturally endowed with EQ. We see this in families, schools, and workplace: how women seem to make friends with other women far more easily, even if it starts with gossip and shared tips on fashion and make up. When joint families were more common, girls tended to bond with cousins (cousin sister is our unique Indianism) and younger aunts: for shared fun, exchange of confidences, and sometimes guidance when a girl felt diffident or shy to go to her mother. Anyone travelling in a Mumbai local for any length of time can see and vicariously experience the camaraderie that exists between groups of women taking the same train practically every day. It almost compels eavesdropping: they talk about husbands, in-laws (specially the mother-in-law, no surprises here), water problem, unreliable maids, interfering neighbours, jealous colleagues, hard to discipline kids, even as they admire the new sari one of them is wearing, exchange recipes ... the list can be endless. We see this even in easily exchanged information at doctors' waiting rooms or a short stop for gossip while buying vegetables in the market. Given this almost genetic/gender propensity for easy bonding, it is surprising to find this emotional sisterhood missing in popular cinema. What we see instead is kitchen politics at its most scheming, be it on TV (soaps cannot function without this narrative prop) or family melodramas. Bromance is celebrated in myriad ways but sisterhood as integral to the story—unless it is a feminist tract—is hardly even acknowledged.

Generally, the heroine has a best friend and confidante among the gaggle of giggly girls that hangs around her—as part of the set decor, which would otherwise look empty? Seriously speaking, such an important part of a woman's social and emotional life gets short shrift in mainstream cinema. The *sakhi* is so integral to classical literature and our traditional theatre; it is surprising her updated avatar is so often missing from film narrative. Bromance, that formed such a big sub-textual part of the Amitabh Bachchan era, now occupies the centre and front. A tentative effort is taking the first necessary steps to redress the balance. Some significant films have made female bonding the centre—emotional, structural—of their stories.

Nagesh Kukunoor's *Dor* (2006) weaves an exquisite narrative—like an *ikkat* that entwines threads of many hues into an intricate pattern—that joins a young Muslim woman from the green hills of Himachal and a rustic Rajasthani girl in a bond as unexpected as it is uplifting. It is a small, beautifully made film where not a single frame appears extraneous and everything—theme, images, editing, cinematography, music, and acting—fall into perfect place, as if they were preordained. *Dor* has the delicacy of a single muslin thread and the tensile strength of steel, a jeweller's eye for detail and a panoramic clarity of vision. It is a sensitive story of the intertwined lives of two completely dissimilar women, so movingly told that it doesn't have to shout its feminist message. A poignant and inspiring anthem to sisterhood, the narrative uses multiple journeys as insightful metaphors.

Dor draws its basic story from the Malayalam film *Perumazhakkalam* (2004) and duly acknowledges it, though the ignorant flayed Kukunoor for plagiarism. What Kukunoor does to the original melodrama is remarkably imaginative. He is like the skilled craftsman fashioning an exquisite vase from a lump of clay. The original story was centred on the Saudi concept of justice: a person guilty of killing another person can escape the prescribed death penalty if the bereaved wife gives *maafinama*, a written pardon. It is a faceoff between two women: the widow and the wife of the man who killed her husband. To add an edge of perceived prejudice, the widow is from an orthodox Hindu family and the woman seeking pardon is Muslim. How much more fraught can a story get? In the Malayalam original, Kerala's monsoon rains—referred to in the title—are an evocative element and a plot device. Kukunoor's daring leap of imagination sets the story in the burning sands of Rajasthan, the vast sandy stretches dotted with a solitary temple, a fluttering red banner adding a touch of colour. The *havelis* and stray pavilions, the arches and bylanes of Jodhpur add an architectural detail etched against the vast, seemingly unending landscape. There is also the added contrast of Zeenat's home set in mountains covered in lush green vegetation, to highlight Rajasthan's desert splendour.

In this varied landscape, unfold parallel lives of two very different women. In the Malayalam film too, the women were from different religions but both were Malayalis and shared the larger linguistic and cultural ethos. Recognizing Bollywood's all-India reach and appeal, Kukunoor uses popular elements to touch common ground. *Dor* creates a haunting, Sufi inspired theme song, *Ye hausla* that invokes courage in Shafqat Amanat Ali's voice; it is a recurring leitmotif that heightens various moods of Zeenat's journey.

Zeenat (Gul Panag) is a fiercely independent teacher from a Himachal Pradesh village. It is implied she is an orphan and Baig Sahib, the kindly village elder is a father figure who supports her. She finally gives in to her importunate suitor Aamir on the eve of his departure to Saudi where he has found a job. His parents are not in favour of this marriage. The simple *nikah* is set against verdant mountains. The film cuts intermittently, from Zeenat's self-reliant ways to teenaged Meera (Ayesha Takia) and her stolen moments with her brand new husband Shankar. A bashful bride sheds her inhibitions to dance to Bollywood songs for her own pleasure and that of her besotted husband on Rajasthan's golden sands. Shankar too leaves for Saudi so that he can send money to reclaim their ancestral *haveli* from mortgage. For the father, the proud patriarch Randhir Singh (Girish Karnad) getting the *haveli* back is equal to restoring family honour.

Aamir and Shankar are roommates in Saudi. Shankar is accidentally killed and there are no witnesses but Aamir is the accused. An official from the Indian external ministry informs Zeenat that Aamir's only hope is to get pardon from Shankar's wife, her signature on the *maafinama*. Otherwise, he must face the death sentence. All Zeenat has is a photograph of Aamir with Shankar. Aamir's parents have now embraced Zeenat. She has been giving them the money Aamir sends. Zeenat's faith in Aamir is firm: she loves and knows him; he could never kill anybody.

Zeenat sets out for Rajasthan, on the slender basis of a photograph and no proper address. Her journey from the hills to the desert is an adventure fraught with dangers, known and unknown. Zeenat travels on, undeterred by men accosting her because they know she is an outsider. Like a minor naughty but helpful deity in a mythological play, or a comic relief in puppet theatre, appears the chameleon-like Bahroopiya—the traditional performer who changes costumes and can act any part. This con man is an artist. Shreyas Talpade relishes the opportunity to display various modes of speech, disguises, and take offs on Bollywood heroes. After stealing her bag, the Bahroopiya without a name befriends Zeenat, returns her stuff and helps locate Meera.

Meera is shattered. Covered in the widow's garb of dark blue, her bangles broken, bindi erased, and all colour leached out of her clothes and life as per prescribed rites, Meera sits in a dark room. Only a shaft of light falls across, to shows her ravaged face. Zeenat locates the village on Jodhpur's outskirts with Bahroopiya's help, thanks to his instant changes of persona—from police inspector to income-tax officer to street astrologer and many amusing disguises.

Zeenat decides to meet the family upfront. She is first welcomed as the wife of Shankar's friend, also in response to her courteous behaviour. But when she informs who she is and what she wants from Meera, they are so enraged that Shankar's mother spits on Zeenat's face. Meera is sweeping the stairs at the back of the house. Randhir Singh orders that no one will speak of this to Meera. Zeenat is still determined to somehow meet Meera and appeal directly to her. Meera is a virtual prisoner and domestic slave. She is allowed to leave the fortress-like home only to visit the temple. Zeenat waylays Meera and befriends her. Zeenat is moved by Meera's seclusion and hesitates to talk of the *maafinama*. Her empathy for Meera makes her reluctant to tell the innocent teenager the truth. Something intangible connects the two—Meera, all wrapped in blue, unadorned and vulnerable; Zeenat in her serviceable salwar suits, her eyes not lined with kohl as is her normal practice, and a tentative smile held out as a promise. The close ups emphasize the unmade up faces; two women stripped of superficial veneers for a close encounter.

This burgeoning friendship between a lonely Meera and far more self-assured and older Zeenat is fraught with guilt. Zeenat knows she is encouraging Meera to meet her for self-serving purpose. But friendship between strangers can bloom even in the desert, given Zeenat's genuine concern for the young girl trapped in orthodoxy and Meera's gratitude that her gloomy life is lit by a ray of real conversation with someone, the promise of simple fun at least for a short while. It gradually deepens to unalloyed attachment and concern for each other. Sometimes, Bahroopiya joins them. The three of them spontaneously dance to *Kajra Re* with abandon on undulating sand dunes and dissolve into laughter. Zeenat is often distressed by her mixed emotions and hesitates to tell Meera who she is and what she wants. She doesn't want to lose the friendship that takes root so naturally like a plant that has found water at last in the desert.

Finally, when Zeenat learns that Aamir's execution might be imminent, she musters up courage to tell Meera the truth. Expectedly, Meera is angry. Zeenat leaves the decision to the young girl. Meera angrily asks herself: God decides who lives and who dies. Why should I be burdened with this decision? She is torn between affection for Zeenat and hurt that her trust was betrayed. She is a simple girl, with a zest for life that is crushed out by the in-laws' unfeeling attitude. They had initially blamed her for bringing bad luck to the family. Brought up traditionally, obedience to elders is ingrained. Yet, she yearns for affection and someone who shares her feelings. Even something so routine like listening to her favourite songs is denied. Another trial of her fortitude awaits Meera.

Her father-in-law is offered a way out of his debt. Chopra (Kukunoor in a cameo) is a local factory owner who holds the *haveli*'s mortgage. He is willing to waive the debt if Meera can 'serve' him and meet his needs. The patriarch is at first aghast at this discreet demand couched in polite words but decides getting the *haveli* back is worth more than Meera's honour. No one dares murmur a word of protest. This finally triggers Meera's resolve to leave.

There is a beautiful, silent scene between Meera and the embittered old grandmother. She would routinely chastise the young bride whenever she neglected chores to be with her husband. It seems as if she resented Meera's effervescence and joie de vivre. Now, the same sour-faced Dadi hides the keys to the main door and wordlessly gives it to Meera in the dark of the night. Meera creeps out, the heavy gate creaks open and lets her escape to freedom.

Zeenat is on the way back home, mission unaccomplished. She leaves a goodbye letter and a talisman for Meera. As she reads the letter that is contrite, caring, and stoic in accepting whatever is in store for Aamir, Meera is moved to tears. She signs the pardon paper left in the temple—their meeting place—and desperately runs to the station where Zeenat is waiting for the train. The climax makes words superfluous. Their faces so nakedly expressing their emotions speak with unmatched eloquence. Zeenat is already in the train and finally when Meera sees her and hands over the paper—there are smiles on both faces; of gratitude and understanding. As the train starts to move, Zeenat comes to the door and stretches out her hand. For a few moments, a startled Meera stands still. Then decision made, she runs alongside until the two outstretched hands clasp each other. Meera is pulled inside and they are locked in the embrace of sisterhood. It is one instance where the over used symbolism of boarding a running train gains fresh meaning and you feel like cheering the two women now bound together with the silken threads of friendship. *Dor* means thread. A seemingly tenuous but tensile thread of hope, redemption and liberty.

Dor courts and breaks stereotypes. Kukunoor makes the point simply, without clamouring for attention. He reverses our prejudiced perceptions and ingrained stereotyping. Zeenat is the supposedly 'oppressed' Muslim woman but she is blessed with an inborn independence of mind and spirit that nothing can cow down. Meera has to realize that it is far more difficult to take control of her life and not let the patriarchal system crush all joy and colour out of her young life. This kind of realization and subsequent transformation comes with a heavy dose of didacticism in our films that spout a cause. *Dor* makes the whole process organic and seamless. Kukunoor invites us to share the joy and agony, tenderness and simple fun that punctuate the film. There are moments of joy that indulging in normal everyday things brings. So assured is Kukunoor of the depth of his characters and the persuasive power of his authentic milieu that he can salute and celebrate the sheer enjoyment Bollywood brings to the remote corners of India. The performances are delicately nuanced, complementing each other's pitch with a musician's finesse. Ayesha Takia lives her role, taking us into all that Meera feels—her bubbling joy when we first see her dancing to *You are my Sonia* with such abandon, and her gut-wrenching grief as she clutches Shankar's belongings, the quiet fortitude and tentative happiness as she makes a new friend. Gul Panang conveys with fine restraint Zeenat's self-reliance and self-contained dignity. Her gnawing conscience breaks through on occasions, furrowing a face that is expressively mobile. Shreyas Talpade steals every scene he is in and brings hope and infectious enjoyment that are so essential to the narrative that could otherwise be grim. *Dor* ranks among the finest films of Hindi cinema.

Sometimes word of mouth publicity can backfire. *Parched* (2015) was preceded by expectations of explicit sexual content—curious are the ways the unseen publicity machine works. There were leaked images on YouTube before the film came to theatres after being feted on the festival circuit. In the small theatre where I saw the film, gangly teenagers present were there just because of their prurient interest. Hopefully they took away some lessons of how not to be brutal, mean men. Leena Yadav tells a gutsy, earthy story of three women linked by deep friendship as they battle abuse in a Rajasthan village where patriarchal practices of child brides, dowry, and routine subjugation of women are unquestioned. She spices the grim tale with raunchy humour (with a female subversion of the *Ma Behen gaalis*[1]) and the unexpected discovery of what a vibrating mobile can do to pleasure a sexually frustrated woman.

Rani (Tannishtha Chatterjee) is a widow with a surly, horny teenaged son Gulab (Riddhi Sen) and a bedridden old mother-in-law to care for. She mortgages her house to pay the bride price for an educated 15-year-old bride Janki (Lehar Khan) from a neighbouring village. Janki has a high school sweetheart, a gentle and educated young man. Desperate to avoid being married off, Janki cuts her long hair. Despite that, Rani accepts her and takes home the child bride. What Yadav doesn't make an effort to explain is why Gulab is so vicious and has imbibed the worst traits of patriarchy. Patriarchal society shows at least token respect for a mother, more so if she has a son. Raised without a father by a hardworking mother who does all she can to make him happy, Gulab turns out to be a loutish bully hanging out with equally loutish friends who routinely visit prostitutes. His idea of sex and relationship with women is warped. His treatment of the young bride is tantamount to rape, after beating her up.

Rani's best friend Lajjo (Radhika Apte) is branded barren by her chronically drunken, abusive husband. The third in this trio is Bijli (Surveen Chawla) who is part of a touring troupe of entertainers. Bijli is the dancer with swag whose performances—including pole dance's desi version—has the men drooling. She also entertains paying customers afterwards but is choosy about the men she will entertain sexually. This annoys the

---

[1] Abuse with sexual innuendo directed at mothers and sisters to insult a man.

owner of the troupe and he brings in a younger dancer. The potential rival's appeal is coarse whereas Bijli's charm is joyously erotic. The village men who throng the fair-like revelry generated by the troupe's visit are thwarted by Bijli's choosy ways. They equate her with a prostitute who has no right to refuse any client. Bijli's reign is under threat by the younger rival Rekha who is more compliant.

Bijli's days are spent with her friends Rani and Lajjo. She is not only more worldly wise but knowledgeable too, about a man being infertile. Bijli introduces Lajjo, whose burning desire is to be a mother, to the fantasy figure of a cave-dwelling sadhu whose lovemaking is tender, sensuous, and homage to womanhood. Lajjo is pregnant to her utter joy.

Gulab's generalized anger is not satisfied with beating up his wife. It finds a special target. His ire is directed at Kishan, the educated young man who runs an NGO. Kishan's wife is not local. She is an educated outsider and their marriage is one of equals—something that annoys the village men. Kishan is truly helpful—not a fantasy figure like the cave-dwelling sexpert sadhu—and his NGO provides an income to women skilled in traditional embroidery. The narrative presents the full range of ethnic crafts kept alive by women. Shot by Oscar winning cameraman Russell Carpenter (*Titanic*), the colours and moods of ethnic aesthetics of the location add a sheen that stops short of exotica as a selling point. It is not easy to find a location in Rajasthan that is not colourful. The village women are paid for what they love to do, the first step to economic independence. It is this very independence that threatens men, weaned on patriarchal values that get entrenched over time.

When the Panchayat meets to consider problems that the village faces, the first case is that of Champa, a girl who has run away from her husband and returned to her parents. The elders decree that she must return to her marital home even when Champa reveals that all the men in the family rape her. Kishan and his wife try to intervene in protest but they are ridiculed for their modern ideas that are anathema to the way the village lives—and has lived for centuries. Kishan's polite but firm attempt to speak up for Champa provokes general hostility of the men and confuses some of the women. A man speaking on their behalf is something they have never known.

This incident further reinforces Gulab's almost visceral dislike of Kishan. Gulab's spurts of violence are inexplicable. Is he a psychotic young man who takes out his frustration at his inadequacies through increasing levels of violence? He and his goon friends attack Kishan's shop and beat him up until he is almost dead. Shaken to the core, Kishan and his wife leave the village. A source of income and pride in their expertise are snatched away from these women.

Gulab steals all the money Rani has. When Rani confronts him, he tells her he is leaving the village, his mother and wife can fend for themselves. The director leaves it to our reading, to surmise from the narrative's lack of any explanation for why Gulab behaves the way a crucial character like him does. Is it just a generic portrayal of male anger and machismo that a boy learns from those around him?

Multiple events lead to a concerted resolution. Rekha displaces Bijli as the dancer. Angry and needing money, Bijli starts sleeping with many men and permits rough sex. This leads to her being raped and Bijli can't take this humiliation. Meanwhile, when Lajjo informs her husband Manoj of her pregnancy, she is mercilessly beaten up by her husband who knows his inadequacy. While venting his anger and humiliation, Manoj accidentally falls into the kitchen fire and burns to death. Lajjo's mourning is perfunctory.

Rani is at last forced to be decisive after Gulab abandons her. She sells her house to pay off the mortgage. She now turns a caring woman, not a mother-in-law. She sets Janki free from this meaningless marriage, urging her to unite with her sweetheart and most importantly, to resume her education. Bijli comes to take her two friends and they drive off in a carriage—symbolically a victorious chariot—into the metaphorical sunset. Their joy is contagious even though lingering questions remain. What kind of freedom do these lifelong friends envisage? In terms of imagery, the ending is perfect. We remain content for the moment. Together, the resilient women can perhaps find a new life of dignity. Lajjo's child will be born in a new dawn.

The serious flaw in Yadav's storytelling is the lack of any grey in her characterization. All the men in the village, with the exception of the sadhu and Kishan, are stereotypes of various degrees of brutality. The worst offender is Gulab the son who is so coarse, selfish, and ruthless it is unbelievable. Yadav evades the question of motivation: why is this young man is so resentful, violent, and vicious? It is a convenient ploy for Rani to bond with the young daughter-in-law and set her free. Feminism doesn't mean you make men into caricatures of cruelty in order to expose the rigid patriarchy that denies women their needs, wants, worth, and dignity to live as individuals. Feminist discourse has moved beyond these stereotypes decades ago. Yadav is often guilty of giving an exotic gloss to everyday things. It smacks of catering to a foreign gaze that can't accept India—even poverty and women's oppression—minus exoticism. The fantasy figure of sadhu-in-a-cave is the prime example. It makes us wonder even if naive foreigners can swallow a sanitized version of sexual mumbo jumbo.

From rural India, the sisterhood narrative moves to a city that is both modern and deeply traditional: the spick and span lakefront Bhopal can flaunt its museums and Arts Centre that will do any Indian city proud while the inner old city clings to orthodoxy. Bhopal is perhaps the most appropriate city that mirrors the flux Indian society is caught in. Alankrita Srivatsava has found the perfect locale to set her incendiary *Lipstick under My Burkha* (2016) that has made an impact at home and abroad. The poster has a lot going for it with its clever graphics: a woman showing her middle finger is a morphed lipstick. And the Burkha of the title stands for the cloak of hypocrisy that patriarchy wraps over women, denying them desire, autonomy, dignity. A visible symbol making women invisible, something that applies to women at large and not just Muslims. The action is set in Hawai Manzil, a sprawling, decaying building in the old city where many families—Hindu and Muslim—live amicably. It is a crumbling structure, more like a tenement house—airless and cramped rooms that belie the meaning of Hawai Manzil, a breezy, storied mansion. Buaji (Ratna Pathak Shah) co-owner along with her nephews dismisses brokers and municipal officers who want to tear it down and build a mall. It survived the gas tragedy[2], she tells him.

Srivastava tells the stories of four women who live there, each battling a personal problem as best as she can. 55-year-old widow Usha universally called Buaji has been depersonalized to such an extent that she has even forgotten her name. She is secretly addicted to erotic fiction. Her voiceover narrates Rosie's fantasies from *Lipstick Dreams*, as a recurring motif to underline whatever is happening in her monotonous life; or a

---

[2] The Union Carbide explosion in Bhopal in 1984 that killed over 3000 people and 16,000 plus survivors battling incurable illnesses.

bridge to the happenings in other women's lives. It is an ingenious device that connects the intimate emotional lives of very different women who live in the same building and yet, are more than neighbours and less than friends. As Usha reads sizzling parts of the book, she fantasises about Jaspal, the hunky swim coach where he saves her from near drowning. She takes her nephew's kids for their swim lesson and has this near drowning episode because one of the kids plays a prank. We see Usha's gaze riveted on Jaspal's rippling muscles. She just can't look away and lines from her favourite book, of Rosy gazing at the tenant across bathing with the window open, describe her yearning. Unfocused fantasies now find a focus. Jaspal tells her to sign up for swim lessons. Usha's mishap-ridden adventure, of trying to buy a swimsuit by pretending it is for her niece, is both sweet and funny. The director takes care that we don't laugh at Usha.

Shirin Aslam (Konkona Sen Sharma) her neighbour who happens to be at the mall, guesses it's for Usha and helps her buy a suitable swim suit in a matter of fact way. When Usha broaches the pending rent, and offers to waive it, Shirin quick to catch the unsaid, assures her she will not tell anyone. Thus begin Usha's swim lessons that further fuel her fantasies and leads her to assume the young man is interested in her. She starts having erotic conversations with him under the assumed name Rosie. Her initial hesitancy when she calls and hangs up tells us how she longs for erotic contact, considered unthinkable for a post-menopausal woman by our censorious society.

Shirin is a married woman with three kids and always scared of another pregnancy now that her Saudi-based husband Rahim (Sushant Singh) is home. He is the worst kind of male chauvinist; refuses to use a condom, a bully in bed who thinks foreplay is wasted on a wife, brusque with children, and thinks his word is law. Shirin secretly works as door-to-door saleswoman for a consumer products company. Her hesitant manner gives way to quiet confidence when she thinks of inventive ways to barge into a home and pitch her product. She is so good that her company wants to promote her to trainer. That would involve telling her jobless husband about her job but she is afraid of his anger. Shirin's doctor tells her plainly that the condom is the only way to ward off pregnancy. Three secret abortions and three deliveries, the rough sex all make any other contraceptive method unsuitable. She gets a prescription for condoms and passes it on to the salesman: he asks, *Topi chahiye? Kaunsa brand?*[3] Her sons with her don't know *topi* is slangy code for condom and clamour for one. Srivastava's humour is germane to the situation. There is no forced humour. Sharp observation and superb ensemble performances bring out the nuances of satire, changing moods, and tensions of all the women we identify with—their problems are so common and yet, each one is individualized.

The feisty Leela (Aahana Kumra) is a beautician with far out dreams. She has no hang ups about sex and has an on-going affair with Arshad (Vikrant Massey) the local photographer. She pitches the idea of a package deal for couples: she will be the makeup expert who will make every bride look like Katrina Kaif while Arshad will put together a special album of the couple from wedding to honeymoon. They have a portfolio to show would-be investors—Leela and Arshad in various costumes, cosying up against posters of tourist spots across the world—but there are no takers for Leela's deal. Her dream of travelling all over the world remains a dream, leading to quarrels with Arshad. Her widowed mother has forcibly got her engaged to Manoj, an eligible, if boring, young man. During the engagement ceremony, there is a power outage and Leela has a quickie session with Arshad—photographer for the occasion—and records it on her phone camera. Caught in the act by her outraged mother, Leela is dragged back to stand beside the fiancé and paste a plastic smile on her glum face.

The dancing during the engagement shows off Rehana's (Plabita Borthakur) sensuous moves even in her loose salwar suit, head decorously covered. Her mother, embarrassed and angry, drags her home. Shut up in her room with a poster of her idol Miley Cyrus on the wall, Rehana continues dancing to the music in her head. 18-year-old Rehana Abidi may be from an orthodox Muslim family, stitching burkhas by the dozen for their family-run shop. But when she sets out for college in her Burkha, she signals her rebellion. She wears jeans and a Tee underneath, strolls into a swanky mall, and picks up a lipstick to slip it under her Burkha and walks away, her shoplifting undetected. Rehana stuffs the Burkha into her backpack, lets her hair loose, and puts on red lipstick before she saunters into college. Rehanna reminds you of *Gully Boy*'s Safeena, who takes off

---

[3] You want a cap? Which brand?

the head scarf once she is in college. Rebellion is a matter of what you wear. It is not just a superficial assertion of fitting in with college peers. Jeans are the uniform of the young, be it Bhopal or Bombay.

Rehana is an aspiring singer (her American-English pronunciation is good, yet another surprise from a girl full of surprises), she wants to audition for the college band but the cool crowd that runs the show cuts her short. Rehana gets noticed when she joins the protest against the proposed ban on jeans. She speaks passionately to the reporter about these restrictions on personal freedom. Her punch line, *Hamari azaadi se aap itna darte kyun hai*? (Why does our freedom frighten you so much?) It sums up what the film says again and again, and in many voices. It gets Rehana noticed and gets her entry into the cool crowd where Dhruv Bose is the unofficial boss. To attend his party, Rehana has to resort to shoplifting again (for a bronze dress and boots). Once more, the Burkha comes to her aid. Unbeknownst to her, the act has been caught on CCTV camera. Namrata, her rival for Dhruv's attention, is pregnant and uses the incriminating footage to expose Rehana in public. The Diwali celebration, a big carnival actually, at Hawai Manzil's compound is where things come to a head.

Rehana's question is perhaps what disturbed the Censor Board. The hilarious and illiterate objections need to be preserved for their crass stupidity. 'The story is lady oriented, their fantasy above life. There are contanious (sic) sexual scenes, abusive words, audio pornography and a bit sensitive touch about one particular section of society, hence film refused under guidelines (sic),' reads the letter issued by CBFC (Central Board of Film Certification). Rehana's question—like Buaji's right to her erotic fantasies—is addressed to society at large. Expression of female desire and assertion of freedom strike at the pillars of patriarchy.

Public protest and the lead role taken by sensible filmmakers left the Censor Board no option but to let the film be seen in India. It had won plaudits on the festival circuit: *Lipstick under My Burkha* won the Oxfam Award for the Best Film on Gender Equality at the Mumbai Film Festival and the Spirit of Asia prize at the Tokyo International Film Festival. The general Indian public found nothing objectionable; even the portrayal of Rehana's orthodox parents was not criticism of specifically Muslim society. Buaji's extended family is even more vicious, when they throw her out after they find erotic books and a swimming costume (a decorous one, like a frock) in her room. She has been the family elder looking after the mithai shop.

Shirin on her sales rounds comes upon her husband all cosy and attentive with a young woman who doesn't wear a burkha. She follows the other woman home and confronts her when she is entertaining guests. This helps her decide she must take up the job but she avoids confronting Rahim. Shirin's colleague spills the truth at the Diwali celebration. Rahim, all cold fury, tells her: you are a wife, be like one. He orders her to give up her job.

Leela vacillates between the two men in her life. Marriage to Manoj means a conventional, unadventurous life in Bhopal with a mother-in-law in tow. Her attempt to initiate sex with Manoj is met with a hesitant suggestion that they wait for the wedding night. When she goes to Arshad's place and drags him to bathroom for a quickie, he pushes her away. All you want from me is sex is his accusation. He sounds as if he wants emotional commitment from her. Meanwhile, Manoj has found the sex video with Arshad on her phone. Leela has made plans to leave Bhopal for Delhi. Will it materialize? Yet another question in the volley of questions let loose. Rehana's shoplifting and her alternate life in college are now known to her parents. The father's reaction is a mixture of hurt and anger: hurt that she has rejected her culture and anger that she has misused the freedom of being allowed to go to college. As for Usha, her dream of revealing Rosie's identity to Jaspal ends in pathetic, public humiliation. The family's reaction is extreme. It is rather hard to accept that they are bent on throwing her out, Usha being part owner of the property. Ratna Pathak Shah gives such a perfect performance that she makes you feel Usha's yearning, the hope of something exciting happening, that life is not over for a woman over fifty. She can't be condemned to attend *satsangs*[4] for the rest of her life. Shah validates female desire whatever age she is.

The four women sit in the dark, passing a cigarette in mute commiseration. The cigarette is a worn out cliché but we share the pain, anger, and frustration they feel. There are no easy answers to their problems … Sisterhood doesn't always find answers or even look for them. Sometimes, it is enough to just sit in companionable silence and feel

---

[4] Gathering of the devout to listen to a sermon.

each other's pain. Even as we watch them wrapped in ambiguity, hope curls up like a whiff from the shared cigarette smoke. Perhaps Rehana will find new ways to rebel. She is too spunky to accept being cloistered at home. Leela's energy—her sexual appetite and business plans attest to its resilience—will hit the target someday. We fervently hope that Shirin finds the strength to walk away from the tyrannical Rahim. It is Usha and her broken dream that haunt us with its sadness.

Certain stories are so derivative in their theme and narration that they need special pleading for critical scrutiny. The trope of friends meeting for an important occasion—a wedding, a class reunion, or any other celebration—is a Hollywood staple. The reunion is layered with old resentments confronted, suppressed secrets spilling out for a sort of catharsis, new understanding that heals old hurts ... variations are many and the location of the reunion is as much a character as the people present. Mira Nair's *Monsoon Wedding* (2001) is a pioneer of this genre in India. Of not only the celebration of the big fat Punjabi wedding that has become a part of Indian cinema's narrative tradition but also an occasion to question apparently happy families and the simmering grievances pushed under the *shor sharaba*—delightfully shortened to *sho sha*—of noisy jollity. *Monsoon Wedding* also brought in an outsider's gaze to examine all that goes into the event, with objectivity and also undeniable affection of a homecoming insider—but without the enveloping rosy tint of nostalgia. Nair has made the first crossover film without exoticizing India and made an upper-class Delhi wedding intimate and yet probing, revealing the worm at the core of the happy-families facade. This blend of comic tone with expose of dirty secrets—a child molester uncle—has set the template for a new genre. Bollywood has dispensed with the serious intent and taken up the big fat Indian wedding gleefully to its grateful heart. *Monsoon Wedding* is an international film—in style and ironic tone—set in India with Indian actors.

Pal Nalin who made his mark with documentaries draws from *Monsoon Wedding*'s comic zest and the Hollywood trope of a bunch of friends reuniting after years to come up with India's first female buddy film—the tagline to advertise *Angry Indian Goddesses* (2015). The film premiered at Toronto to good audience and critical response. You can trust our Censor Board—especially when the notoriously film-illiterate Pahlaj Nihalani presided over it—to ask for 16 additional cuts after giving the film an adult certificate. So much of crucial dialogue, specially of Nargis Nasreen (Tannishtha Chatterjee) who plays a political activist fighting for Adivasi rights, has been incised to mutilate the ideological argument in a film full of arguments that goes hand in hand with high-spirited fun.

Six years in gestation according to the makers, *Angry Indian Goddesses* is remarkable for the way it introduces seven different women, involves us in their dynamics and keeps us engaged with *all* of them. *All* is the crucial word though the central character is Frieda. The way Pal Nalin creates a montage of the women is guaranteed to ignite interest. We have Frieda Da Silva (Sarah-Jane Dias) walking off from an ad shoot for a fairness cream as the client thinks it's his mansplaining right to talk down to an ace fashion photographer. 'Jo' Joanne (Amrit Manghera) an aspiring Indo-British actress is told she is not cast for acting but to show off more sex appeal in her ethnic costume on the sets of a B-grader. She storms off. Pammy (Pavleen Gujral) a Delhi trophy wife drops a bar bell on a loudmouth's foot as she reacts to his vulgar comments on her figure at the gym. 'Mad' Madhurita (Anushka Manchanda, the singer) is a rocker who gets off the stage to tackle a heckler who wants her to sing a Bollywood raunchy hit. 'Su' Suranjana (Sandhya Mridul) a tough businesswoman fires her staff for asking her to rethink her stand on a land dispute and cools off in the pool. Laxmi (Rajshree Deshpande) the house help at Frieda's Goa house has to deal with constant harassment from a bike-rider ... all the women have reasons to be angry. All anger is left behind as they head to Goa for a holiday at Frieda's family home. She has invited them for a celebration ... It is to celebrate Frieda's forthcoming wedding but to whom is the secret to be revealed much later.

When Goa beckons, can anyone stay away? Su, a workaholic single mother brings her 6-year-old daughter Maya along. Pammy brings her designer saris—to be ribbed about appropriate beach-wear—along with her grouse at having to be the perfect bahu of a rich family all the time. Jo is torn between her desire to be a Bollywood star and coping with jibes about her fake Indo-Brit accent. Mad is depressed and will vent her anger at how her last album was a dud but cheers up to sing for her friends who love her and her music. Laxmi will serve them meals with a smile and is drawn into their fun. She will also grab her harasser by his testicles and squeeze them. She is actually Frieda's friend and support system. Laxmi is also fighting a case against her brother's killers.

Pal Nalin says he found characters with voices during his years of living with the story. Sandhya Mridul claimed in publicity interviews that 'collectively we are playing every woman.' Perhaps a tall claim considered that all, except Laxmi, are privileged women. In essence, the problems they face are common to women across class: like Suranjana feeling guilty of not giving enough time to her young daughter Maya; Pammy, a topper in college, has to sacrifice her entrepreneurial ambition even though she is married to a businessman; Jo having to put up with her sex object image; Frieda finally giving up her glamorous job to pursue photography as art. The friends do the usual girly things: indulge in facials, gorge on chocolates and cupcakes, do Bollywood *thumkas* with gusto. Teasing and laughing over truth or dare games veers off into confessional mode of desires, disappointments, sex, and lust ... The actors improvised much of the dialogue for it to flow with the spontaneous digressions of real conversation. Sandhya Mridul the most articulate of them says: 'it was like a retreat and therapy for us'.

They can uninhibitedly give the female gaze its play, drooling at the hunky neighbour washing his car bare-chested. They have a good laugh over it. There is desultory talk about Shiva and Parvati, of how Kali is the only Angry Indian Goddess. After establishing the relevance of the film's title, the director has freeze shots of them posing like Kali—tongue out, fierce demeanour, and Bharatanatyam mudras to denote her wrath. Though the connection is rather obvious, the actual scene flows along like a lively group dance, each improvising a step. What is remarkable is that the reference to Kali is not in the usual religious terms of Indian cinema. It is done in a casual way—rather self-consciously at times—with enough information for a foreign audience but indicating to Indians that these cosmopolitan girls know about Kali without attaching too much religious significance to it.

Finally, the secret of Frieda's betrothed is revealed when Nargis Nasreen enters late into the narrative after Frieda shows her friends the heirloom-wedding gown. Frieda is marrying Nargis at a time when gay relationships were criminal according to India's regressive laws unchanged from British times. Her friends have apparently no issue with it though you can see their awkwardness with its actual implications. Nargis doesn't fit in easily. Su of course has an issue when she meets her opponent in the land acquisition issue. The capitalism versus rights of the displaced argument is heated but not ugly. Hostilities cease after some wine and good food. They can all see the love between the two women. Frieda actually requests Su to wear her black suit and give her away at the church ceremony. It is time for drama to intervene to give the film its serious turn and bring the feminist issue to the fore. The intent is admirable but the execution looks like a deliberate imposition to showcase the film's feminist credentials when it has already been established by the women most naturally by being who they are: bright and independent at the core.

We see it when they are accosted by bunch of obnoxiously sexist bikers while the friends are driving around. The girls retaliate. They continue to harass the girls at a bar but they don't take these men seriously. They are out celebrating the night before the wedding and it is here that the film hits a jerky bump in the narrative. Jo is angry after an argument about her accent and walks off to the beach. The others continue partying. When Jo doesn't return, they go looking for her. They find her dead body, obviously raped before being killed. The cops start their investigation and the shaken girls go back home. Maya, Su's rather lonely daughter given to taking photographs, had followed Jo and taken pictures. They see the rapists are the habitual harassers who have been following them. Su goes back to the spot with a gun and shoots three men before Nargis stops her. Mad snatches the gun and shoots the other two.

The grieving friends are in shock. To add to their distress, the local policeman (Adil Hussain) speaks insultingly to them, disparaging their clothes and 'immoral' behaviour. The classic blame the victim syndrome spouted by a man who is supposed to uphold the law. The implied criticism is racist. It is allright for foreign tourists (mainly 'loose' White women) to go around in skimpy clothes but that is ruled out for good Indian girls—*sanskari*[5] in short. It is the new word of approbation used by the Hindutva brigade that espouses cultural nationalism.

This unspoken Hindu criticism is rebutted by the spontaneous response of the congregation where a funeral service is being held for Jo. The sneering cop walks into the church and asks the guilty person to stand up. One by one, the friends stand up. Then follows the cliché?

---

[5] Virtuous and wellbred.

Expected closure? The entire congregation slowly rises to its feet. A community taking collective responsibility for the crime committed in their midst. Without splitting theological hairs, *Angry Indian Goddesses* can be read as a simplistic face off that contrasts appropriation of Hinduism by Hindu fundamentalists who reject pluralism, and Christian charity that submits to the concept of collective guilt and expiation. This leads to the feel-good statement that is imposed on a film that falters towards the end, after being so intelligent, witty, warm, and engaging for such a large part of the narrative.

The same thing can't be said about *Veere di Wedding* (2018), a sorry reprisal of *Sex and the City* that diehard fans of the popular American series will not forgive. Derivatives from a genre can lead to good storytelling with believable characters you can identify with if you don't slavishly stick to a formula. Pal Nalin could do it in *Angry Indian Goddesses*. Director Shashanka Ghosh can't decide whether he wants to make a comedy, satire, or drama high on female hormones all under the umbrella of a female buddy film. He crams every current cliché into an unwieldy narrative that suffers from a start and stop malfunction. The four young women who have been friends since school days now live on different continents and have different lifestyles. Each has a different problem.

Kalindi (Kareena Kapoor) develops a rash that comes on with stress. The stress is caused by her live-in boyfriend Rishabh (Sumeet Vyas) wanting to get married. Kalindi is scarred by her parents' unhappy marriage and her adored mother's death. She is happy living with her understanding, compatible boyfriend in Australia where no one is bothered whether they are married or not. She gives in because his parents in Delhi want their son to be married—which means an over-the-top Punjabi wedding they really can't afford. Two of her buddies live in Delhi anyway. Avni (Sonam Kapoor Ahuja) wants to get married—rather desperately after a high school crush marries someone else—even though she is a divorce lawyer. A classic case of hope triumphing over second hand experience. Sakshi Soni (Swara Bhaskar) is a rich girl who flaunts attitude as she does her designer bag. She has come home to her parents who don't ask her anything, after she leaves her husband in London. Sakshi is the object of speculative gossip for the bunch of nosy aunties who she seeks to rile and shock at every chance she gets. Sakshi gets the best lines and the best scenes in the predictable film. The girl we can relate to is Meera

(Shikha Talsania) because she behaves most normally despite doing the most 'abnormal' thing for a well brought up conservative Sikh girl: she has gone and married an American against her family's wishes and lives in New York, coping with a baby plus disgruntled husband who feels neglected.

The scene is set for fireworks and girly re-bonding but most of the time is taken up with Kalindi's obsession with her ancestral house—a lovely bungalow set in a charming garden. She is close to an uncle who is gay and lives with his partner. One progressive element, ticked off. Estranged from a philandering father and his new wife; ticked off for the emotional trauma angle. For satire, there is the overbearing mom-in-law-to-be with the most showily vulgar taste for fastidious Kalindi's pretty nose to scrunch up in distaste. The poor fiancé caught between a mother's emotional blackmail and his bride-to-be's look of long-suffering patience that can snap any minute. All other troubles are those of satellites orbiting princess Kalindi's sun.

Sakshi gets the scene to pull off the shocker that is the film's talking point. We see her masturbating (under the sheet) when her husband walks in unexpectedly. She holds up her hand like a cop at a traffic signal to stop him for interrupting her orgasm that is just coming. Swara Bhaskar was reviled by social media trolls and outraged puritans. That is the truly funny moment in the film. For genteel satire, there is a desperate Avni meeting potential mates on awkward dates. After a night of revelry, she ends up with a stranger in bed. Not a total stranger but a guest at the pre-wedding parties who tries to hit on her. After the expected breaking off of the wedding, followed by a therapeutic holiday in Thailand, Kalindi is talked into getting married by her buddies. So it all ends well, including Kalindi inheriting her childhood home, her uncle and father reconciled, and she gets her tasteful low key wedding in her mother's lehenga. The in-laws have to submit to her superior taste because the father-in-law is arrested for bank fraud. It is a monotonous, cheerless narrative with no surprises coming from characters that are one-line sketches.

The criticism is flippant because there is nothing in the shallow, bland writing that merits a serious look. It's meant for would-be fashionistas to drool over Sonam Kapoor's clothes and accessories. After all, she wears the fashionista crown. The writing does not dare go down the casual, experimental sex path set by the long-running series. Instead, what we get is Meera confessing that she and her husband haven't had sex for a year. The forced abstinence could lead to a divorce but John Stinson (Edward Sonnenblick) is the sensible and caring sort who follows his wife to Delhi and sets the stage for reconciliation with her Bade Papa. Even with the divas taking centre stage most of the screen time, we like the unfashionable Meera and John best. They ring true. The rest are unfortunately as fake as designer rip-offs.

We have to look back to parallel cinema for a truly inspirational film where women bond to save one of their own from a lustful tyrant. That classic is Ketan Mehta's *Mirch Masala* (1987), which is part operatic, part parable and combines these elements seamlessly in a heightened realistic narrative. It is deliberately flamboyant but also muted by design to create magic. The authentic milieu of a Gujarat village in pre-Independent India creates a wide cast of credible characters from the Mukhiya (Suresh Oberoi) to the Gandhian teacher (Benjamin Gilani) trying to explain the concept of Independence to bewildered men who know nothing but feudalism and the distant British Sarkar whose representative comes periodically to collect taxes. Over all of them towers the proud, beautiful Sonbai (Smita Patil) whom the idling louts fear and desire. Her husband, another idler (Raj Babbar) finally finds a job in the railways and leaves a distraught wife behind. The shiftless gossipers, all men, say with a knowing smirk that his demanding wife wears him out at night and that explains his lethargy. Sonbai disdainfully ignores them and goes about her work. Most of the women pound chillies in the factory owned by one of the villagers. It is fortress-like compound on the village outskirts guarded by the old chowkidar Abu Miya (Om Puri). Saraswati (Deepti Naval) the Mukhiya's submissive wife overlooks his infidelity but defies him to send her little daughter to the Masterji to be educated. The Mukhiya puts an end to her bid for independence most humiliatingly. She bides her time...

Into this village comes the swaggering, luxuriously moustachioed Subedar (Naseeruddin Shah playing the villain with operatic grandeur). His retinue pitches a well-equipped tent, including a gramophone that astounds bedazzled villagers with the magic of music coming out of a box. His wandering eye falls on Sonbai and it is lust at first sight. But Sonbai is different from other women who willingly submit to being summoned by him. When he accosts her repeatedly, she slaps him and this insult enrages the Subedar puffed up with his own pomp. He orders her to be captured. Sonbai running through fields chased by his horsemen, hiding behind mounds of chillies, is on par with any other iconic scene from *Mother India* (1957) to *Mughal-E-Azam* (1960). Sonbai is fiery as a red chilli and escapes her hunters to hide in the chilli factory. Faithful Abu Miya shuts the massive door and all the women are inside. The Subedar sends an ultimatum. Hand over Sonbai or the village will have to face the consequences of her defiance. The other women grumble about their enforced captivity and are initially hostile to Sonbai. Even within captivity, life goes on. A woman goes into labour. The birth of a new life infuses a collective spirit of defiance. Saraswati hides from the village men, to bring them bundles of rotis, handed over through an opening in the high wall. Women inside agree that only a woman will think of practical things like food.

The men of the village are cowards. They plead with Sonbai to surrender to save the village. 'I will not go even if my husband asks me to' she declares. 'I will die rather than go' is Sonbai's final word. By now, the women are united and want to take a stand. Subedar's men lay siege and batter down the huge wooden door locked from inside by Abu Miya. The grey-haired guard gets his rusty rifle ready. He is the first to be killed on duty as the soldiers rush in.

Something spectacularly unimaginable unfolds before our mesmerised eyes. A surging crowd of women rushes forward and throws chilli powder at the men, blinding them. The screen is awash in red. I can only quote from the impact the scene had from my book *Smita Patil, A Brief Incandescence*. 'In retrospect, you know this is a temporary triumph. But the moment sweeps you up to a mythic level of blinding splendour, a choreographed act becomes the victorious dance of woman- power. It gives birth to the legend, of once upon a time lived a strong, passionate woman, Sonbai.'[6]

Film images have a resonance beyond the particular time of its making. The image of Abu Miya's resistance and his body riddled with bullets connect subliminally to the scene from Rajat Dholakia's *Parzania* (2005) made in the aftermath of 2002 massacre of Muslims in Gujarat. In *Parzania*, a colony's gate is battered down by a murderous mob. A Parsi boy goes missing forever. *Parzania* is based on the reality of the grieving

---

[6] Smita Patil, A Brief Incandescence. P.189 HarperCollins (2015)

Parsi family. It tells you the story of an enclosed neighbourhood of mostly Muslim families terrorized and killed by rampaging Hindu mobs—as they also did to Gulbarg society.

Mirch Masala's influence can be traced in *Mrityudand* (1997) made exactly 10 years later by Prakash Jha. Jha goes back to his native terrain of Bihar, its caste and class politics that establishes its rule everywhere. The whole economy and people's lives are controlled by the nexus of priest-politician-businessman. The focus is on two brothers, Abhay Singh (Mohan Agashe) and Vinay Singh (Ayub Khan), scions of a once wealthy landlord family now living on faded glory. The brothers are at the mercy of the powerful businessman Tirpat working in tandem with the local politician. Abhay Singh, married for 17 years to Chandravati (Shabana Azmi), seeks to hide his impotence by branding her barren. Then in a diabolical move, he colludes with Tirpat to get the temple priest killed and takes over as priest. He is now a celibate sanyasi.

Younger brother Vinay marries Ketki (Madhuri Dixit) an educated girl from a small town. Seeing how her husband is indebted to the evil duo, Ketki encourages Vinay to set up as a contractor. Soon, Vinay becomes a pawn in the hands of Tirpat. The early part of the film is confusing in its delineation of caste, class, and religious power centres and the nefarious nexus born of it. Vinay is the latest, rather willing victim who walks into their net. He will not heed Ketki's warnings and takes on the role of the authoritarian, abusive husband. Kekti is not the meek sort. You are my *pati*, not my *parmeshwar*[7], is her ultimatum to Vinay. She takes the ailing Chandravati for whom she sincerely cares for to the hospital in the nearby town with the help of Rambaran (Om Puri), a lower caste trader who has been lending money to the erstwhile landlord family. Ramabaran talks sense into Vinay and gets him out of Tirpat's coils. Chastened, Vinay woos Ketki back. But Tirpat gets Vinay killed.

The ever-dependable Rambaran tends to Chandravati with care and soon their emotional attachment turns physical. Jha films this mature love with tenderness. Chandravati gets pregnant. Instead of shame, she declares to her celibate husband that she had borne enough abuse from him. She will now let desire rule her life. It is a revolutionary statement to make in a feudal patriarchal society. She and Ketki unite as the fount

---

[7] You are my husband, not my God.

of empowerment, starting with their maid who had for years met Tirpat's demand for sexual favours to pay off her husband's debt.

Tirpat decides that the time has come to silence the voices of rebellion. He enters the ancestral house to intimidate them but is stunned to see a rifle-wielding Ketki, surrounded by all the women who have been exploited by him and his cronies. *Mrityudand* doesn't reach, or even aspire to, *Mirch Masala*'s epic scale. Jha shows that you can tell an impactful story about the bonding of women who have suffered under patriarchy by using a mainstream narrative with restraint.

7

The Subversives

Subversion is no longer a covert operation. Subversives flaunt their iconoclasm with pride. The very ethos and raison d'être of indie films invites such subversions—of not just the garden variety of parodying actors or scenes from old favourites. No, these intrepid filmmakers touch the Untouchables of Hindi cinema. Bimal Roy and Guru Dutt are not off limits; nor the literary classics on which their iconic films are based. *Dev D* (2009) and *Sahib Bibi Aur Gangster* (2013) have been recast in modern idiom and their ethos altered to suit the frenetic hurly burly of India on the go.

The new generation directors create a welcoming space for women, where they can be themselves, shed inhibitions to express what they want and feel. These filmmakers are fearless, convinced that classics are not holy cows. Classics can be remade on *their* terms, reflecting their vision of what cinema can be when one dares to recast inherited icons. Subversion is the name of the remake game so obviously enjoyed by directors like Anurag Kashyap and Tigmanshu Dhulia. They have the quirky sensibility and audacious talent to make edgy cult films for the millennial generation. *Dev D* and *Sahib Biwi Aur Gangster* fit in right with the zeitgeist where the past is invoked as a quotation minus the nostalgia, where the present is sought to be captured in all its urgent frenzy. The classic is not treated with the reverence due to an unsurpassable landmark; its codes and signifiers are acknowledged and reinterpreted. It goes beyond mere updating to reflect contemporary mores. The eye behind the camera is caught in the paradox of mirroring the past while raptly engaged in navel gazing on an unapologetic ego trip. The result can infuriate the outraged purist, titillate the *aam janta* in search of something novel and challenge the deconstructionist's love affair with semiotics. *Dev D* and *Sahib Biwi Aur Gangster* become filmmakers' films for this generation, standing out amidst the clutter of niche films searching for an urban audience. You get the rare opportunity to cherish a loved classic and yet respond to the compelling new avatar it has taken, braced for the assault of brazen chutzpah and calculated charm.

Anurag Kashyap's *Dev D* has forever changed our perception of the hallowed, rather adolescent archetype that had anyway outstayed its time. *Devdas* had degenerated into a literary and film cliché. The time for reinventing the characters was seized by Kashyap with disruptive glee. Displacement of the original milieu is the preferred starting point. That adds an enormous initial advantage to the unfolding of the film, because it helps in shedding a lot of accumulated cultural baggage.

To millions of fans over the decades, *Devdas* and *Sahib Bibi Aur Ghulam* cannot be uprooted from their Bengali ethos. Of the two, *Devdas*—a narcissistic hero trapped in self-pity created by an immature Saratchandra when he wrote it in his late teens—has been translated and then transplanted into many languages. There are Devdas films in Telugu, Tamil, Malayalam, Assamese, Urdu (two films were made in Pakistan). The transplantation survived, because the paralysed will of the vacillating hero spoke to the collective subconscious of a colonised people still grappling with the notional freedom of individual will. Individual will versus Karmic inevitability was—and continues to be—a question that provokes anxiety, fear of the new, and capacity to deal with change. It also became a crucible of creativity. A freed creativity that was eager to explore the consequences of this debate through literature and intellectual discourse.

The timeframe of the novel is early twentieth century when Calcutta was the centre of not only Bengali culture but the seat of British power. The city and its cultural ethos became trendsetters for the entire country. The reformist Brahmo Samaj was established in 1828 and its monotheistic faith had consciously discarded *Kulin*[1] Brahmanical practices of Hinduism. Subaltern historians question the validity of the term Bengal Renaissance as it is an elitist construct that does not address the plight of the marginalized nor their grassroots contribution to the evolution of cultural practices. But most people connect the reformed faith and

---

[1] Bengali Brahmins who can trace their lineage to the five families who had migrated from Kanauj (Kanyakubj in Uttar Pradesh).

acceptance of rationalism as prime facilitators of renaissance in every field—social change, Western education for the middle class too, not just the aristocracy, women's burgeoning freedom, literature, painting, theatre, and a revival of traditional arts with new ways of seeing and depicting. Then, the coming of the railways that made travel to distant corners of the country easy. In Bimal Roy's *Devdas* (1955), the train plays a crucial role in the narrative as the wandering hero on the verge of death travels miles before he gets to Paro's home—to die anonymously outside the gates of her marital mansion. In Sanjay Leela Bhansali's *Devdas* (2002), more than his death, what you remember is Paro's royal pallu trailing queen-like behind her on the ground as she rushes to the gate that has been ordered to be closed. These are images embedded in collective memory.

What does Kashyap do? He dispenses with a whole segment of the well-loved story and even the famous climax. Paro disappears from the story in the second half, except as a name and that is less frequently mentioned. It is an audacious incision from a cherished text—written and visual. What he replaces it with is not self-pity and despair but hope of a new beginning. His Dev is a selfish jerk, if you have to use the more accurate slang to describe him. The subliminal association of Hamlet's angst with a lovelorn Devdas drinking himself to death is not allowed to come anywhere near the millennial Dev. The ending is the best place to look at the beginning to appreciate how daringly Kashyap has subverted a classic.

Kashyap not only transplanted his story from Bengal's languorous countryside to the earthy rusticity of Punjab but also banished the hero to England. He follows Bhansali's lead here. In the Bimal Roy *Devdas,* the childhood of a truculent, violence prone Devdas and an adoring yet wilful Paro is dwelt upon at length. It establishes their bond for life. Kashayp also starts with an adolescent Dev waiting for Paro to bring him some food and quarrels with her. Paro is feisty, gives him back word for angry word. Dev is sulking because he is caught smoking by his teacher. Dev is impudent. He calls his father by name—the shortened nickname used by his grandmother—and is unrepentant when reprimanded. That arrogance stays with him all his life, even when he is down and out. It is a case of arrested adolescence.

For the vast majority, Dilip Kumar is the perfect Devdas and he is not to be imitated. Parody would be blasphemy. Perfection is beyond the reach of even the most daring actors and directors. His lines are invoked with reverence: *kaun kambakht bardasht karne ko peetha hai, main to peetha hu, ki saans le saku*.[2] Kashyap, in a way, plays safe and takes his cue from the Bhansali version. But the intent is not parody: either of the easily parodied Shah Rukh Khan or Bhansali's operatic excess. It is reinvention of an angst-ridden romantic as a self-destructive, selfish egoist with a sense of entitlement. The world owes him the woman he wants. He lost her purely because of his immature distrust and condescension for a girl he thinks is his social inferior. Dev (Abhay Deol, who is credited with the concept) is an irresponsible wastrel supported by his long-suffering family—monetarily—but he is an emotional outcast. Even more so when his rather indulgent father (belying the reputation of strict disciplinarian) dies.

Kashyap's Dev is banished to London for his own good and the family's peace of mind. Instead of aristocratic *zamindari*, the family is part of industrial India's new rich: it owns sugar mills among other things. When Dev returns, the most urgent thing on his mind is to have sex with Paro, his childhood sweetheart. Paro is equally impatient. She is not the coy country girl waiting to be wooed but a hot-blooded young woman who sent her topless picture to Dev when he demanded it. When talking to him on the phone, she is so aroused she touches herself seeking pleasure. Dev's brother is getting married; the bustling household gives them no privacy. Every encounter is interrupted. Frustrated, Dev tells Paro to do something about it. The arresting image of Paro cycling through the fields with a mattress behind her speaks of her passionate commitment, uncaring if they are caught. Passionate and practical. But the assignation is doomed. A rejected suitor tells Dev that Paro is insatiable in bed; she left him exhausted for two days. When Paro initiates foreplay and comments on how hairy he is, Dev gets up and stalks out in disgust. He does not bother to answer the distraught Paro. When she accosts him later, Dev is dismissive. She is beneath him and can never be his wife. Meanwhile, he is having it off on the side with Rasika, a wedding guest, a girl from a rich Delhi family destined to play a large part in Paro's life.

Paro in her earlier versions is a proud woman, hurt by Dev for not making an effort to defy caste and social inequalities. In Roy's film, a dignified Suchitra Sen risks discovery and disgrace by visiting Devdas late at

---

[2] Which wretched man drinks to bear pain, I drink so that I can breathe.

night in his home. It is Dev who is afraid and sends her home. It was appropriate for the time in which the film is set. Bhansali's penchant for operatic magniloquence reduced the issue of class difference to a farce, with Kirron Kher's vindictive over-the-top dance. Paro makes her own decisions in *Dev D*. She quickly agrees to marry Rasika's rich older brother, a widower with children; not grown up children who are deferential as in both the earlier versions but young kids whose affection she can win. Instead of wallowing in heartbreak, we see her abandon the bashful bride's decorum to dance with wild abandon at her own wedding.

In Mahie Gill, Kashyap found his perfect Paro: spirited, sexy, who gives as good as she gets, and completely pragmatic in moving on quite happily with her life. There is none of the ridiculously sighed *Issh* ... or Aishwarya Rai's coy coquetry as she is ensconced with queenly grace on a swing. Bhansali never lets us forget that he is presenting Miss World in a different avatar. The millennial Paro is a sturdy Punjabi lass. She doesn't weep over a lost love like Dev who loiters around her new house to spy on her. For a woman with self-respect, the mooning ex is an insult if he descends to stalking.

Kashyap is scrupulously unsentimental. He sets Paro's pragmatic acceptance of her choice against Dev wandering around the sleazy district of cheap lodges, business-like sex workers, seedy bars, and drug dealers made even more lurid under the smoky ambience of neon lights. Kashyap's tribute-cum-subversion is not hidden away in the subtext. He flaunts it with élan. A poster of Shah Rukh Khan as Devdas—sporting a Fedora at a jaunty angle—looms at the entrance of a dingy joint frequented by a jeans and tee clad Abhay Deol while he wastes away in a drug haze. The half-French teenaged Chanda, now a sex worker, watches Madhuri's *maar dala* on TV with total absorption. Madhuri's Chandramukhi has the sexual swag of a sought-after courtesan that hides her vulnerability. Bhansali is so awed by Madhuri that the focus is on her dancing—sensuous and yet decorous. There is a hint of melancholy under the practiced charm and courtly ways expected of a cultured *tawaif*. Bhansali has no rationale to bring Chandramukhi to Paro's marital home for Durga Puja except to star them for a dance face off: *dolare* that became the Bhansali brand trendsetter for rivals in love to duel in a dance-off. That defines his Chandramukhi. There is no hint of how she ended up in a kotha.

Bimal Roy's *Devdas* starred another diva, Vyjayanthimala. The more Devdas heaps scorn upon her, the deeper she falls in love with him. Her wistful song *jise tu kabool karle woh adaa kahan se laoon* voices her regret of lacking the charm to win his acceptance. She renounces her life of pleasing others and leaves Calcutta. She lives austerely in a village. Here comes Bimal Roy's first departure from the literary text, something alien to his sensibility. The two women in the hero's life cross each other's path: Paro a wealthy chatelaine is being carried in a palanquin and Chandramukhi dressed in a simple sari walks by her as she comes from the opposite direction. They look at each other for a longer time than such a casual meeting warrants. Kashyap pays tribute to this memorable brief encounter in an even briefer, even more random encounter, not once but twice. The first time is when Paro gets into a train to collect her nude photograph print. She sits across from Chanda seen in profile. Later, when we are absorbed in Chanda's story, we see her escaping from her rural incarceration. The same shot but slightly different. It is a fleeting acknowledgement of an old master that passes under the radar if we are not alert. It is a quiet moment, an echo of the deliberate quietude of a classically correct auteur.

The biggest departure of Kashyap's film is the story he creates for Chanda, a character on par with the hero. He builds up Chanda's (Kalki Koechlin) whole persona and backstory using topical events to ground the trauma that a 17-year-old schoolgirl undergoes. Chanda is the professional name she adopts. In fact, she is Leni from a privileged background: rich Indian father and a French mother. Her indiscretion is getting her act of giving oral sex to an older boyfriend filmed. The video is downloaded by half of Delhi and she is slut shamed. The family flies off to Europe to perhaps let the scandal die down. Leni is under strict watch, not even allowed to go for a walk. Typical of an outraged teenager, she is crudely graphic in insulting her father for watching the offending video. Her shocked father shoots himself. The grieving mother abandons Leni, packing her off to her paternal grandmother's home in a Punjab village. The economy of the narrative is eloquent; it is poignant and brutal. There was an infamous video of a girl of a top Delhi school fellating a fellow student that had gone viral. Leni's youthful lapse is based on that scandal.

Leni's desperate call to her mother is not answered. Her uncle and grandmother treat her like a moral outcaste. The uncle's admonition

Aankhe neeche is eerily similar to what happens to Anushka Sharma in *NH10*. It is forbidden for a woman to look at a man, even her uncle, in the eye. At the end of her tether, Leni runs away to Delhi. Not one of her fellow students helps her. Hungry and with limited money, the vulnerable young girl is easy prey for the pimp and brothel owner who seems very supportive. Chunni the pimp helps Leni write her school board exam, and then enrol in college for a BSc honours course. She is being groomed for higher-end clientele who will pay for the privilege of having sex with a posh young girl.

Leni, now Chanda, can command her price. Her boudoir is girly pink; mannequins in bikinis wear bizarre wigs. Props for Leni's expertise in role-play and kinky sex are suggestively strewn around. Dev too lands in Chunni's clutches. Alcohol is not enough to get stoned. He needs drugs to dull his pain. A barely sober Dev is brought to Leni's boudoir when she is dispensing phone sex in Tamil, then French, and finally English. When she learns Dev studied in London, she switches on her Brit accent till he asks her to stop it. That first meeting ends in Dev getting irritated and Chanda intrigued. It is the beginning of a complex relationship where Dev is free to talk of Paro at length. Chanda is a good listener. She can also joke about her profession. She mentions a client who will say escort, the high-sounding word for a prostitute but can't bring himself to say the Hindi equivalent of whore.

Chanda is an enigma. She is obviously good at what she does: dressed in costumes, from a baton-wielding nurse to a schoolgirl in uniform. Dev seems to be able to talk to her, sinking as he is into sloth and a perpetual drug haze. He calls up Paro's husband late at night and demands to talk to her. A few days later, Paro comes to his grimy unkempt room in a seedy joint. She is disgusted at how he stinks, the litter of bottles around and mound of unwashed clothes. The homemaker in her rises to the occasion; she gets fresh towels and detergent, orders Dev to bathe like an authoritative matron. Paro washes his clothes, including underwear and tells him some home truths. You love only yourself is her comeback to his plaintive declaration, I love you. Marry your image in the mirror is her mocking advice, a tinge of bitterness in her tone. Incidentally, Chanda too tells Dev he can't love anyone but himself (minus marry your image bit). It is not surprising how well they can read Dev. The problem is for him to read his own mind and feelings—he is a long way from that maturity.

Dev attempts to make love to Paro. It is an act of desperation. She turns her face away, lips compressed in a straight line when he tries to kiss. She is furious when he asks her about her sex life with an older man. Paro leaves, her face masked by huge glares as she goes away in a cycle rickshaw. That is the last time we see her. Images of Paro making love to her husband haunt Dev's fevered brain. Almost totally sozzled, Dev drives his brand new BMW (his father's last gift disregarding his older son's objections) mowing down some pedestrians. Kashyap's colour palette is attuned to the mood. The bars and drug joints are shot under a diffused red light. The graffiti and posters on the walls add up to post-modern grunge. When Dev sets out on his fatal drive, images are superimposed and the screen is awash in pale cold blue.

The accident coincides with his father's heart attack. It is another connection with Chanda. They are both responsible for the death of their fathers. The police let him out for four days to attend the funeral. Except his mother who first slaps him in anger and sorrow, no one speaks to him. The brother thrusts a wad of cash into his hands, to be given to the lawyer who is trying to get him bail. What about me?, Dev asks. It is a question not answered.

Dev is a slave to his impulse. He asks the old Sardarji taxi driver to drive around for binge drinking. Having seen the cash wrapped in paper, what happens next is foregone. Dev is left stoned and stranded with hardly any money. Dev's last wandering—part of the original text—is hitchhiking with a biker along lonely mountain roads. He finally gets back to Delhi, sick in body and mind when he is thrown out of a bar since he can't pay for his drink. Rescued by a waiter he had tipped lavishly, he finally contacts Chanda. She takes him home—a spartan room—and cleans him up. As if the cleansing has cleared his mind, Dev admits: I am a slut. Chanda is wearing a ring he had bought in London for Paro. She is taking him to the police station where he is asked to report daily. Dev has confessed he loves Paro forever. And casually adds to Chanda, I love you too. Is that enough for a tentative new beginning? Dev has read Chanda's diary when she is away at college. She has endured far more than he did and has come out stronger. Unlike her cinematic predecessors, this Chandramukhi does not opt for renunciation. She embraces life—even when ugly and painful—with the tenacity to survive and the satisfaction of educating herself. Is this their road to redemption? The soundtrack doesn't throw the recurring musical motif of *tera ye emotional atyachar*[3] in your face now. This burgeoning relationship is full of ironies and unexpected epiphanies.

Irony is beyond Tigmanshu Dhulia. Dhulia has already proved his credentials with *Haasil* (2003). UP's lawless hinterland is the new favoured terrain where the rule of the *lathi*[4] is the state of normalcy, violent eruptions are endemic and corrupt networks—of netas, contractors with armies of hoodlums and feudal remnants—are all busy playing lethal double-crossing games. Both the physical and mental landscape are now recognizable terrain where smalltown hunger to get somewhere fast fuels internecine blood feuds, simmering sexuality explodes to shatter metropolitan India's patronizing perceptions of the vast unknown grey area beyond its ken. Dhulia adopts a more slam bang, in your face approach that drains away the elegiac elegance and hypnotic languor of the Guru Dutt/Abrar Alvi classic. In hindsight, that is the only possible approach when you are face to face with cinematic perfection.

Guru Dutt/Alvi wrought cinematic perfection from imperfect characters. *Sahib Bibi Aur Ghulam* (1962) mourns the passing of a decadent late nineteenth century culture of landed aristocracy while the educated middle class claims its rightful place in the new hierarchy. It is not a lament but a sympathetic overview of history told in mainstream narrative style with sensitivity to nuance. The mise en scene is an eloquent testament to the masterly collaboration between an auteur's artistry of creating poetry out of his internalised angst with the magical camera of V.K. Murthy. Based on Bimal Mitra's classic novel *Shaheb Bibi Golam*, Dutt's film is a broad and deep narrative that conveys sweeping changes when one era yields to the next. Satyajit Ray's evocative *Jalsaghar* (1958) portrayed profundity with an austere brush, focusing on a lonely zamindar awaiting his end in the crumbling mansion by the river. Irony is the key element in a narrative that balances empathy and objectivity with finesse. Dutt's film contains all the popular elements of storytelling but the atmospherics and acting raise it to unrivalled mastery. Meena Kumari, of the intoxicating wine drenched voice and eyes that look into the soul, created the unforgettable tragedy of Choti Bahu. It is a character (and

---

[3] Your emotional violence.
[4] Heavy club.

performance) that ranks among the greats in the pantheon of Indian cinema.

We see history unfold through the eyes of middle-aged Bhoothnath (Guru Dutt) who is supervising the demolition of the Chowdhury Rajbari. Labourers digging up the rubble find a woman's skeleton with a gold *kangan* on her wrist. Bhoothnath recognizes it as the *kangan* that adorned Choti Bahu's winsome wrist. Choti Bahu's tragedy is narrated in flashback, from the vantage point of her death.

It is a haunting song that first introduces Choti Bahu to the naive newcomer to the city. Bhoothnath is educated but coming from a village, the splendours of the Rajbari overwhelm him. His brother-in-law works for the Chowdhury family. They live in the quarters meant for the retinue of retainers. At night, an eerie beckoning voice mesmerises with the call, *koyi door se awaaz de chale aao*[5] in Geeta Dutt's mellow, seductive voice. A victim of this changing class structure is the beautiful, lonely Choti Bahu; a middle-class woman married to the younger son Chote Babu (Rehman) who spends all his time at either a tawaif's kotha or rearing pigeons. An indolent lifestyle devoted to the pursuit of pleasure is de rigueur for the aristocracy. Choti Bahu wants the intimacy of marriage, not fritter away her time in making and remaking jewellery as women of the *zamindari* are expected to do. She is a stunningly sensuous woman who claims the rights of a wife.

The psychology of Chote Babu is a curious case of desire dependent on transgressing norms: his desire is fuelled by alcohol in the company of *tawaifs* who are the Other. He is addicted to this stimulation. His beseeching beautiful wife is rejected. The pathos of *na jao saiyan chhuda ke baiyan, qasam tumhari main ro padungi*[6] expresses her yearning.

Bhoothnath begins work as a clerk as Mohini Sindur factory owned by Subinoy Babu, a staunch member of the reformist Brahmo Samaj. His vivacious, educated daughter Jaba (Waheeda Rehman) takes great pleasure in mocking the awkward naff who doesn't know how to respond to her teasing. Jaba is modern, mixing with men in her father's drawing room: a total contrast to Choti Bahu who is traditional and lives in the segregated women's section.

---

[5] From afar someone calls out, come to me
[6] Don't go my love, don't free your hand from my clasp. I swear on you, I will weep bitterly.

Bhoothnath is summoned into Choti Bahu's presence. Curiosity and trepidation make him nervous as he approaches her chamber, led by a trusted servant. We hear her mellifluous voice before we sight her. Come, she says kindly and her maid places food before the bashful young man. His first sight of Choti Bahu is akin to a paean of worshipful adoration. The camera makes adoring love to her. We first see her feet adorned with *altaa*, the gaze travels upwards slowly like a caress, taking in the silken folds of her sari; then the jewel-encrusted, bedecked bosom; and finally the face worthy of a goddess with her big bindi emblazoned on her forehead, past those fathoms deep eyes. A slightly amused smile lingers on her lips. Bhoothnath is mesmerized and so are we. The camera is a brush painting an icon. Choti Bahu manages to disarm the awkward Bhoothnath with her kindness. She wants him to get her a box of Mohini Sindur. This sindur is reputed to possess magical power, to keep a husband faithfully by her side.

The power of advertisement even in those days! Soon, Bhoothnath has shed his shyness and pours out his complaints against Jaba, always laughing at him. Choti Bahu and Bhoothnath have found a friend and confidante in each other. If she wanted, Choti Bahu could easily seduce Bhoothnath but she has no desire to do so. She is too traditional a Hindu wife to do it even out of boredom, or even curiosity. There is always an undercurrent of attraction that is not acted upon. This erotic frisson adds another layer, though the emotion Choti Bahu expresses is one of maternal concern—the untranslatable *vatsalya bhava*.

The sindur fails to live up to its magical power. Choti Bahu's plaintive lament, *na jao saiyan chuda ke baiya kasam tumhari main ro padungi* has no effect on her impatient husband. She accosts him, am I not beautiful? To that, his answer is brutally honest. Can you drink with me, entertain me? Picking up the gauntlet, Choti Bahu has her first taste of alcohol ... and she begins to like it.

Bhoothnath starts responding to Jaba's teasing—it is actually flirting—with either a show of mild anger or ignoring her. He is hurt in a bomb explosion in the city—early nationalists fighting against the British—and Jaba tends to him with care and kindness. Soon afterwards, Bhoothnath is on the way to upward mobility. He leaves Calcutta to train with an architectural firm. When he comes back, Subinay Babu is dead. Jaba is alone, refusing to marry the proper Brahmo groom her father had found. She has been waiting...

More disturbing is the news at Rajbari. Chote Babu is paralysed and Choti Bahu is addicted to alcohol. She turns to Bhoothnath and he brings her liquor, often selling a piece of jewellery she gives to pay for it. The Chowdhury fortunes have declined. Bad management and investments have dimmed their glory days. Bade Babu, the older son, one day overhears Choti Bahu ask Bhoothnath to accompany her on a visit. She wants to go to the temple to pray for her husband's wellbeing and recovery. Bade Babu suspects an affair and summons his henchmen. They way lay the carriage. Bhoothnath is beaten up till he is unconscious and Choti Bahu has disappeared... the mystery had not been cleared.

Flashback ends. Jaba drives up in a carriage to pick up Bhoothnath. Obviously the two have got married. It is natural when it is revealed they were betrothed as children before Subiyan Babu embraced Brahmo Samaj. Choti Bahu interred along with the derelict marital home. Can we read it as poetic justice or a victim of history that changed in a generation?

Given the multi-layered classic that Dhulia has dared to subvert, he wisely chooses to pick up hints from the original and build on it to the farthest extent possible. So the sexual frisson straight away sparks into blazing sex. Turn of the century setting of feudalism destroyed by its own decadence and the rise of the educated middle class is now recast as the rise of the smalltown mafia playing an important part in the power game of political patronage. Dhulia has anyway confessed in an interview to *MW* October 2011 issue that Vijay Anand is more his mentor than Guru Dutt.

Sahib Biwi Aur Gangster is superior pulp fiction crossed with an all-time classic, clever, and contemporary with crackling dialogue and frenetic action. The focal point is the entry of Babloo (Randeep Hooda), a cocky young man coming to hide in the hinterland from cops. He had beaten up a rival badly enough to send him into a coma. He has a short fuse and it ignites when an uppity girlfriend dumps him because he has 'no class'. The journey is reversed in this film: from big city to the countryside, where a person ready to break the law has many who need such services. He comes as the replacement for a driver who has had an accident. He is to drive the tempestuous Choti Rani around since her husband doesn't have time for her. He comes to this unnamed place where the Raja Sahib's *haveli* is the landmark. He meets Suman, the rather impudent English-speaking daughter of Kanhaiya, the faithful right-hand man of the local lord of the manor.

The calculated riffs on the original start with Suman's mocking drawl. She modernizes the arch raillery of Waheeda Rehman's Jaba. She lengthens out the vowels of the gangster Babloo's name with the skill of a ghazal singer enunciating a single word with many variations. This burgeoning flirtation does not go anywhere, except that Babloo once uses Suman to make Choti Rani jealous after she has rebuffed him.

Choti Rani is all fire and ice. She enjoys her drink, the cigarette in her hand is not just a style statement. Her boudoir is her private, if restricted, kingdom where she summons the new driver to check him out. There is a fleeting image of the Choti Rani's *payal*-clad ankle as she sits regally on her bed, holding court. It is an insider's nod to the inimitable build up to our first glimpse of Choti Bahu, from her *altaa*-decorated feet to the iconic face with her soulful gaze. There is an immediate spark between the bored, restless Rani looking for excitement and the quick-witted Babloo with a knowing gleam in his eye. The stage is set for seduction. Anticipation only makes the pleasure more frantic.

If the narrative opts for the breakneck pace of a thriller, where motives, murder plans, double and treble crosses are only to be expected, Dhulia wisely takes time over the ambience—which was such an integral part of Guru Dutt's film. Aseem Mishra, the talented cinematographer, knows that he can come nowhere near the magic of V.K. Murthy's B&W wizardry. He sensibly captures the decaying ambience of the imposing *haveli*, its peeling paint and age-smudged photographs, huge rooms bereft of rich carved furniture, thereby conveying the sense of scaled down magnificence. Decadence is not poetic anymore.

Instead, its representative Aditya Pratap Singh (Jimmy Shergill, a superbly underplayed blend of hauteur and unexpected vulnerability) is lethally practical, using his 'royal' status to win contracts in the cutthroat business of government tenders for roads and bridges. That is the only way he can survive in this unnamed—but easily guessable—state where ministers are in the pay of contractors who will use blackmail and murder to get their way. This Sahib is a stickler for English table manners, as is his mentally unstable wife Choti Rani (Mahie Gill) who insists that the new driver Babloo eat his breakfast served in her room with a fork. The Raja

Sahib's wry self-knowledge of his status makes him a clear-eyed realist. It is articulated by Suman's pithy summing up: *rutba hai, rupaya nahin*[7]. Glory minus the means is hardship for a proud man who has to beg for money from the Badi Rani (his father's mistress legitimized by marriage to Ranihood) to maintain not only his retainers (now dwindled to the lone Kanhaiya who is deadly with guns) but also the avaricious mistress Mahua (Shreya Narayan). Mahua is ensconced in another *haveli*, to the chagrin of the sex-starved Choti Rani who frets that her husband too might follow his late father's example. Unlike the anonymous dancers, with the exception of one who tends personally to Chhote Babu in *Sahib Bibi Aur Ghulam*, Mahua is a demanding mistress. She is not exactly a courtly *tawaif* trained in aristocratic courtesies. She is more like the Nautanki performer of raunchy dances. Her relationship with the possessive Raja Sahib is more than sexual. Besides being possessive of what he owns like a true feudal lord, Raja Sahib seems to have some genuine emotional connection with his mistress. That is why he is furious at her betrayal though in fact Mahua has been framed, to ambush Raja Sahib.

If the Raja has his fun and games openly, Rani's affair has to be kept discreet. What motivates her blatant seduction of Babloo is hazy but credible, given Mahie Gill's uninhibited yet nuanced performance. Choti Rani has been banished to her quarters, sent on long drives because the Sahib has no time for her, nor the inclination. There is a hint of an earlier indiscretion as she goes into a crazy rant when she learns of Babloo's real name but Dhulia doesn't elaborate. Their mutual sexual attraction is palpable. The stormy seduction and frenetic couplings are pretty graphic. There are ample opportunities to indulge in alfresco sex near a rock as well as assignations in her boudoir.

It is revealed that Babloo is playing a deep game. He is planted in the Sahib's mansion as a temporary driver by the rival Gainda Singh. Babloo is the pivotal go-getter, the planner, and executor of escalating action. For all his scheming, there is a lingering innocence of the original Bhoothnath in Babloo. He thinks Choti Rani is his ladder up the social scale, once the Sahib is conveniently dispatched in a carefully hatched shoot-out at a shikar party. Rani also attends the elaborately planned outing, because Babloo has a compromising video that he may just show her husband.

---

[7] There is status but no money.

Her suspicions prove right. The plot goes horribly wrong for Babloo. He is shot dead, Raja Sahib is shot and survives. The plot unravels to Choti Rani's advantage. Babloo has the naked hunger of the social climber. But what he doesn't know is his place in the Rani's scheme of things. For her, sexual gratification is temporary. Class loyalty is permanent. Babloo was only for her bedroom. In public, she is the Rani.

Dhulia's preoccupation with violent action and intrigue does lead to a confused unfolding without offering sufficient dramatic justification for the plot spiralling out of control in the second half. Sheer energy, the sustained engaging quality of the characters, and the paradox of polished rawness give *Sahib Bibi Aur Gangster* its throb and thrust. The denouement may be weak but the postscript is brilliant.

The postscript turns all our expectations topsyturvy. Choti Rani is truly big game player for all her volatility and mood swings. She knows when there is an opportunity and grasps it before anyone can snatch it away. After the shootout, it is election time. Choti Rani is in charge now, waving regally to her *praja* from the terrace. She wheels out Raja Sahib in his chair, lifting his hand for the obligatory wave. She now has him doing her bidding, payback time for all the subtle—and not so subtle—humiliations she has endured. In the game of king, queen, and knave, Rani emerges the winner, holding all the aces. She stakes her claim in the game of thrones. Unlike Choti Bahu, Choti Rani escapes being a victim.

This is the only way Dhulia could subvert a classic: change the tragic for the satirical, moral absolutes for amoral gamesmanship. He gains in thrills and humour, since he does not even aspire to replicate tragic grandeur. Dhulia left room for sequels but sadly, not one has come close to the first.

Subversion works only once. Repetition kills it, voiding it of new insights and inventive tropes. Yet, the audacity of successful subversion needs not only to be acknowledged but applauded.

8
Subversion in Retro Mode

Subversion does not always have to be in your face, challenging us as *Dev D* and *Sahib Bibi Aur Gangster* do. It can be more subtle and spring surprises without alarming the audience. It can have a ripple effect that goes back in time and bring acclaimed older actors to the forefront. It is like rain over a few monsoons trickling down to replenish depleting ground water. Some of it is sucked up to the surface and rejuvenates fading careers.

There is something liberating in the air with the arrival of the millennial woman in our cinema. The concept of the millennial woman is not—and should not be—a Procrustean bed. Any non-formulaic film and non-stereotypical heroine should not be stretched, shrunk, and twisted to fit the rigid Procrustean bed. Films like *Maqbool, Haidar, English Vinglish, Dedh Ishqiya, Cheeni Kum, Andhadhun, De De Pyar De* perhaps needed the invigorating millennial air to take birth and more importantly, succeed.

Tabu always made us feel that her vast reservoir of talent was not fully explored after the bilingual *Astitva* (2000, Hindi and Marathi) and *Chandni Bar*. *Astitva* sought to affirm a middle class, lonely wife's right to not feel guilty about her brief affair with a musician when she was a young woman. Now a middle-aged matron with a grown up son, she has to explain why she is the beneficiary of her late music teacher's will. The husband with a calculator for a mind and freezer for a heart is made an unfeeling, entitled chauvinist to justify Aditi's quiet rebellion years ago. It is a film from a predictable male point of view: Mahesh Manjrekar is just not able to people Aditi's world with credible, non-stereotypical men in conservative Pune. Both the husband and son are judgemental and reject her explanation of one rainy night's transgression. It is suggested the son is the result of that night, as the husband calculates back in time, of when a conception was possible since he keeps track of his travel dates as well as when he had sex with his wife: a ridiculous situation and even more ridiculous resolution. Two other token women represent progressive attitudes and sympathise with Aditi. Aditi finds support from the insensitive son's girlfriend. Tabu's finely calibrated performance, of refusing to feel guilty for that night of passion with a sympathetic man who understood her, is *Astiva*'s sole virtue. It is textbook feminism by a director who made his reputation with action dramas centred on violent, misguided macho men, the prime example being *Vastav* (1999).

Tabu is known for her whimsical choices: of films and voluntary absence from the screen. Her absence made her presence even more wanted. It is serendipity that brought Tabu and Vishal Bharadwaj together. We cannot imagine anyone else in *Maqbool* (2004) and what Tabu brought to *Haider* (2014) is exceptional. *Haider* extends *Hamlet* to daringly relevant contemporaneity both political and psychological. A decade apart ... from ambitious, guilt-wracked Nimmi to Ghazala, a far more intriguing character than *Hamlet*'s Gertrude, Tabu's skills as an actor unafraid to venture into even more forbidden territory grow sharper and deeper. Tabu brings maturity and depth to the transgressive mother's redemption in *Haider*.

A modern Lady Macbeth first. Bharadwaj transposes Shakespeare's Scotland to the murky Bombay underworld ruled by the seemingly benign Abbaji (Pankaj Kapur). Similar to Macbeth's opening, *Maqbool* encapsulates both the plot and mood with two corrupt, cynically funny cops: the veteran duo of Naseeruddin Shah and Om Puri reprise their parallel cinema camaraderie with brilliant dark humour. They go beyond the prophesying witches; they engineer the plot along with timely interventions.

Another departure from Shakespeare is Nimmi (Tabu). Her Lady Macbeth is a young, restless, sensuous mistress of the patriarch Abbaji. Maqbool (Irrfan) is Abbaji's right hand man, treated with fatherly affection by the otherwise canny Don. Nimmi is in love with Maqbool and he is equally smitten but needs repeated urging from her to dispatch Abbaji to his maker and claim Nimmi. Tabu plays Nimmi as a passionate, determined young woman who has ambitions of being more than a pampered mistress of an old man. Her decorous demeanour while dancing along with the other women at a family celebration is artfully underlaid with subtle flirtation with the stoic Maqbool. Even when they are all walking to the dargah with many others, she boldly brushes against his hand before holding it. She is no shrinking violet in love and crime. Nimmi is instigator and participant with a matchless sense of timing.

When quiescent conscience wakes up to guilt, Nimmi's fear, desperation, and remorse reach a crescendo of great cinematic expression. Tabu makes this modern version of Lady Macbeth her own, in nuance and understanding, giving it the edge of a wronged mistress who cajoles with coquetry and strikes like a vengeful cobra. Maqbool and Nimmi are together when they pay for their crimes. Tabu is so identified with her Lady Macbeth role that in the noir thriller *Andhadhun*; one of the characters refers to Tabu's Simi by the Shakespearean moniker.

In a country that deifies mothers and motherhood, *Haidar* was almost blasphemous for making Ghazala sensuous and playful. She almost displaces the eponymous hero from centre stage. It is intriguing how and why Bhardwaj departs so drastically from Shakespeare. *Haidar* is not only brave—almost foolhardy—in its setting: Bharadwaj's version of *Hamlet* is rooted in deeply troubled Kashmir where an alienated people—not all of them separatists—want autonomy. *Azaadi* is a far, forlorn cry while India and Pakistan 'play border border' as Haidar says with mocking despair. Bharadwaj makes his narrative unequivocally political, not evasive when it comes to where his sympathies lie. This, in the ethos of triumphalist nationalism, with the RSS setting the agenda of equating nationalism with Hindutva, is exhilaratingly courageous.

Ghazala's enlarged role makes you wonder: did Vishal Bharadwaj read T.S. Eliot's seminal essay on *Hamlet* in his critical collection *The Sacred Wood*? All this is pure speculation of course but Ghazala's centrality in the dramatic and emotional tone of the narrative justifies the reference to Eliot's influential critique that drove generations of English literature students to wrestle with this critical puzzle. Yes, Tabu is a fabulous actor who can give credence to a complex character with strong negative vibes. That could be part of the reason but I am searching for something far more fundamental to Bharadwaj's adaptation of Shakespeare's longest play that has probably attracted more interpretations and tomes of criticism than any other.

English literature students have had to grapple with the dictum laid down by T.S. Eliot, as formidable a critic as he was iconic poet of classical modernism. Eliot pronounced *Hamlet* an 'artistic failure' because the 'intractable material' failed to find its 'objective correlative'. He goes on to elaborate. *Hamlet* belonged to the very popular Elizabethan genre of the revenge play where a son avenges the betrayal and death of his father. The revenge motive and Hamlet's notorious inability to act for a variety of psychological and ethical reasons become more complex by the additional difficulty of dealing with the effect of a mother's guilt upon her son. Hamlet is disgusted by *an enseamed bed* when he sees Gertrude happy with his uncle she married in unseemly haste. Eliot finds a problem with Hamlet's excessive abhorrence and Gertrude's placidity. He goes on to say that Shakespeare 'was unable to impose this motive successfully upon the "intractable" material of the old play'. (Critical consensus is that the Bard reworked an existing template.) 'Probably more people have thought *Hamlet* a work of art because they found it interesting, than have found it interesting because it is a work of art. It is the "Mona Lisa" of literature.' For those who don't have to critique the critique, it is best to further quote what Eliot meant by his obiter dicta of 'objective correlative'. 'The only way of expressing emotion in the form of art is by finding an "objective correlative"; in other words, a set of objects, a situation, a chain of events which shall be the formula of that *particular* emotion; such that when the external facts, which must terminate in sensory experience, are given, the emotion is immediately evoked. If you examine any of Shakespeare's more successful tragedies, you will find this exact equivalence.'

The crux of the problem is that Gertrude is a wishy-washy woman who is simply unable to sustain the level of Hamlet's disgust—an emotion that he is unable to come to terms with. To quote Eliot for the last time, 'his disgust envelops and exceeds her. It is thus a feeling which he cannot understand; he cannot objectify it, and it therefore remains to poison life and obstruct action'.

Cut to *Haidar*. As a political narrative, it enlarges the individual tragedy into the collective tragedy of a people denied full autonomy. If something was rotten in the state of Denmark, to Haidar (Shahid Kapur), the whole of Kashmir is a prison. Yes, Haidar is the protagonist, yet he is not always central. That place is slowly taken up by Ghazala—tender, sensual, imperious, grieving, and finally, decisive—who is flirting gaily with her slightly comical yet sinister brother-in-law within weeks of her idealistic husband's disappearance. The undertone of the Oedipal complex in the play is a given. I have not seen an image more evocative of nascent oedipal love in our cinema: Haidar bending down to kiss Ghazala's neck when she is adorning herself before the mirror. Is the mirror reflecting self-knowledge to both or only Haidar?

This is crucial to the unfolding subsequent action. Haidar's mocking soliloquy in Lal Chowk, of India-Pakistan 'playing border border' when all are trapped in existential angst, is prelude to donning the self-deprecatory clown persona. Haidar's antic disguise, of feigned madness is mirrored by Ghazala's deepening introspection, of how she has damaged the son she loves so much. It is for her to intervene and atone for the wrong she has done—unwittingly perhaps but she is more sensitive than the placid queen given to shallow lamentations. In that sense, Bharadwaj restores dramatic equilibrium, finding the objective correlative for a film where the personal does become truly political.

Hamlet's damning words: '*O most wicked speed ... to post/With such dexterity to incestuous sheets!*' is answered by the willing martyrdom of a suicide bomber that Ghazala opts for, to pay with her '*too too sullied flesh*'. A fitting, flaming end that echoes the violent bomb blasts of contemporary times, unlike death by poison. Poetic justice, or the flourish of the wholly unexpected wrought so brilliantly by Bharadwaj? The answer is implicit in the question. Tabu's Gazala demands understanding, if not empathy. She is tragically widowed—accidentally or by design is left ambiguous. We don't see much of her with her husband, the hardworking, humanitarian doctor. Instead, Ghazala teases us to surmise that she finds the flirtatious brother-in-law (Kay Kay) more lively and marries him with indecent alacrity. We see a beautiful mature woman who makes no apologies for fulfilling her needs, emotional and sexual. Widow re-marriage in the context of Kashmir and its Muslim population is acceptable, unlike in a conservative Hindu setting.

It is when Gazala sees how irreparably she has damaged her darling son that she rouses herself from languorous indulgence. Tabu transforms her body language, from luxurious lassitude to purposeful action. She invigorates the narrative with an almost feral, female flair. *Maqbool* and *Haidar* may not have been box-office hits but they are cult films, counted among the best adaptations of Shakespeare. Original interpretation married to the strength of rootedness is a winning combination. '*Absent thee from felicity awhile,/And in this harsh world draw thy breath in pain, To tell my story.*' Hamlet's parting injunction to Horatio reminds us as much of Haidar's tragedy as Ghazala's in Bharadwaj's brilliant film. The words resonate with every viewing. The grandeur of tragedy is not for women in our cinema. Choti Bahu is the only other tragic figure in Hindi cinema but she fades away into death and oblivion. Ghazala opts for a fiery, blazing death to incinerate her sins of omission and commission.

Shades of grey become Tabu and enhance her elusive appeal. They unleash the powerhouse in her. In Sridhar Raghavan's *Andhadhun*, the sleeper hit of 2018, Tabu's relish of her casual psychopathy does the impossible: suspension of moral judgement. Raghavan is indubitably Bollywood's Nawab of noir. Spiced with sinful black humour, he has changed our taste buds. The outrageous is the new normal. We are weaned off cloying sentimentalism to savour the sharpness of wicked wit. It is a piquant crime thriller centred around blind pianist Akash's (pretending to be blind) dilemma of being a witness to murder and yet unable to do anything about it. Akash (Ayushman Khurrana) is preparing for a competition in London and thinks being blind gives him cachet, an un-spelt out advantage. Meanwhile, he plays at a local upmarket bar/club where he becomes the favourite of Pramod Sinha (Anil Dhawan). Sinha is an amiable Bollywood star of the 80s now living a retiree's life in Pune with a high maintenance diva for his second wife, the much younger Simi (Tabu). Sinha invites Akash home for a private performance (of his popular hits) to celebrate his anniversary. Simi is bored out of her pretty head with Sinha's narcissistic obsession with watching his hit songs on a loop. She doesn't see it as an endearing, rather harmless preoccupation: a congenital affliction expected of a once popular hero.

Simi is having an affair with a macho police Inspector. An unlikely pair if there ever was one. Who knows just how lust for kicks works? She is to the manor born and he a middle-class Maharashtrian married to a wife who coddles him with healthy food to maintain that muscular body. Raghavan throws in these contrasts like an oblique aside to pepper his narrative with delectable ironies. Simi and her cop lover murder Pramod who turns up inopportunely from a trip for a planned anniversary surprise. Akash blunders blindly into this overwrought scene as the guilty lovers are trying to dispose of the body. Trigger-happy Simi then goes on a casual killing spree. She tosses her elderly, inconvenient neighbour over the balcony of the high rise because she might give incriminating evidence. The old lady next-door has a terribly inquisitive nose and remarkable memory for details.

Tabu plays Simi with fascinating amorality. She is sharp and uncovers Akash's pretence. It is a cat and mouse game now, with Simi the relentless pursuer, who can think on her running feet and has absolutely no qualms of killing anyone who comes in the way. Hence the sobriquet Lady Macbeth, from Akash's friend who is helping him to escape. The pace doesn't allow for questions of plausibility because it becomes a headlong chase, Akash trying to get to Bombay and then to London with Simi in hot pursuit. The point of a noir thriller is that it allows for audience identification with only the nominal protagonist who too leaves us with ambivalent feelings. Simi rises from being the chief antagonist/murderer to an extremely interesting character whose lightning moves and malign motives capture our imagination. We are almost powerless to resist this black widow's lethal skills as survivor and hunter. Simi has the charm to momentarily disarm Akash's suspicion. She almost succeeds in making him the latest prey but fate/destiny/karma (call it what you will) intervenes with precision that gives a surreal spin to accidental justice.

Tabu delights, with the poise and sophistication she brings to a new age family drama, *De De Pyar De* (2019) that flirts with the outré and yet manages to be acceptable because it avoids moralizing like the coronavirus. The film crossed the 100 crore mark (to merit the status of a hit), revealing that the audience is receptive to hitherto unacceptable (on moral grounds) relationships. Tabu is Manju, separated wife (but not divorced) who has to deal with the messy situation when her London-based husband Ashish (Ajay Devgn) turns up at the Manali family home with Ayesha (Rakul Preet Singh) the new squeeze he wants to marry. His elderly parents and 25-year-old daughter Ishika are shocked. Manju is cool, as if she expected something like this, and bored with the outrage this May-December romance causes. Ayesha is barely older than Ishika, who is on the verge of introducing the family to her boyfriend's father. She has told them she has no father.

Standing on the periphery but edging to the centre is VK (Jimmy Sheirgill) an amused onlooker of a risqué situation fast getting out of control. He is the *shairi*-spouting, gift-bearing suitor bent on wooing Manju who pretends to be too busy to take him seriously. VK suggests Ashish pass off as Manju's brother, the Mama who has every right to be present at this important family conclave. To her chagrin, Ayesha is relegated to Ashish's secretary status. Frayed tempers, misunderstandings, catfights between Manju and Ayesha with claws unsheathed and veiled insults flying, Ishika's routine hysterical breakdowns … all follow as expected while director Akiv Ali keeps the touch light even as he firmly holds the skeins from getting tangled.

De De Pyar De is a non-judgemental family drama that starts on a high note of cynicism and ends in a family celebration that sensibly stops short of gooey sentimentality. The tone borrows from the popular American series *Modern Family,* with tacit tribute to vintage Woody Allen (persona non grata now but his influence can't be wished away by Me Too indignation). Luv Ranjan is the anti-rom com guru of acerbic comedies. Some of that cynicism comes through in *De De Pyar De* to give the mating game blues its bite. Co-written and co-produced by Luv Ranjan, his attitude to romance, sex, love, and marriage finds a new focus. A 50-year-old separated man falling hard for a 26-year-old woman confident of her sexuality and its power. Ashish, a successful businessman, is not looking for commitment while Ayesha is a tease: she is flattered but keeps telling him he is too old for a hot girl like her even as she playfully tests out his muscular body. She is an engineer during the week but a bartender on weekends because she enjoys the sexy banter with her clientele. She is no coy virgin who has to be wooed into an affair. This no fuss openness to sex without the promise of marriage is contemporary—with the proviso, that it is all happening in London, not in censorious Delhi. The irony is that Ishika wants to live with her fiancé in this same Delhi where both of them work.

In deference to the star power of his leads, Ranjan gives considerable time and screen space to the separated couple where we can see the residue of affection and shared experience of parenthood under all the exasperation. When Manju is exhausted from dealing with Ishika's hysterics, Ayesha's offended barbs and everyone looking to her to solve the intractable situation, she and Ashish have comfort sex. Something that a couple who have gone through the demanding emotional cycle of marriage take recourse to without it meaning anything or altering newer relationships. Ayesha is too immature to understand this. She scoots back to London. After Ashish sets things right with Ishika's boyfriend and his conservative father, Manju flies off to London to placate Ayesha with the divorce papers signed.

Tabu makes her Manju sharp-tongued who can shoot off accurate salvos at the bouncy, fresh-faced Ayesha and yet be unexpectedly generous. Experience has made her wiser and not grudge her ex-husband this new love. There is no hankering to rekindle romance of their college sweetheart days. Manju has many things to keep her more than busy. She has been de facto mistress of this lovely old house, her in-laws giving her the responsibility of running the family hospitality business. Now she truly grows into a gracious chatelaine, a warm person at heart who is also fun loving.

Tabu has also been on the other side of the May-December romance, as the 30-something visitor from Delhi falling in love with Amitabh Bachchan's London-based 60-plus master chef-cum-snooty restaurateur. The film was *Cheeni Kum* (2007) Balki's debut that made gastronomy as central as the unlikely chemistry between the leads. Instead of a spicy Hyderabadi zaafrani pulao (the dish over which the amateur and the professional squabble), the film collapses like a wobbly soufflé with the infusion of a terminally ill child and Bachchan's cantankerous mother (the delightful Zohra Saigal). One of the risqué scenes has Tabu demanding her boyfriend to run to the tree at the other end of the park: to test his stamina for other things on her mind. Otherwise, the eyebrow-raising romance limped to a tame end.

There could not have been a more heartwarming comeback for Sridevi than *English Vinglish* (2012). Gauri Shinde has spoken of the film being a sort of apology to her mother—like many middle-class women of her time, she could not speak English making the children squirm in school. Shashi Godbole (Sridevi), in cotton saris and a long braid, is a Pune homemaker who is famous for her laddoos. It is a business she runs from home with her mother-in-law's blessing. It is very revealing that Shashi's culinary speciality is making laddoos. It is a humble, ubiquitous sweet to celebrate all occasions, has a long shelf life unlike pricier and more exotic mithais. *Man mein laddu phoot rahe hai* (literally, laddoos are bursting in the heart) is the idiom to connote overwhelming happiness. Shashi puts away a decent amount with her small business but is constantly put down by her adolescent daughter who is ashamed of her mother. The trip to the US, five weeks before the rest of the family joins her for her niece's forthcoming wedding, acts as a catalyst of change. Her embarrassing experience of inability to order coffee galvanizes Shashi to put her stashed away cash (she changes them to dollars in India) into a spoken English class. She does it secretly, commuting from her widowed older sister's suburban home to New York and becomes the star pupil of the small group of internationals grappling with the vagaries of syntax and pronunciation.

These are the best scenes in the film, funny and warm as the small group interacts, exchanges confidences and anxieties. The rather dishy French chef is attracted to Shashi and they happily chat away—he in French and she in Hindi—but they seem to understand each other from the tone of voice and expressive gestures. It is an ego booster for Shashi but she is too sweet and committed to her marriage to even indulge in mild flirtation. She realizes watching English movies with subtitles is a quick way to learn the language.

Her husband—given to taking Shashi for granted—and chastened daughter learn to appreciate her. The most important line in the film is Shashi saying rather wistfully: respect is worth more than just love. Sridevi lives the role: vulnerable, hurt, determined, and strong by turns. We even overlook the shrill voice that had caged her into the vivacious, sexy child-woman stereotype (Sridevi made it uniquely her own, to give her credit). Shashi gave Sridevi the actor a second innings. Sadly, her untimely death cut the second innings short.

Madhuri Dixit Nene, her rival all through their parallel careers, came back as the dancing diva. Somehow, the image of the forlorn *tawaif*—Chandramukhi in Sanjay Leela Bansali's over the top *Devdas*—refused to leave Madhuri's screen persona. Even in *Dedh Ishqiya* (2014), Abhishek Chaubey's delicious riff on *nawabi* niceties and courtly courtesies, Madhuri is the elegant, aristocratic widow who dances divinely in private for her own pleasure (and for the besotted Khalu, peeping through chinks in the glass doors, as Naseeruddin Shah reprises the petty criminal from the first *Ishqiya*). Begum Para (Madhuri Dixit) spins an elaborate ruse of hosting a competitive *mushaira*, summoning aspiring poets to a decaying *haveli* so that she can pick a suitable consort to fulfil her late husband's wishes. The charade is a con game to cheat the assembled guests under the spell of the exquisite Begum and her saucy attendant Muniya (Huma Qureshi) who has Khalu's nephew-cum-sidekick Babban (Arshad Warsi) under her thrall. There is a missing necklace worth millions in play and a screwball comedy finale where the enterprising women make a getaway. A delicious decadence pervades the narrative and the comedy veers from irony to zany, as the director enjoys subverting the Muslim Social genre with unexpected finesse. In the game of outwitting smitten men, Begum Para and Muniya are more than partners in crime. There is just a tantalizing hint of sexual chemistry between the women to perk up the decorum with subtle sizzle. Madhuri queens over *Kalank* (2019, a spectacular debacle) as the noble, misunderstood *tawaif* in the love-cum-political saga set during Partition.

It is rather unfair to stereotype a good actor and great dancer as the eternal *tawaif*. Madhuri has turned producer—of Marathi films initially—but she might choose a script that does her talent justice. Now Katrina Kaif too is reportedly joining the producer bandwagon to find roles that are different. With Deepika Padukone's deglamourized *Chapaak* and Priyanka Chopra playing mother to a teenager in her own production, *The Sky Is Pink*, two huge stars decided it was time to give creativity its place under the arc lights. Marriage has not confined their ambition. Vanity is not all. Things are definitely changing with the A list stars taking the lead.

Social media and its many platforms bring stars down from the stratosphere, making them more human and accessible. It enables them to depart from the given script, to articulate concerns and preoccupations that they hold dear. Padukone confessed to depression and how she coped with it. She has not just stopped with her confession. She is also engaged in outreach programmes: Padukone featured in a news report that showed her interacting with small town and rural women of Karnataka, encouraging them to come out and get help for depression that is so common and yet is hidden from, and by, families.

Most recently, Vidya Balan made a gutsy video on body shaming—*Dhun Badal Ke Toh Dekho*[1]. It gives new meaningful words to familiar tunes, to drive home the essential point: how damaging body shaming is to a person's self-worth and self-image. In one shot, Balan appears with smudged lipstick and tears streaming from mascara-smeared eyes to convey deep anguish. The other non-conformist (who has now gone shrill with her support to Hindutva and its conservative values) had earlier savagely spoofed the Item Song and divas who are reduced to item girls. '*Cos I have a vagina re is* the refrain of an elaborate parody of how an item

---

[1] Change the tune and then see.

song is shot: back dancers dissolving into anonymity, the choreographer's instructions to heave the breasts some more and the voyeuristic eye behind the camera. Ranaut is defiantly unrepentant and is visibly enjoying the gig. The popular dance number, *chittiya kalayiya Ve*—an automatic must have at wedding sangeets and desi parties—is the target of this rambunctious take off. Ranaut skilfully walks the razor's edge of slut shaming item girls and don't give a damn defiance even if it attacks top heroines who have shimmied, shaken their breasts while thrusting the derriere for the camera. You can see her being bitchy without apology, having a blast dancing to outrageous lyrics. Streaming platforms have blazed a scorching trail of not only graphic crime series but also lust stories where women's sexually is expressed with no apologies.

It seems there are no holy cows left in Bollywood that had stepped warily between so many written and unwritten taboos. Will the third decade of this millennium take this freedom further? There is a post-millennial Generation Z waiting in the wings. The auguries are all encouraging. It will not be the old story of two steps backward for every progressive step forward. One hopes the changes will be nuanced and take root for lasting impact. The evolution of the millennial woman is a continuum that Bollywood seeks to grasp and portray. Will this new Indian woman as portrayed in popular culture cut free from the moorings mired in patriarchal norms? She has come far but there is a still a long way to go.

Afterword

Even as this book was being proofed, changes in how we consume visual content demanded acknowledgement, if not detailed analysis. I am sure many media mavens are feverishly engaged in keeping track of the frenetic pace at which cinema has, and is changing. Streaming platforms are the new frontier—beckoning directors, producers, actors, and viewers. Covid is the marker of the big change in many aspects of life, including entertainment.

The West could boast of trendsetting series that birthed fanatic followers. Each season waited with bated breath and wild speculation by an addicted audience—*Homeland* and *Game of Thrones* being two examples familiar to anyone who has not been living under a rock. Hindi cinema has coped rather adroitly with globalization but now the demands of keeping up with the transformation have grown even more challenging.

Indian entertainment industry, in all languages, is running in place, because the time it takes to nurture a concept to fruition poses the danger of redundancy by the time we see it on our screens. There is much clamour for difference for the sake of difference. Coming to Bollywood, it is a case of Bollywood is dead, long live Bollywood. Moghuls of the movie screen dipped their toes in the OTT ocean rather gingerly but now have caught on to the game. They need to enter this vast contentious space if they have to survive. The lure is lack of any defined censorship laws that can be applied to this content. The government, aware of the subversive nature of this unfettered creative freedom, is mulling over drafting rules that protect 'Indian values' and threat to national security. Vague but ominous threats.

Indian OTT content did not wait till Covid confined audience to their homes. As early as 2018, the anthology *Lust Stories* flaunted its intent with the title. The anthology featured young women as far apart as a domestic servant servicing her bachelor employer and an attractive, unconventional teacher sailing close to the stormy hormones of teenaged boys. *Four More Shots Please* began streaming in 2019, with its desi-take on *Sex and The City*. Four young women—from early 30s to mid-20s—reveal their flaws and ambitions, bonded into the sisterhood of urban women who work hard and party harder. Zoya Akhtar, the most successful woman filmmaker of her generation, led a pack of women writers to create *Made in Heaven*. Sobhita Dhulipala (ex-Miss USA) is one half of a pair of wedding planners spinning out extravagant celebrations for upper crust Delhi society. Her business partner is a closet gay and she is a middle-class working girl married into a high-profile business family, carrying the mixed baggage of ambition, insecurities, and compromises.

Delhi Crime scored as the best drama series at the 48th International Emmys. At the centre of the story is Shefali Shah (liberated from playing mother to strapping heroes) as the no-nonsense, committed South Delhi Assistant Commissioner of police. In record three days, she tracked and arrested the infamous rapists of Nirbhaya: the gruesome, misogynistic crime that shocked a nation's conscience. Older actors like Sushmita Sen and Raveena Tandon played meaty, action packed roles in thrillers *Aarya* and *Aranyak*. Who can overlook the stunning impact of Samantha in the hugely popular *The Family Man*, Season 2? She was the antagonist who made the audience understand, if not empathize with the torn and turbulent life of an LTTE commando.

Then came Madhuri Dixit, the diva who really did not retire, holding centre stage in the deconstruction of a female star's persona in *The Fame Game*. Many are ready to follow in her path-breaking wake, whatever the flaws of the series poised for its second season. Where the dancing queen leads, can others resist following? Mafia dons and gunslingers in the badlands of UP and Bihar are slotted into stereotypes while women are no longer content to be confined to a niche. They demand and get space of their own—pre, post, and deemed millennial—with panache.

Select Filmography—Chapterwise

Some films like *Duniya Na Mane, Mirch Masala, Dev.D, Sahib Bibi Aur Ghulam, Devdas* recur in many chapters

Introduction

Mother India (1957)
Producer...Mehboob Khan
Director...Mehboob Khan
Screenplay...Wajahat Mirza, S. Ali Raza (Dialogues)...S. Ali Raza...
Music...Naushad
Lyrics...Shakeel Badayuni
Cinematography...Faredoon A. Irani...
Editing...Shamsudin Kadri
Sound...Koushik
Art Direction...V.H. Palnitkar
Cast...Nargis, Sunil Dutt, Rajendra Kumar, Raaj Kumar, Kanhaiyalal, Jilloo Maa, Kumkum, Chanchal...

Godmother (1999)
Producer...Rajat Sengupta (executive producer)
Director...Vinay Shukla
Screenplay...Vinay Shukla
Cinematography...Rajan Kothari
Editing...Renu Saluja
Music...Vishal Bharadwaj (as Vishal)
Sound...Narinder Singh
Art Direction...Rajat Pathare. Prasad Phadte

Cast... Shabana Azmi, Milind Gunaji, Nirmal Pandy, Govind Namdeo, Raima Sen, Sharman Joshi

---

Hum Aapke Hai Kaun (1994)
Producer... Rajshri Films
Director... Sooraj Barjatya
Screenplay... Sooraj Barjatya
Cinematography... Rajan Kinagi
Editing... Mukhtar Ahmed
Sound... C.S.Narayan Rao
Music... Raamlaxman
Lyrics... Dev Kohli, Ravindra Rawal
Art Direction... Bijon Das Gupta
Cast... Salman Khan, Madhuri Dixit, Mohnish Bahl, Renuka Shahane, Alok Nath. Anupam Kher, Reema Lagu

---

Dilwale Dulhania Lejayenge (1995)
Producer... Yash Raj Films
Director... Aditya Chopra
Screenplay... Aditya Chopra
Cinematography... Manmohan Singh
Editing... Keshav Naidu
Sound... Anuj Mathur
Music... Jatin- Lalit
Lyrics... Anand Bakshi
Art Direction... Sharmishta Roy
Cast... Shah Rukh Khan, Kajol, Amrish Puri, Farida Jalal, Anupam Kher, Parmeet Sethi, Mandira Bedi, Himani Shivpuri

---

Ki & Ka (2016)
Producer... R.Balki, R.Damani, Sunil Lulla
Director... R.Balki

Screenplay... R.Balki, Rishi Virmani
Cinematography... P.C.Sriram
Editing... Chandan Arora
Sound... Debasish Mishra, Premsankar S.
Music... Ilayaraja
Lyrics... Yo Yo Honey Singh, Meet Bros (and others)
Art Direction... N.Madhusudan
Cast... Kareena Kapoor Khan, Arjun Kapoor, Rajit Kapoor, Swarup Sampat, Amitabh Bachchan (cameo), Jaya Bhaduri (cameo)

Bandini (1963)
Producer... Bimal Roy
Director... Bimal Roy
Screenplay... Nabendu Ghosh, Jarasandha (story)
Cinematography... Kamal Bose
Editing... Madhu Prabhavalkar
Sound... Dinshaw Bilimoria
Music... Sachin Dev Burman
Lyrics... Shailendra, Gulzar
Art Direction... Sudhendu Roy
Cast... Ashok Kumar, Nutan, Dharmendra, Raja Paranjpe, Asit Sen. Tarun Bose

---

Badhai Ho!
Producer... Hemant Bhandari, Vineet Jain
Director... Amit Sharma
Screenplay... Akshat Ghildial
Cinematography... Sanu John Varughese
Editing... Dev Rao Jadhav
Sound... Amarjit Barman
Music... Abhishek Arora
Lyrics... Vayu Kumar, Mellow D
Art Direction... Koushal Chowdhary

Cast ... Ayushman Khurrana, Neena Gupta, Gajraj Rao, Surekha Sikri, Sania Malhotra, Sheeba Chaddha, Shardul Rana

---

Guide (1965)
Producer ... Dev Anand
Director ... Vijay Anand
Screenplay ... Vijay Anand, Pearl S Buck (US) (R.K.Narayan novel))
Cinematography ... Fali Mistry
Editing ... Vijay Anand, Babu Sheikh
Sound ... J.M.Barot
Music ... Sachin Dev Burman
Lyrics ... Shailendra
Art Direction ... Ram Yedekar
Cast ... Dev Anand, Waheeda Rehman, Kishore Sahu, Leela Chitnis, Anwar Hussain, Gajanan Jagirdar

---

Chakra (1981)
Producer ... Manmohan Shetty, Pradip Uppoor
Director ... Rabindra Dharmaraj
Screenplay ... Rabindra Dharmaraj, Jaywant Dalvi (Story)
Cinematography ... Barun Mukherjee
Editing ... Bhanudas
Music ... Hridaynath Mangeshkar
Lyrics ... Madhosh Bilgrami
Art Direction ... Bansi Chandragupta
Cast ... Smita Patil, Naseeruddin Shah, Kulbhushan Kharbanda, Ranjit Chowdhry, Rohini Hattangadi, Salim Ghouse, Savita Bajaj

---

Arth (1982)
Producer ... Kuljit Pal
Director ... Mahesh Bhatt

Screenplay ... Mahesh Bhatt, Sujit Sen
Cinematography ... Pravin Bhatt
Editing ... Keshav Hirani
Sound ... Hitendra Ghosh
Music ... Chitra Singh, Jagjit Singh
Lyrics ... Kaifi Azmi
Art Direction ... Madhukar Shinde
Cast ... Shabana Azmi, Kulbhushan Kharbanda, Smita Patil, Rohini Hattangadi, Raj Kiran, Dina Pathak, Kiran Vairale

---

Damini (1993)
Producer ... Aly Morani, Karim Morani, Bunty Walia
Director ... Rajkumar Santoshi
Screenplay ... Sutanu Gupta, Dilip Shukla
Cinematography ... Ishwar Bidri
Sound ... Rakesh Ranjan
Music ... Shravan, Nadeem
Lyrics ... Sameer
Cast ... Rishi Kapoor, Meenakshi Seshadri, Sunny Deol, Amrish Puri, Kulbhushan Kharbanda, Rohini Hattangadi, Sulabha Arya

---

Lajja (2001)
Producer ... Rajkumar Santoshi
Director ... Rajkumar Santoshi
Screenplay ... Rajkumar Santoshi, Ranjit Kapoor, Ashok Rawat
Cinematography ... Madhu Ambat
Editing ... V.N.Mayekar
Sound ... Pradeep Suri
Music ... Ilaiyaraaja (background score), Anu Malik
Lyrics ... Sameer
Art Direction ... Nitish Roy

Cast... Manisha Koirala, Jackie Shroff, Madhuri Dixit, Rekha, Ajay Devgn, Anil Kapoor, Mahima Chaudhry, Danny Denzongpa

---

Chapter 1—No Means No

Pink (2016)
Producer... Ronnie Lahiri, Rashmi Sharma, Shoojit Sircar (creative producer)
Director... Aniruddha Roy Chowdhry,
Screenplay... Ritesh Shah, Aniruddha Roy Chowdhry (story), Shoojit Sircar (story)
Cinematography... Avik Mukhopadhyay
Editing... Bodhaditya Banerjee
Sound... Pragyan Gogoi, Elias Issa
Music... Shantanu Moitra, Faiza Mujahid, Anupam Roy
Lyrics... Tanveer Ghazi
Art Direction... Meghna Gandhi
Cast... Amitabh Bachchan, Taapsee Pannu, Kirti Kulhari, Andrea Tariang, Piyush Mishra, Angad Bedi

---

Anaarkali of Aarah (2017)
Producer... Priya Kapur, Sandip Kapur
Director... Avinash Das
Screenplay... Avinash Das
Cinematography... Arvind Kannabiran
Editing... Jabeen Merchant
Sound... Arun Nambiar
Music... Rohit Sharma
Lyrics... Prashant Ingole, Avinash Das, Ravinder Randhawa, Dr.Sagar, Ramkumar Singh
Art Direction... Ashwini Shrivatsav

Cast... Swara Bhaskar, Pankaj Tripathi, Sanjay Mishra, Mayur More, Ishtiyak Khan

Precedents from the past

Duniya Na Mane (1937)
Producer... Vishnupant Damle, Sheikh Fattelal
Director... V.Shantaram
Screenplay... Narayan Hari Apte
Cinematography... V.Avadhoot
Editing... A.R.Sheikh
Sound... Shankarrao Damle
Music... Keshavrao Bhole
Lyrics... Munshi Aziz
Art Direction... Sheikh Fattelal
Cast... Shanta Apte, Keshavrao Date, Vimala Vasishta, Shakuntala Paranjpye, Raja Nene

Insaaf Ka Tarazu (1980)
Producer... B.R. Chopra
Director... B.R. Chopra
Screenplay... Shabd Kumar
Cinematography... Dharam Chopra
Editing... S.B.Mane
Sound... B.K.Chaturvedi
Music... Ravindra Jain
Lyrics... Sahir Ludhianvi
Art Direction... Shanti Dass
Cast... Dr.Shreeram Lagoo, Zeenat Aman, Raj Babbar, Padmini Kolhapure, Deepak Parashar, Iftekhar, Simi Garewal

Angaaray (1986)
Producer ... Gurdip Singh
Director ... Rajesh Seth
Screenplay ... Salim Khan
Cinematography ... Ravi Kiran
Editing ... Dilip Kotalgi, Zafar Sultan
Music ... Anu Malik
Lyrics ... Rajendra Krishan
Cast ... Smita Patil, Rajesh Khanna (special appearance), Raj Babbar, Shakti Kapoor, Bindu, Iftekhar

---

Mirch Masala (1987)
Producer ... National Film Development Corporation
Director ... Ketan Mehta
Screenplay ... Ketan Mehta, Tripurari Sharma, Hriday Lani, Shafi Hakim
Cinematography ... Jahangir Chowdhury
Editing ... Sanjiv Shah
Music ... Rajat Dholakia
Cast ... Smita Patil, Naseeruddin Shah, Suresh Oberoi, Om Puri, Deepti Naval, Raj Babbar, Benjamin Gilani, Dina Pathak, Ratna Pathak, Supriya Pathak

---

Chapter 2—Rom com Revamped

Dil Deke Dekho (1959)
Producer ... S.Mukerji
Director ... Nasir Hussain
Screenplay ... Nasir Hussain
Cinematography ... Dilip Gupta
Editing ... S.E.Chandiwale
Sound ... Ishan Ghosh

Music ... Usha Khanna, Sonik (background score)
Lyrics ... Majrooh Sultanpuri
Art Direction ... Shanti Dass
Cast ... Shammi Kapoor, Asha Parekh, Sulochana, Raj Mehra, Rajendra Nath

---

Love in Simla (1960)
Producer ... S. Mukerji
Director ... R.K. Nayyar
Screenplay ... Agha Jani Kashmiri
Cinematography ... D.K.Dhun
Editing ... Indu Kumar
Sound ... Ishan Ghosh
Music ... Iqbal Qureshi
Lyrics ... Rajendra Krishan
Art Direction ... Shanti Dass
Cast ... Joy Mukherjee, Sadhna, Azra, Kishore Sahu, Shobhna Samarth, Durga Khote

---

Junglee (1961)
Producer ... Subodh Mukerji, Probodh Mukerji
Director ... Subodh Mukerji
Screenplay ... Subodh Mukerji, Agha Jani Kashmiri
Cinematography ... N.V.Srinivas
Editing ... V.K.Naik
Sound ... Kuldip Singh
Music ... Shankar-Jaikishan
Lyrics ... Hasrat Jaipuri Shailendra
Art Direction ... Shanti Dass
Cast ... Shammi Kapoor, Saira Banu, Lalita Pawar, Shashikala, Anoop Kumar

---

Hum Tum (2004)
Producer... Yash Raj Films
Director... Kunal Kohli
Screenplay... Siddharth Anand, Kunal Kohli
Cinematography... Sunil Patel
Editing... Ritesh Soni
Sound... Dileep Subramanian
Music... Salim Merchant, Sulaiman Merchant, Jatin-Lalit
Lyrics... Prasoon Joshi
Art Direction... Sharmishta Roy
Cast... Saif Ali Khan, Rani Mukerji, Rishi Kapoor, Kiron Kher, Rati Agnihotri, Jimmy Sheirgill (special appearance), Abhishek Bachchan (special appearance)

Socha Na Tha (2005)
Producer... Dharmendra
Director... Imtiaz Ali
Screenplay... Imtiaz Ali
Cinematography... Ravi Yadav
Editing... Imtiaz Ali, Sirish Kunder
Sound... Zahir Bandukwala
Music... Sandesh Shandilya
Lyrics... Irshad Kamil
Cast... Abhay Deol, Ayesha Takia, Ayesha Jhulka, Apoorva Jha, Rati Agnihotri, Sandhya Mridul

---

Bunty Aur Babli (2005)
Producer... Yash Raj Films
Director... Shaad Ali
Screenplay... Jaideep Sahni, Aditya Chopra (story)
Cinematography... Avik Mukhopadhyay
Editing... Ritesh Soni
Sound... Anuj Mathur

Music... Shankar, Ehsan, Loy
Lyrics... Gulzar
Art Direction... Sharmishta Roy
Cast... Abhishek Bachchan, Rani Mukerji, Amitabh Bachchan, Raj Babbar, Kiran Juneja, Prem Chopra, Puneet Issar

---

Salaam Namaste (2005)
Producer... Yash Raj Films
Director... Siddharth Anand
Screenplay... Siddharth Anand
Cinematography... Sunil Patel
Editing... Ritesh Soni
Sound... Rishi Oberoi
Music... Vishal Dadlani, Shekhar Ravjiani, Salim-Sulaiman
Lyrics... Jaideep Sahni
Art Direction... Prakash Nambiar
Cast... Saif Ali Khan, Preity Zinta, Arshad Warsi, Javed Jaffrey

---

Jab We Met (2007)
Producer... Dhilin Mehta
Director... Imtiaz Ali
Screenplay... Imtiaz Ali
Cinematography... Nataraja Subramanian
Editing... Aarti Bajaj
Sound... Dileep Subramaniam
Music... Pritam. Sandesh Shandilya, Sanjoy Chowdhury (Background score)
Lyrics... Irshad Kamil, Faiz Anwar
Art Direction... Teddy Maurya
Cast... Shahid Kapoor, Kareena Kapoor, Tarun Arora, Dara Singh, Pavan Malhotra, Kiran Juneja

Love Aaj Kal (2009)
Producer ... Dinesh Vijan, Saif Ali Khan
Director ... Imtiaz Ali
Screenplay ... Imtiaz Ali
Cinematography ... Nataraja Subramanian
Editing ... Aarti Bajaj
Sound ... Faisal Majeed
Music ... Pritam, Salim-Sulaiman
Lyrics ... Irshad Kamil
Art Direction ... Gobinda Baidya
Cast ... Saif Ali Khan, Deepika Padukone, Rishi Kapoor, Rahul Khanna Giselli Monteiro

---

Band Baaja Baraat (2010)
Producer ... Yash Raj Films
Director ... Maneesh Sharma
Screenplay ... Habib Faisal, ... Maneesh Sharma (story)
Cinematography ... Aseem Mishra
Editing ... Namrata Rao
Sound ... Indrajit Neogi
Music ... Salim-Sulaiman
Lyrics ... Amitabh Bhattacharya
Art Direction ... Aditya Kanwar, Rashmi Sethi
Cast ... Anushka Sharma, Ranveer Singh, Manmeet Singh, Niraj Sood, Karan Sagoo, Kanishka

---

I Hate Love Stories (2010)
Producer ... Karan Johar, Ronnie Screwwala
Director ... Punit Malhotra
Screenplay ... Punit Malhotra
Cinematography ... Ayanaka Bose
Editing ... Akiv Ali
Sound ... Ali Merchant

Music ... Vishal-Shekhar, Salim-Sulaiman
Lyrics ... Anvita Dutt
Art Direction ... Amrita Mahal
Cast ... Imran Khan, Sonam Kapoor, Sammir Dattani, Samir Soni, Bruna Abdullah, Kavin Dave

---

Shudh Desi Romance (2013)
Producer ... Yash Raj Films
Director ... Maneesh Sharma
Screenplay ... Jaideep Sahni
Cinematography ... Manu Anand
Editing ... Namrata Rao
Sound ... Sarit Chatterjee
Music ... Sachin-Jigar
Lyrics ... Jaideep Sahni
Art Direction ... Rashmi Sethi
Cast ... Sushant Singh Rajput, Parineeti Chopra, Rishi Kapoor, Vaani Kapoor

---

2 States (2014)
Producer ... Karan Johar
Director ... Abhishek Varman
Screenplay ... Abhishek Varman, Chetan Bhagat (novel)
Cinematography ... Binod Pradhan
Editing ... Namrata Rao
Sound ... Ali Merchant
Music ... Shankar, Ehsan, Loy
Lyrics ... Amitabh Bhattacharya
Art Direction ... Kshamata Sachin, Gurav, Amrita Mahal
Cast ... Arjun Kapoor, Alia Bhatt, Revathy, Amrita Singh, Ronit Roy, Shivkumar Subramaniam

---

Dum Lagake Haisha (2015)
Producer... Yash Raj Films
Director... Sharat Kataria
Screenplay... Sharat Kataria
Cinematography... Manu Anand
Editing... Namrata Rao
Sound... P.C. Vishnu
Music... Andrea Guerra, Anu Malik
Lyrics... Varun Grover
Art Direction... Navin Chand, Naveen Lohara, Mahto Mohang
Cast... Ayushman Khurrana, Bhumi Pednekar, Sanjay Mishra, Sheeba Chaddha, Seema Pahwa

---

Shubh Mangal Savadhan (2017)
Producer... Krishika Lulla, Anand K. Rai
Director... R.S. Prasanna
Screenplay... Hitesh Kewalya, R.S. Prasanna (story)
Cinematography... Anuj Dhawan
Editing... Ninad Khanolkar
Sound... Arun Nambiar
Music... Tanishk, Bagchi, Vayu, Rachita Arora
Lyrics... Vayu
Art Direction... Laxmi Keluskar, Sandeep Meher
Cast... Ayushman Khurrana, Bhumi Pednekar, Seema Bhargava, Anshul Chauhan, Brijendra Kala, Jimmy Sheirgill (Cameo)

Toilet: Ek Prem Katha (2017)
Producer... Hitesh Thakkar
Director... Shree Narayan Singh
Screenplay... Siddharth-Garima
Cinematography... Anshuman Mahaley
Editing... Shree Narayan Singh
Sound... Debasish Mishra

Music ... Manas Shikhar, Vickey Prasad, Sachet Parampara
Lyrics ... Siddharth-Garima
Art Direction ... Krishna Thakur
Cast ... Akshay Kumar, Bhumi Pednekar, Sudhir Pandey, Anupam Kher, Divyendu Sharma, Shubha Khote

---

Qarib Qarib Singlle (2017)
Producer ... Sutapa Sikdar
Director ... Tanuja Chandra
Screenplay ... Tanuja Chandra, Gazal Dhaliwal, Kamna Chandra (story)
Cinematography ... Eeshit Narain
Editing ... Chandan Arora
Sound ... Shankarnarayanan Ramachandran
Music ... Anu Malik, Rochak Kohli, Vishal Mishra, Naren Chandavarkar (background score), Benedict Taylor (background scoe)
Lyrics ... Husaain Haidry, Rajshekar
Art Direction ... Seema Kashyap
Cast ... Irrfan, Parvathy Thiruvothy, Neha Dhupia, Brajendra Kala, Rishabh Kumar, Luke Kenny

---

Sonu ke Titu Ke Sweety (2018)
Producer ... Bhushan Kumar, Krishan Kumar, Luv Ranjan
Director ... Luv Ranjan
Screenplay ... Rahul Mody, Luv Ranjan
Cinematography ... Sudhir K. Chaudhary
Editing ... Akiv Ali
Sound ... Kaarthic Senthil
Music ... Zack Knight, Rochak Kohli, Amal Mallik, Rajat Nagpal, Ranghava, Yo Yo Honey Singh, Saurabh Vibhav, Hitesh Sonik (background score)
Lyrics ... Singhsta, Yo Yo Honey Singh, Swapnil Tiwari

Art Direction... Aashish Porwal, Tarpan Shrivastava
Cast... Karthik Aryan, Nushrat Bharucha, Sunny Singh Nijjar, Alok Nath, Madhumalti Kapoor

---

Chapter 3—Non-conformists Are the New Cool

Bhumika (1977)
Producer... Bhisham M. Bijlani, Lalit M. Bijlani, Freni M. Variava
Director... Shyam Benegal
Screenplay... Girish Karnad, Satyadev Dubey, Shyam Benegal (based on Hansa Wadkar's memoir Sangte Aika)
Cinematography... Govind Nihalani
Editing... Bhanudas
Sound... Hitendra Ghosh
Music... Vanraj Bhatia
Lyrics... Majrooh Sultanpuri
Art Direction... Shama Zaidi
Cast... Smita Patil, Amol Palekar, Naseeruddin Shah, Anant Nag, Sulabha Deshpande, Amrish Puri, Baby Ruksana

---

Fashion (2008)
Producer... Ronnie Screwwala, Zarina Mehta, Madhur Bhandarkar
Director... Madhur Bhandarkar
Screenplay... Ajay Monga, Madhur Bhandarkar, Anuradha Tiwari, Niranjan Iyengar
Cinematography... Mahesh Limaye
Editing... Devendra Murdeshwar
Sound... Jayant Vajpayee
Music... Salim-Sulaiman
Lyrics... Sandeep Nath, Irfan Siddiqui
Art Direction... Nitin Chandrakant Desai

Cast... Priyanka Chopra, Kangana Ranaut, Mughda Godse, Arbaaz Khan, Arjan Bajwa, Raj Babbar, Kiran Juneja, Samir Soni, Kitu Gidwani

Ishqiya (2010)

Producer... Vishal Bharadwaj, Raman Maroo
Director... Abhishek Chaubey
Screenplay... Vishal Bharadwaj, Sabrina Dhawan, Abhishek Chaubey
Cinematography... Mohana Krishna
Editing... Namrata Rao
Sound... Sushant Amin, Abhishek S. Bhattathiri
Music... Vishal Bharadwaj, Hitesh Sonik (background score)
Lyrics... Gulzar, Ajinkya Iyer
Art Direction... Nivedita Shastri
Cast... Vidya Balan, Naseeruddin Shah, Arshad Warsi, Salman Shahid, Adil Hussain, Rajesh Sharma

Tanu Weds Manu (2011)

Producer... Vikram Malhotra, Sanjay Singh, Shailesh R. Singh, Surya Sonal Singh
Director... Anand L. Rai
Screenplay... Himanshu Sharma
Cinematography... Chirantan Das
Editing... Hemal Kothari
Sound... Tony Babu
Music... Krsna Solo, Pritesh Mehta (background score)
Lyrics... Raj Shekhar
Production Design... Wasiq Khan
Cast... Madhavan, Kangana Ranaut, Jimmy Sheirgill, Deepak Dobriyal, Swara Bhaskar, Eijaz Khan, K.K. Raina

The DirtyPicture (2011)

Producer... Ekta Kapoor and Shobha Kapoor
Director... Milan Luthria
Screenplay... Rajat Arora
Cinematography... Bobby Singh
Editing... Avik Ali
Sound... Ajay Kumar P.B.
Music... Vishal-Shekar, Sandeep Shirodkar
Lyrics... Rajat Arora
Art Direction... Mohan Bingi and Sandeep Suvarna
Cast... Vidya Balan, Emraan Hashmi, Tushar Kapoor, Naseeruddin Shah, Rajesh Sharma

---

Cocktail (2012)

Producer... Saif Ali Khan, Dinesh Vijan
Director... Homi Adajania
Screenplay... Imtiaz Ali, Sajid Ali
Cinematography... Anil Mehta
Editing... A. Sreekar Prasad
Sound... Dileep Subramanian
Music... Pritam, Salim-Sulaiman
Lyrics... Amitabh Bhattacharya, Irshad Kamil, Arif Lohar, Yo Yo Honey Singh
Art Direction... Sandeep Sharad Ravade
Cast... Deepika Padukone, Saif Ali Khan, Diana Penty, Dimple Kapadia, Rahul Khanna, Randeep Hooda, Boman Irani

---

Queen (2013)

Producer... Viacom 18 Motion Picture, Anurag Kashyap, Vikramaditya Motwane, Madhu Mantena
Director... Vikas Bahl
Screenplay... Vikas Bahl, Chaitally Parmar, Parveez Shaikh, Anvita Dutt Guptan

Cinematography... Bobby Singh, Siddhart h Diwan (Additional cinematography)
Editing... Abhijit Kokate, Anurag Kashyap
Sound... Saumit Deshmukh
Music... Amit Trivedi, Rupesh Kumar Ram
Lyrics... Anvita Dutt
Art Direction... Kishen Dagar
Cast... Kangana Ranaut, Rajkumarr Rao, Lisa Haydon, Yogendra Tiku, Sabeena Imam, Jeffrey Ho, Marco Canadea, Guithob Jospeh, Mish Boyko

Margarita with a Straw (2014)
Producer... Ishan Talkies, Shonali Bose, Nilesh Maniyar, Jyoti Kapur Das
Director... Shonali Bose, Nilesh Maniyar (co-director)
Screenplay... Shonali Bose, Atika Chohan
Cinematography... Anne Misawa
Editing... Monisha R. Baldawa, Bob Brooks (co-editor)
Sound... Vijay Kumar
Music... Mikey McCleary
Lyrics... Prasoon Joshi
Art Direction... Avinash Lalwani, Boishali Sinha
Cast... Kalki Koechlin, Revathy, Sayani Gupta, Hussain Dalal, Kuljit Singh, Malhar Khushu, William Moseley

Piku (2015)
Producer... Ronnie Lahiri, Sneha Rajani, N.P. Singh
Director... Shoojit Sircar
Screenplay... Juhi Chaturvedi
Cinematography... Kamaljit Negi
Editing... Chandrashekhar Prajapati
Sound... Tony Babu
Music... Anupam Roy

Lyrics ... Manoj Yadav
Art Direction ... Sanket Ghag
Cast ... Deepika Padukone, Amitabh Bachchan, Irrfan, Moushmi Chatterjee, Raghuvir Yadav, Jishu Sengupta, Balendar Singh, Sajal Bhattacharya, Swaroopa Ghosh

---

Tanu Weds Manu Returns (2015)
Producer ... Sunil Lulla, Anand L. Rai
Director ... Anand L. Rai
Screenplay ... Himanshu Sharma
Cinematography ... Chirantan Das
Editing ... Hemal Kothari
Sound ... Anish P. Tom
Music ... Krsna Solo
Lyrics ... Raj Shekhar, N.S. Chauhan
Production Design ... Wasiq Khan
Cast ... Madhavan, Kangana Ranaut, Jimmy Sheirgill, Deepak Dobriyal, Swara Bhaskar, Eijaz Khan, K.K. Raina. Mohammad Zeeshan Ayyub,

---

Manmarziyan (2018)
Producer ... Madhu Mantena Varma, Anand L. Rai
Director ... Anurag Kashyap
Screenplay ... Kanika Dhillon
Cinematography ... Sylvester Fonseca
Editing ... Aarti Bajaj
Sound ... Sanjay Mongia, Allwin Rego
Music ... Amit Trivedi
Lyrics ... Shelle
Art Direction ... Lavanya Grover
Cast ... Taapsee Pannu, Abhishek Bachchan, Vicky Kaushal, Ashnoor Kaur, Jasmin Bajwa, Swairaj Sandhu, Neelu Kohli

Gully Boy (2019)

Producer... Excel Entertainment
Director... Zoya Akhtar
Screenplay... Zoya Akhtar, Reema Kagti, Vijay Maurya
Cinematography... Jay Oza
Editing... Nitin Baid
Sound... Ayush Ahuja
Music... IshQ Bector, Divine, Kaam Bhaari, Raghu Dixit, The Savage Audio Collective, Karsh Kale, Mikey McCleary, Chandrashekhar Kunder, Naezy, Rishi Rich, Jasleen Royal, Dub Sharma, Spitfire
Lyrics... Ace, Aditya Sharma, Javed Akhtar, Kaam Bhaari, Divine, Karsh Kale, Bhinder Khanpuri, Naezy, Gaurav Raina, Tapan Raj, Spitfire, Ankur Tiwari
Art Direction... Maria L. Baker, Roshan Vichare
Cast... Ranveer Singh, Alia Bhatt, Siddhant Chaturvedi, Vijay Raaz, Amruta Subhash, Vijay Varma, Kalki Koechlin, Ikhlaque Khan, Sheeba Chaddha

---

Thappad (2020)

Producer... Bhushan Kumar
Director... Anubhav Sinha
Screenplay... Anubhav Sinha, Mrunmayee Lagoo
Cinematography... Soumik Mukherjee
Editing... Yasha Ramchandrani
Sound... Pragyan Gogoi
Music... Mangesh Dhakde (background score), Anurag Saikia (songs)
Lyrics... Shakeel Azmi, Sanah
Production Design... Nikhil S. Kovale
Cast... Taapsee Pannu, Pavail Gulati, Ratna Pathak Shah, Kumud Mishra, Tanvi Azmi, Maya Sarao, Ram Kapoor, Manav Kaul

Chapter 4—Woman the Hero

Kahani (2012)
Producer... Kushal Goda, Sujoy Ghosh
Director... Sujoy Ghosh
Screenplay... Sujoy Ghosh, Advaita Kala (story)
Cinematography... Satyajit Pande
Editing... Namrata Rao
Sound... Imran Shaikh
Music... Vishal-Shekhar
Lyrics... Vishal Dadlani, Anvita Dutta, Sandeep Srivatsava
Production Design... Kaushik Das
Cast... Vidya Balan, Parambrata Chattopadhyay, Indraneil Sengupta, Nawazuddin Siddiqui, DhritimanChatterjee, Saswata Chatterjee, Darshan Jariwala

---

NH10 (2015)
Producer... Vikas Bahl, Anurag Kashyap, Krishika Lulla, Madhu Mantena Varma, Anushka Sharma
Director... Navdeep Singh
Screenplay... Sudip Sharma
Cinematography... Arvind Kannabiran
Editing... Jabeen Merchant
Sound... Subash Sahoo
Music... Karan Gour
Lyrics... Varun Grover, Neeraj Rajawat, Manoj Tapadia
Production Design... Mustafa Stationwala
Cast... Anushka Sharma, Neil Bhoopalam, Darshan Kumar, Deepti Naval, Sidharth Bharadwaj, Tanya Purohit

---

Mary Kom (2014)
Producer... Sanjay Leela Bhansali, Jyoti Kapur Das, Sandeep Singh
Director... Omung Kumar

Screenplay ... Saiwyn Quadras
Cinematography ... Keiko Nakahara
Editing ... Sanjay Leela Bhansali, Rajesh Pandey
Sound ... Chiranjibi Bipin Nanda
Music ... Rohit Kulkarni, Shivamm, Shashi
Lyrics ... Prashant Ingole, Biju Thaangjam, Sandeep Singh
Art Direction ... Vanita Omung Kumar, Ram More
Cast ... Priyanka Chopra, Sunil Thapa, Robin Das, Rajni Basumatary, Darshan Kumar, Biju Thaangjam

---

Nil Battey Sannata (2015)
Producer ... Anand L.Rai, Ajay Rai, Sanjay Shetty, Nitesh Tiwari, Alan McAlex
Director ... Ashwiny Iyer Tiwari
Screenplay ... Ashwiny Iyer Tiwari, Neeraj Singh, Pranjal Choudhary, Nitesh Tiwari (story)
Cinematography ... Gavemic Ary
Editing ... Shekhar Prajapati,
Sound ... Kunal Sharma
Music ... Rohan-Vinayak
Lyrics ... Shreyas Jain, Nitesh Tiwari, Manoj Yadav
Production Design ... Laxmi Keluskar
Cast ... Swara Bhaskar, Ratna Pathak Shah, Riya Shukla, Pankaj Tripathi, Vishal Nath, Prashant Tiwari, Sanjay Suri

---

Neerja (2016)
Producer ... Atul Kasbekar, Shanti Sivaram Maini
Director ... Ram Madhvani
Screenplay ... Saiwyn Quadras, Sanyuktha Chawla Shaikh
Cinematography ... Mitesh Mirchandani
Editing ... Monisha Baldawa
Sound ... Subhash Sahoo, Ravi Soni
Music ... Vishal Khurana

Lyrics ... Prasoon Joshi
Production Design ... Priti Gole, Anna Ipe, Aparna Sud
Cast ... Sonam Kapoor, Shabana Azmi, Yogendra Tiku, Abrar Zahoor, Jim Sarbh, Ali Baldiwala, Shekhar Ravjiani, Vikrant Singta

---

Akira (2016)
Producer ... A.R.Murugadoss
Director ... A.R.Murugadoss
Screenplay ... A.R.Murugadoss, Santha Kumar(story). Arun Shekhar
Cinematography ... R.D.Rajasekhar
Editing ... A.Sreekara Prasad
Sound ... Saumit Deshmukh
Music ... Vishal-Shekhar, John Stewart Edun (background score)
Lyrics ... Manoj Muntashir, Kumaar
Production Design ... Aparna Sud
Cast ... Sonakshi Sinha, Anurag Kashyap, Konkona Sen Sharma, Amit Sadh, Atul Kulkarni, Nandu Madhav, Smita Jaykar, Rai Laxmi

---

Secret Superstar (2017)
Producer ... Kiran Rao, Allen Liu
Director ... Advait Chandan
Screenplay ... Advait Chandan
Cinematography ... Anil Mehta
Editing ... Hemanti Sarkar
Sound ... Pritam Das
Music ... Amit Trivedi
Lyrics ... Kausar Munir
Production Design ... Pallavi Bagga, Suman Roy Mahapatra
Cast ... Zaira Wasim, Meher Vij, Raj Arun, Tirth Sharma, Kabir Sajid, Farrukh Jaffar, Aamir Khan (Special appearance) Monali Thakur(self), Shaan (self)

SELECT FILMOGRAPHY 251

Raazi (2018)
Producer ... Karan Johar, Vineet Jain, Hiroo Johar, Apoorva Mehta
Director ... Meghna Gulzar
Screenplay ... Harinder Sikka (book *Calling Sehmat*) Meghna Gulzar, Bhavani Iyer
Cinematography ... Jay I. Patel
Editing ... Nitin Baid
Sound ... Kunal Sharma
Music ... Shankar- Ehsan- Loy, Tubby
Lyrics ... Gulzar
Art Direction ... Pallavi Pethkar
Cast ... Alia Bhatt, Vicky Kaushal, Rajit Kapoor, Shishir Sharma, Ashwath Bhatt, Jaideep Ahlawat, Soni Razdan, Arif Zakaria, Amruta Khanvilkar

---

Chhapaak (2020)
Producer ... Meghna Gulzar, Deepika Padukone, Govind Singh Sandhu
Director ... Meghna Gulzar
Screenplay ... Meghna Gulzar, Atika Chohan
Cinematography ... Malay Prakash
Editing ... Vini N. Raj
Sound ... Yogesh Nehe
Music ... Shankar-Ehsan-Loy
Lyrics ... Gulzar
Art Direction ... Pallavi Pethkar, Nilesh Vishwakarma
Cast ... Deepika Padukone, Vikrant Massey, Vishal Dahiya, Madhurjeet Sarghi, Ankit Bisht, Pallavi Batra, Geeta Agarwal, Anjana Om Kashyap

---

Panga (2020)
Producer ... Fox Star Studios
Director ... Ashwiny Iyer Tiwari

Screenplay ... Nikhil Mehrotra, Ashwiny Iyer Tiwari, Nitesh Tiwari (additional script and dialogue)
Cinematography ... Archit Patel, Jay I. Patel
Editing ... Ballu Saluja
Sound ... Satish Solanki
Music ... Shankar-Ehsan-Loy, Ankit Balhara (background score) Sanchit Balhara (background score)
Lyrics ... Javed Akhtar
Art Direction ... Sandeep Meher
Cast ... Kangana Ranaut, Jassie Gill, Richa Chadha, Neena Gupta, Yagya Bhasin, Megha Burman, Rajesh Tailang

---

Blast from the past

Hunterwali (1935)
Producer ... Wadia Movietone, The Bombay Talkies Studios
Director ... Homi Wadia
Screenplay ... Homi Wadia, Joseph David
Cinematography ... Balwant Dave
Music ... Master Mohammad
Lyrics ... Joseph David
Cast ... Fearless Nadia, Sharifa, Gulshan, Boman Shroff, John Cawas, Master Mohammad

---

Diamond Queen (1940)
Producer ... Wadia Movietone
Director ... Homi Wadia
Screenplay ... J.B.H. Wadia, Munshi Sham
Cinematography ... R.P.Master
Editing ... S.R.Gaikwad
Sound ... K.M.Contractor

Music ... Madhavlal D. Master
Lyrics ... Munshi Sham
Art Direction ... Pestonji D. Mistri
Cast ... Fearless Nadia, Radharani, Nazira, Fatma, John Cawas, Sardar Mansur, Sayani Atish, Dalpat

Chapter 5—Woman at Work

Chandni Bar (2001)
Producer ... Lata Mohan
Director ... Madhur Bhandarkar
Screenplay ... Mohan Azad, Madhur Bhandarkar, Masud Mirza
Cinematography ... Rajeev Ravi
Editing ... Hemal Kothari
Sound ... Prakash Bhatia
Music ... Raju Singh
Art Direction ... Prasanna Karkhanis, Yeshwant Patil
Cast ... Tabu, Atul Kulkarni, Rajpal Yadav, Shri Vallabh Vyas, Vinay Apte, Ananya Khare, Suhas Palshikar, Vishal Thakkar, Meenakshi Sahani

Lakshya (2004)
Producer ... Excel Entertainment
Director ... Farhan Akhtar
Screenplay ... Javed Akhtar, Karan Kashyap
Cinematography ... Christopher Popp
Editing ... Anand Subaya
Sound ... Vic Kaspar, Sardia Wong
Music ... Shankar-Ehsan-Loy
Lyrics ... Javed Akhtar
Art Direction ... Sunil Babu, Suzzanne Merwanji, Sonal Sawant

Cast ... Hrithik Roshan, Preity Zinta, Amitabh Bachchan, Om Puri, Sharad S. Kapoor, Raj Zutshi, Sushant Singh, Ranvir Shorey (self), Amrish Puri

---

Corporate (2006)

Producer ... Sahara One
Director ... Madhur Bhandarkar
Screenplay ... Ajeet Ghorpade, Madhur Bhandarkar, Manoj Tyagi
Cinematography ... Mahesh Limaye
Editing ... Devendra Murdeshwar
Sound ... Ashish Manchanda
Music ... Shameer Tandon, Raju Singh (background score)
Lyrics ... Sandeep Nath
Art Direction ... Omung Kumar
Cast ... Bipasha Basu, Kay Kay Menon, Raj Babbar, Rajat Kapoor, Lillete Dubey, Harsh Chaya, Bharat Dabholkar

---

Page 3 (2005)

Producer ... Bobby Pushkarna, Shailendra Singh
Director ... Madhur Bhandarkar
Screenplay ... Nina Arora. Madhur Bhandarkar, Manoj Tyagi
Cinematography ... Madhu Rao
Editing ... Suresh Pai
Sound ... Parikshit Lalwani, Kunal Mehta
Music ... Raju Singh (background score), Shamir Tandon
Lyrics ... Sandeep Nath, Ajay Jhingran
Art Direction ... Sailesh Mahadik
Cast ... Konkona Sen Sharma, Atul Kulkarni, Sandhya Mridul, Tara Sharma, Boman Irani, Bikram Saluja, Soni Razdan, Anju Mahendru, Jai Kalra

Wake up Sid (2009)

Producer ... Hiroo Yash Johar, Karkan Johar
Director ... Ayan Mukherjee.
Screenplay ... Ayan Mukherjee, Niranjan Iyengar
Cinematography ... Anil Mehta
Editing ... Shaan Mohammad
Sound ... Baylon Fonseca
Music ... Shankar-Ehsan-Loy, Amit Trivedi (music, background score)
Lyrics ... Javed Akhtar
Art Direction ... Kabir Chowdhry
Cast ... Ranbir Kapoor, Konkona Sen Sharma, Supriya Pathak, Rahul Khanna, Anupam Kher, Kashmira Shah, Namit Das, Shikha Talsania

---

Luck by Chance (2009)

Producer ... Excel Entertainment
Director ... Zoya Akhtar
Screenplay ... Zoya Akhtar, Javed Akhtar
Cinematography ... Carlos Catalan
Editing ... Anand Subaya
Sound ... Manik Batra, Baylon Fonseca
Music ... Shankar-Ehsan-Loy
Lyrics ... Javed Akhtar
Art Direction ... Abid T.P
Cast ... Farhan Akhtar, Konkona Sen Sharma, Rishi Kapoor, Dimple Kapadia, Juhi Chawla, Anurag Kashyap, Isha Sharvani, Hrithik Roshan (cameo) Aamir Khan(self), Shahrukh Khan (self) and a galaxy of Bollywood stars playing themselves

---

No One Killed Jessica (2011)

Producer ... Ronnie Screwwala
Director ... Raj Kumar Gupta
Screenplay ... Raj Kumar Gupta

Cinematography ... Anay Goswami
Editing ... Aarti Bajaj
Sound ... Sushant Amin, Imran Shaikh
Music ... Amit Trivedi
Lyrics ... Amitabh Bhattacharya
Production Design ... Sukant Panigrahy
Cast ... Rani Mukerji, Vidya Balan, Myra Karn, Neil Bhoopalam, Rajesh Sharma, Satyadeep Misra, Yogendra Tiku

---

Jab Tak Hai Jaan (2012)
Producer ... Yash Raj Films
Director ... Yash Chopra
Screenplay ... Aditya Chopra, Devika Bhagat
Cinematography ... Anil Mehta
Editing ... Namarata Rao
Sound ... Sarit Chatterjee
Music ... A.R.Rahman
Lyrics ... Gulzar
Art Direction ... Toby Riches
Cast ... Shah Rukh Khan, Katrina Kaif, Anushka Sharma, Anupam Kher, Rishi Kapoor, Sharib Hashmi, Andrew Bicknell, Sarika

---

Inkaar (2013)
Producer ... Viacom 18 Motion Pictures
Director ... Sudhir Mishra
Screenplay ... Sudhir Mishra
Cinematography ... Sachin Krishn
Editing ... Archit D. Rastogi
Sound ... Yogi Dholakia
Music ... Shantanu Moitra, Shamir Tandon
Lyrics ... Swanand Kirkire
Production Design ... Gautam Sen

Cast... Arjun Rampal, Chitrangda Singh, Vipin Sharma, Mithun Rodwittiya, Deepti Naval

---

Satyagraha (2013)
Producer... Prakash Jha, Ronnie Screwwala, Sidharth Roy Kapur
Director... Prakash Jha
Screenplay... Prakash Jha, Anjum Rajabali
Cinematography... Sachin Krishn
Editing... Santosh Mandal, Sunder Pathun
Sound... Rakesh Ranjan
Music... Salim-Sulaiman, Indian Ocean, Meet Bros
Lyrics... Prasoon Joshi
Art Direction... Uday Prakash Singh
Cast... Amitabh Bachchan, Ajay Devgn, Kareena Kapoor, Manoj Bajpayee, Arjun Rampal, Amrita Rao, Anjali Patil, Mughda Godse

---

Mardaani (2014)
Producer... Yash Raj Films
Director... Pradeep Sarkar
Screenplay... Gopi Puthran, Vibha Singh
Cinematography... Artur Zurawski
Editing... Sanjib Dutta
Sound... Anilkumar Konakanola, Prabal Pradhan
Music... Salim-Sulaiman, Julius Packiam (background score)
Lyrics... Kausar Munir
Art Direction... Madhu Sarkar, Kuriakose, Bhavani Patel
Cast... Rani Mukerji, Tahir Raj Bhasin, Priyanka Sharma, Mona Ambegaonkar, Gautam Babbar, Vishwa Bhanu

---

PK (2014)
Producer... Vidhu Vinod Chopra, Raj Kumar Hirani

Director ... Raj Kumar Hirani
Screenplay ... Raj Kumar Hirani, Abhijat Joshi
Cinematography ... C.K. Muraleedharan
Editing ... Raj Kumar Hirani
Sound ... Abhishruti Bezbaruah
Music ... Shantanu Moitra, Atul Gogavale
Lyrics ... Swanand Kirkire, Amitabh Verma
Art Direction ... Tanvi Patel
Cast ... Aamir Khan, Anushka Sharma, Saurabh Shukla, Sanjay Dutt, Boman Irani, Sushant Singh Rajput, Parikshit Sahni

---

Drishyam (2015)
Producer ... Kumar Mangal Pathak, Sarita Patil, Abhishek Pathak
Director ... Nishikant Kamat
Screenplay ... Jeethu Joseph (original Malayalam story) Upendra Sidhaye (adaptation)
Cinematography ... Avinash Arun
Editing ... Aarif Sheikh
Sound ... Bulganin Baruah, Vishnu Das, Imran Shaikh
Music ... Vishal Bharadwaj, Sameer Phaterpekar
Lyrics ... Gulzar
Art Direction ... Rita Ghosh
Cast ... Ajay Devgn, Shriya Saran, Tabu, Rajat Kapoor, Ishita Dutta, Mrunal Jadhav, Prasanna Ketkar, Yogesh Sonam, Rishab Chadha

---

Dear Zindagi (2016)
Producer ... Gauri Khan, Karan Johar
Director ... Gauri Shinde
Screenplay ... Gauri Shinde
Cinematography ... Laxman Utekar
Editing ... Hemanti Sarkar
Sound ... Debasish Mishra

Music ... Amit Trivedi
Lyrics ... Kausar Munir
Production Design ... Rupin Suchak
Cast ... Alia Bhatt, Shah Rukh Khan, Kunal Kapoor, Aditya Roy Kapoor, Ali Zafar, Bobby Duggal, Angad Bedi, Ira Dubey

Chapter 6—Sisters under the Hood

Mrityudand (1997)
Producer ... Prakash Jha
Director ... Prakash Jha
Screenplay ... Shaiwal (story) RajanKothari, Anil Ajitabh, Prakash Jha
Cinematography ... Rajan Kothari
Editing ... Prakash Jha
Sound ... Rakesh Ranjan
Music ... Anand-Milind, Raghunath Seth
Lyrics ... Javed Akhtar
Art Direction ... Sharmishta Roy
Cast ... Shabana Azmi, Madhuri Dixit, Om Puri, Ayub Khan, Mohan Agashe, Mohan Joshi, Haraish Patel, Pyare Mohan Sahay

Dor (2006)
Producer ... Elahe Hiptoola, Devika Bahudhanam
Director ... Nagesh Kukunoor
Screenplay ... Nagesh Kukunoor, Mir Ali Husain
Cinematography ... Sudeep Chatterjee
Editing ... Sanjib Dutta
Sound ... Vipin Bhati
Music ... Salim Merchant, Suleiman Merchant
Lyrics ... Mir Ali Husain
Art Direction ... Muneesh Sappel

Cast ... Gul Panang, Ayesha Takia, Shreyas Talpade, Girish Karnad, Prateeksha Lonkar, Rushad Rana, Anirudh Jaykar, Uttara Baokar

---

Angry Indian Goddesses (2015)
Producer ... Pan Nalin
Director ... Pan Nalin
Screenplay ... Pan Nalin, Subhadra Mahajan
Cinematography ... Swapnil S. Sonawane
Editing ... Shreyas Beltangady
Sound ... Manoj M. Goswami
Music ... Cyril Morin (original music)
Art Direction ... Tiya Tejpal
Cast ... Sarah-Jane Dias, Tannishtha Chatterjee, Rajshree Deshpande, Sandhya Mridul, Amrit Maghera, Pavleen Gujral, Anushka Manchanda Adil Hussain

---

Parched (2015)
Producer ... Ajay Devgn, Aseem Bajaj, Leena Yadav, Rohan Jagdale, Gulab Singh Tanwar,
Director ... Leena Yadav
Screenplay ... Leena Yadav, Supratik Sen
Cinematography ... Russell Carpener
Editing ... Kevin Tent
Sound ... Paul N.J. Ottosson
Music ... Hitesh Sonik
Lyrics ... Swanand Kirkire
Art Direction ... Pradip Redij, Aman Mohan Vidhate
Cast ... Tannishtha Chatterjee, Radhika Apte, Leher Khan, Surveen Chawla, Ridhi Sen, Sumeet Vyas, Sayani Gupta, Nancy Nisa Beso

Lipstick under My Burkha (2016)
Producer ... Prakash Jha, JB Angels
Director ... Alankrita Srivastava
Screenplay ... Alankrita Srivastava, Suhani Kanwar, Gazal Dhaliwal
Cinematography ... Akshay Singh
Editing ... Charu Shree Roy
Sound ... Abhinav Agnihotri, Sampath Alwar
Music ... Zebunissa Bangash, Mangesh Dhakde (background score)
Lyrics ... Anvita Dutt
Production Design ... Vikram Singh
Cast ... Ratna Pathak Shah, Konkona Sen Sharma, Ahana Kumra, Plabitha Borthakur, Vikrant Massey, Sushant Singh

Chapter 7—The Subversives

Devdas (1955)
Producer ... Bimal Roy
Director ... Bimal Roy
Screenplay ... Saratchandra Chatterjee(novel) Rajinder Singh Bedi, Nabendu Ghosh
Cinematography ... Kamal Bose
Editing ... Hrishikesh Mukherjee
Music ... Sachin Dev Burman
Lyrics ... Sahir Ludhianvi
Art Direction ... Sudhendu Roy
Cast ... Dillip Kumar, Suchitra Sen, Vyjayantimala, Motilal, Nasir Hussain, Murad, Kanhaiyalal, Moni Chatterjee, Iftekhar, Nana Palsikar

Sahib Bibi Aur Ghulam (1962)
Producer ... Guru Dutt
Director ... Abrar Alvi

Screenplay... Abrar Alvi, BimalMitra (novel)
Cinematography... V.K.Murthy
Editing... Y.G.Chawhan
Sound... P.Thackersey
Music... Hemant Kumar
Lyrics... Shakeel Badayuni
Art Direction... Biren Naug
Cast... Meena Kumari, Guru Dut, Rehman, Waheeda Rehman, Nasir Hussain, Dhumal, Sapru, Harindranath Chattopadhyay, Pratima Devi

---

Dev D (2009)
Producer... Ronnie Screwwala
Director... Anurag Kashyap
Screenplay... Saratchandra Chatterjee(novel), Abhay Deol (concept), Vikramaditya Moatwane, Anurag Kashyap
Cinematography... Rajeev Ravi
Editing... Aarti Bajaj
Sound... Sushant Amin, Imran Shaikh
Music... Amit Trivedi
Lyrics... Amitabh Bhattacharya, Shruthi Pathak
Art Direction... Helen Jones, Sukant Panigrahy
Cast... Abhay Deol, Mahie Gill, Kalki Koechlin, Dibyendu Bhattacharya, Gurkirtan, Satwant Kaur, Parakh Madan, Nawazuddin Siddiqui, Nitin Chainpuri

---

Saheb Biwi Aur Gangster (2011)
Producer... Tigmanshu Dhulia, Rahul Mittra, Jay Patel
Director... Tigmanshu Dhulia
Screenplay... Sanjay Chauhan, Tigmanshu Dhulia
Cinematography... Aseem Mishra
Editor... Aditya Joshi, Rahul Srivastava
Sound... Shankar Singh
Music... Ankit Tiwari, Anuj Garg, Jaidev Kumar, Mukhtar Sahota

Lyrics... Babbu Mann, Sandeep Nath
Art Direction... Dhananjoy Mondal
Cast... Jimmy Sheirgill, Mahie Gill, Randeep Hooda, Shreya Narayan, Deepal Shaw, Rajeev Gupta, Deepraj Rana, Vipin Sharma

Chapter 8—Subversion in Retro Mode

Astitva (2000)
Producer... Rahul Sughand
Director... Mahesh Manjrekar
Screenplay... Imtiyaz Husain, Mahesh Manjrekar
Cinematography... Vijay Arora
Editor... V.N. Mayekar
Sound... Rajendra Hegde
Music... Rahul Ranade, Sukhwinder Singh
Lyrics... Shrirang Godbole
Art Direction... Sudhir Thakkar
Cast... Tabu, Sachin Khedekar, Mohnish Bahl, Smita Jaykar, Ravindra Mankani, Sunil Barve

Maqbool (2003)
Producer... Bobby Bedi
Director... Vishal Bharadwaj
Screenplay... Vishal Bharadwaj, Abbas Tyrewala (adapted from Shakespeare's Macbeth)
Cinematography... Hemant Chaturvedi
Editor... Arif Sheikh
Sound... Shajith Koyeri
Music... Vishal Bharadwaj
Lyrics... Gulzar
Art Direction... Jayant Deshmukh

Cast ... Tabu, Irrfan Khan, Naseeruddin Shah, Om Puri, Pankaj Kapur, Piyush Mishra, Masumeh Makhija, Deepak Dobriyal

---

English Vinglish (2012)
Producer ... R.Balki, R.Damani, Rakesh Jhunjhunwala
Director ... Gauri Shinde
Screenplay ... Gauri Shinde
Cinematography ... Laxman Utekar
Editor ... Hemanti Sarkar
Sound ... Arunav Dutta
Music ... Amit Trived
Art Direction ... Shaibya Rakesh, Maggie Ruder
Cast ... Sridevi, Adil Hussain, Mehdi Nebbou, Priya Anand, Sulabha Deshpande, Navika Kotia, Shivansh Kotia, Sujatha Kumar

---

Haidar (2014)
Producer ... Sidharth Roy Kapur, Vishal Bharadwaj
Director ... Vishal Bharadwaj
Screenplay ... Basharat Peer, Vishal Bharadwaj (adapted from Shakespeare's Hamlet)
Cinematography ... Pankaj Kumar
Editor ... Aarif Sheikh
Sound ... Shajit Koyeri
Music ... Vishal Bharadwaj
Lyrics ... Gulzar
Art Direction ... Shraddha Johri, Rupam Paul
Cast ... Shahid Kapur, Tabu, Shraddha Kapoor, Kay Kay Menen, Narendra Jha, Kulbhushan Kharbanda, Ashish Vidyarthi, Aamir Bashir

---

Andhadhun (2018)

Producer ... Kewal Garg, Sanjay Routray, Ashok Vashodia
Director ... Sriram Raghavan
Screenplay ... Arijit Biswas, Yogesh Chandekar, Sriram Raghavan, Hemanth M.Rao, Pooja Ladha Surti (adapted from Olivier Treiner"s French story)
Cinematography ... K.U.Mohanan
Editor ... Pooja Ladha Surti
Sound ... Madhu Apsara
Music ... Daniel B.George, Amit Trivedi, Raftaar, Girsih Nakod
Lyrics ... Jaideep Sahni
Art Direction ... Amrish Patange, Dayanidhi Patturajan
Cast ... Ayushmann Khurana, Tabu, Radhika Apte, Anil Dhawan, Manav Vij, Ashwini Kalsekar, Zakir Hussain

---

De De Pyar De (2019)

Producer ... Ankur Garg, Bhushan Kumar, Krishan Kumar
Director ... Akiv Ali
Screenplay ... Saurabhi Bhatnagar, Tarun Jain, Luv Ranjan,
Cinematography ... Sudhir K.Chaudhary
Editor ... Akiv Ali
Sound ... Kaarthic Senthil
Music ... Hiten Sonik
Lyrics ... Tanishk Bagchi, Kunaal Varmaa, Shamsher Sandhu, Mellow D
Production Design ... Shashank Tere
Cast ... Ajay Devgn, Tabu, Rakul Preet Singh, Jimmy Sheirgill, Alok Nath, Madhumalti Kapoor, Kumud Mishra, Bhavin Bhanushali, Inayat Sood

Sources of Quotes—Chapterwise

Preface

Amulya Gopalakrishnan—Sunday Times of India 12-1-2020
Gyan Prakash—Sunday Times of India: *Why the protests remind us of Gandhi's Khilafat movement.* 12-1-2020

Introduction

Santosh Desai—(Times of India, 2 July 2018)
Gautam Dalmia—*We Are The World, Times of India*, 3 May 2018
Gautam Dalmia—*We Are The World, Times of India*, 3 May 2018
*Economic Times*s, sourced from: Employment and Unemployment Survey, NSSO

Chapter 1: No Means No

Avinash Das's Interview, Bengaluru Mirror

Chapter 2: Rom Com Revamped

Ira Trivedi—India in Love; Marriage and Sexuality in the 21st Century February 2018, Collider.com, referenced by IMDb.

Chapter 3: Non-conformists Are the New Cool

Abhishek Chaubey's Interview *Bangalore Mirror*, 27 February 2019.
Mrinmayee Lagu, *in Bangalore Mirror*, 3 March 2020

Chapter 5: Woman at Work

Nisha Menon , *afaqs!, Mumbai | In* Media Publishing
Samina Dalwai's article in 24 January 2019, *Indian Express*

Chapter 6: Sisters under the Hood

Smita Patil, A Brief Incandescence. P.189 Harper Collins (2015)

Chapter 7: The Subversives

Man's World—Excerpts from my review of Haidar
Books referred to: The Earth is Flat (by Thomas Friedman)
The Hero with a Thousand Faces (by Joseph Campbell)
In many chapters, I have used a few observations I made in my columns for Man's World